Guthrie to Gotham
The Extraordinary Rides of the Abernathy Boys

Check out
Kent Brooks' other titles
available on
Amazon.com

Old Boston: As Wild As They Come
Letters from Colorado: 1880-1889
Letters from Wyoming: 1880-1889
Letters from Nebraska: 1880-1889
Letters from Indian Territory: 1880-1888
Letters from the Oklahoma Land Run: 1889
Cattle & Cowboys: Letters & More from the 1880s
Letters from Wyoming 1870-1879
When Colorado Was Kansas: Letters from 1859
Letters, Stories and Incidents
from Montana: 1880-1889
Letters, Stories and Incidents from the Santa Fe Trail:
The Bent's Fort Years 1833-1849
Letters, Stories and Incidents
from the Texas Republic: 1836-1846

Guthrie to Gotham
The Extraordinary Rides of the Abernathy Boys

By
Kent Brooks

© Kent Brooks
2025

Cover Image: Undated historical public domain photograph of Bud and Temple Abernathy, on horseback ca. 1910. The original image used for the cover is believed to have been published in a U.S. newspaper around 1910 and is in the public domain. The author digitally restored, and adapted the image above for aesthetic clarity and modern presentation.

ABOVE: Photo of the boys riding in Teddy Roosevelt's return from Africa Parade in New York City.

---

[1] The *Star Press* (Muncie, Indiana) June 20, 1910, Pg. 5.
[2] The *Indianapolis Star* (Indianapolis, Indiana) June 20, 1910, Pg. 1.
[3] The *Washington Times* (Washington, D.C). June 19, 1910, Pg. 4.

All rights reserved: This book or any portion thereof may not be reproduced or used in any manner whatsoever without the express written permission of the publisher except for the use of brief quotations in a book review or scholarly journal.

First Printing: 2025

ISBN: 979-8-9862765-1-9

Address:
849 Main Street
Springfield Colorado 81073

Website www.plainsmanherald.com

Ordering Information:
Special discounts are available on quantity purchases by corporations, associations, educators, and others. For details, contact the publisher at the above listed address.

Trademark Acknowledgement:
"Brush" and "Brush Runabout" are referenced in this work for historical context. Any trademarks used herein are the property of their respective owners.
"Indian Motorcycle" is a registered trademark of Polaris Industries Inc., used in this book solely for descriptive and historical reference. All trademarks, service marks, and trade names are the property of their respective owners. Their use in this book is solely for historical reference and does not imply any affiliation with or endorsement by the trademark owners.

Dedication

While living in Southwest Oklahoma for 15 years, a friend introduced us to a story that never let go of me. Thank you for sharing this true story that inspired this research and compilation.

Contents

Quick Trip Timeline of the Abernathy Boys x

Acknowledgements xi

Preface xv

Introduction 2

Chapter 1: 1908 — Before They Rode Alone 7

Chapter 2: 1909 — The New Mexico Ride 11

Chapter 3: 1910 — From Oklahoma to New York 31

Chapter 4: 1910 — Visiting the Nation's Capital 63

Chapter 5: 1910 — Triumph in New York City 115

Chapter 6: 1910 — Books, Film & Lectures 143

Chapter 7: 1911 — From Saddles to Steering Wheels . 164

Chapter 8: 1911 — The Elephant and Donkey Race 207

Chapter 9: 1911 — Coast to Coast 219

Chapter 10: 1912 — A Lull in the Action? 287

Chapter 11: 1913 — The Indian Motorcycle Ride 292

Chapter 12: The Imitators 303

Chapter 13: School of the Open Road 313

Chapter 14: After the Last Ride 325

Appendix 1 — Timeline of Trips 332

Appendix 2 — Significant 1910 News 335

Appendix 3 — Brush Auto Ads 342

Appendix 4 — Significant 1911 News 346

Appendix 5 — Summary of Abernathy Boys' Journeys 357

Index 359

Glossary 363

Quick Trip Timeline of the Abernathy Boys

Year	Adventure	Key Highlights
1908	White House Visit	Temple, age 3, tours the White House with President Roosevelt.
1909	Ride to Santa Fe, NM	Ages 5 & 9, ride 1,300 miles solo from Oklahoma to Santa Fe.
1910	Oklahoma to NYC	Ride to meet President Taft and greet Roosevelt's return from Africa.
1910	Drive Home	Buy a Brush automobile and drive back to Oklahoma alone.
1911 (Spring)	Donkey vs. Elephant Race	Publicity stunt across several states.
1911 (Summer)	Coast-to-Coast Ride	Cross-country ride from NYC to San Francisco.
1912	Quieter Year	No major publicized journey—reflective pause.
1913	Motorcycle Trip	Ride Indian motorcycles cross-country at ages 9 & 13.

Acknowledgements

This book, like all stories worth telling, stands on the shoulders of many. First, to my teachers—formal and informal—who helped shape the way I think and write. And to my "stabby" editors, red pens blazing—you know who you are—thank you for sharpening both my prose and my perspective.

A heartfelt thank-you goes to my mother-in-law, whose sharp editorial eye, fierce attention to detail, and unflinching honesty made this book stronger in every way. You're not just an editor—you're one of this book's unsung architects.

To my classmates, from kindergarten through grad school, and to the friends and family who've patiently listened to me tell the same stories (over and over again), I'm endlessly grateful. Without your support, encouragement, and occasional eye-rolls, this book would never have made it to the finish line.

I honestly can't imagine compiling a book without today's digital tools—let alone on a typewriter, with nothing but old clippings and a steady hand.

This project joins a growing shelf of my attempts to bring overlooked stories to light—from *Old Boston: As Wild as They Come* to the many volumes of frontier letters. *Guthrie to Gotham* follows that same thread: honoring the extraordinary in the everyday, as well as honoring newspapers that documented these stories and the adventurous in the unlikely.

Preface

We've included many full-text articles in this compilation for the rich detail they offer. These are *italicized*. When we've pulled a quote or excerpt from an article, those are ***bolded and italicized***.

In some cases, we included the transcribed text as well as the news report from the paper for readability or simply because I liked the formatting.

Although Guthrie to Gotham is primarily firsthand accounts and historical newspaper reports, occasionally scenes and dialogue have been lightly adapted or imagined to bring the Abernathy boys' story to life. These moments, inspired by the tone of period sources and the boys' public persona, aim to reflect the emotional truth of their experiences.

We've made every effort to stay true to the historical record. Any interpretive passages are clearly framed and meant to enhance the narrative—not to replace documented fact.

At its core, this book stands on solid ground: the real value lies in the original newspaper coverage, faithfully presented here.

While we've worked to minimize repetition, some articles echo one another—a reflection of how news spread in the early 20th century. Stories often traveled via wire services and were reprinted by various newspapers, each adding their own flair or commentary. We've included some of these similar accounts when they offer unique angles or insights into how the Abernathy boys' adventures were received nationwide.

Introduction

In the early 1900s, when the world was shifting fast and the American frontier still lingered, two young brothers from Oklahoma made headlines across the country. Louis—often called Bud—and his younger brother Temple weren't just playing cowboy. They were living a life many grown men wouldn't dare attempt.

What makes their story even more fascinating is that it's all true. From horseback rides across New Mexico to coast-to-coast treks and early car journeys, these kids tackled some of the wildest challenges you could imagine. And luckily for us, newspapers were there to document just about every mile of it.

This book brings together those original newspaper stories—clippings, quotes, and full articles—to give you a front-row seat. The boy's story struck a nerve with a public that was hungry for stories of courage, grit, and good old-fashioned adventure.

We've organized mostly chronologically, with a handy timeline in the appendix if you want to keep track. Along the way, you'll see just how quickly Louie "Bud" and Temple became national figures—part real-life folk heroes, part headline sensations.

The Abernathy boys' exploits captured the public's attention and were widely covered by the media of the time. They demonstrated resilience and independence at such young ages, becoming American folk heroes.

In these pages, you'll be transported back to a time when newsprint was king and when the adventures of two young boys could captivate an entire nation. Each article, each headline, and each testimonial paint a picture not just of Louis and Temple's incredible rides, but also of a society eager for tales of bravery, resilience, and youthful audacity.

We have tried to limit duplicate articles as much as possible, however, as an article often traveled over the wire, a given newspaper would put their own spin or personality on the story. We have attempted to retain an individual editor's take on a story while at the same time also trying to limit duplication. Whether we got this correct, is up for debate.

As you follow Bud and Temple's story, you'll see how quickly these boys became headline sensations and real-life folk heroes. Their rides weren't just feats of endurance—they reflected the bold energy of a nation on the move, eager for stories of courage and can-do spirit.

Coverage of the boys' 1910 journey was intertwined with the return of Theodore Roosevelt from his African safari. The boys had set out to meet him, and the press was often more interested in Roosevelt's reentry as in the kids blazing their own trail eastward.

After greeting Roosevelt's ship, the boys decided to buy a Brush Runabout and drive it home—alone. They paid for the car with money earned from their newspaper fame[4] and took turns at the wheel. Bud handled most of the driving. Temple, too small to see over the dashboard, peeked through the spokes of the steering wheel.

That blend of truth, boldness, and youthful mischief is what makes the Abernathy story endure. And there's something uniquely compelling about seeing it unfold exactly as readers did more than a century ago—in their own words, through the ink of the day.

So, buckle up—or better yet, saddle up. You're about to ride alongside two boys who captured the imagination of a country and who, more than a hundred years later, still have something to teach us about guts and grit.

---

[4] NOTE: Some sources believe Brush gave them the car as there were Brush banners displayed on the car throughout the trip.

"JACK" ABERNATHY'S TWO BOYS.
LOUIE AND JACK, RIDING INTO TOWN AFTER TRIP FROM OKLAHOMA.

[5] *New-York Tribune* (New York, New York) June 12, 1910, Sun Pg. 3.

6

---

[6] "Abernathy Kids Nearing O.C. from N.Y. Roosevelt Reception", photograph, 1910; (https://gateway.okhistory.org/ark:/67531/metadc229210/: accessed May 5, 2025), The Gateway to Oklahoma History, https://gateway.okhistory.org; crediting Oklahoma Historical Society.

Chapter 1: 1908 — Before They Rode Alone

Little Temple Abernathy, 3 years of age, is one Oklahoma youngster who has the distinction of having seen nearly every nook and cranny of the White House.[7]

When little Temple Abernathy called at the White House with his father...President Roosevelt had the lad shown through the executive house, a distinction probably enjoyed by no other Oklahoma boy three years of age.[8]

In January 1908, an event occurred marking the beginning of the Abernathy boy's travels. Little Temple Abernathy, only three years old, accompanied his father, U.S. Marshal John Abernathy, on a trip to Washington, D.C. What seemed like a routine visit for the senior Abernathy, who was overseeing the extradition of a fugitive and attending his confirmation hearings as a federal marshal, turned into a moment of national curiosity and pride, thanks to young Temple.

The father-and-son duo had traveled to Washington, D.C and during their stay, they were invited to the White House, where Temple captivated the staff and even President Theodore Roosevelt. Wearing a miniature soldier's uniform, young Abernathy was given a full tour of the historic residence. Temple instantly captivated the attention of everyone he met. His charm and confidence were far beyond his years. The story of the young Oklahoman roaming freely

---
[7] The *Wichita Eagle* (Wichita, Kansas) January 14, 1908. Pg. 2.
[8] The *Republican News Journal* (Newkirk, Oklahoma) January 17, 1908, Pg. 2.

through the executive mansion seized the attention of the press, who eagerly reported on how he roamed nearly every hidden corner — a privilege few ever enjoyed.

> **BOY CHIP OFF OLD BLOCK**
>
> **Abernathy's Son in Uniform Visits White House.**
>
> Washington, D. C., Jan. 13.—Little Temple Abernathy, 3 years of age, is one Oklahoma youngster who has the distinction of having seen nearly every nook and cranny of the White House. United States Marshal John Abernathy and Deputy Wiley Haines, of Pawhuska, arrived here this week with Thomas Stutts, wanted here on a charge of grand larceny. They remained here to see to Mr. Abernathy's confirmation. There is no opposition.
>
> This week Marshall Abernathy visited the White House, taking Temple, dressed in the uniform of a soldier. The young man made a hit and was shown through the White House.

[9]

During the tour, Temple's youthful curiosity and boundless energy endeared him to the White House staff. President Roosevelt himself, known for his fondness for children and his close ties to the Abernathy family, took a personal interest in the boy's visit. Temple was not treated merely as a curious toddler but as a guest of honor.

The experience was so unique and heartwarming that it quickly became the talk of both the Oklahoma press and national newspapers.

---

[9] The *Wichita Eagle* (Wichita, Kansas) January 14, 1908, Pg. 2

The bond between Marshal Abernathy and the president added a deeper layer of significance to Temple's White House tour. Known as "Catch-'Em-Alive Jack," John Abernathy was famed for his ability to capture wolves with his bare hands, a skill that fascinated Roosevelt and earned Abernathy a significant place in the President's circle of friends.

The visit marked a pivotal moment for the Abernathy boys as it introduced the younger Abernathy to the public eye and hinted how they would soon capture the curiosity of the public. For the Abernathy boys, it was their first taste of a world that would soon follow their every move with admiration and amazement.

Temple's debut on the national stage also symbolized a broader narrative of the American West. As the country moved into the 20th century, stories of adventure were eagerly consumed by a public longing for heroes of a fading frontier. The Abernathy family, became living embodiments of the change happening in America.

This visit to the White House set the stage for the rides to come. It introduced the world to a family whose story would intertwine with the changing face of America, capturing the hearts of those who longed for tales of courage, audacity, and unyielding spirit and unearthing harsh critics who failed to see merit in letting two small boys make such lengthy trips across country alone.

> When little Temple Abernathy called at the White House with his father, the Oklahoma marshal, President Roosevelt had the lad shown through the executive house, a distinction probably enjoyed by no other Oklahoma boy three years of age. Temple was dressed as a soldier.

10 11 12 13 14 15 16

Through the eyes of a three-year-old boy dressed as a soldier, the nation saw a glimpse of the life that awaited the Abernathy brothers. It was a simple visit to Washington, D.C., but it became the first chapter in a legend that would stretch across the continent and into history books.

---

[10] The *Tonkawa News* (Tonkawa, Oklahoma) January 16, 1908, Pg. 4.
[11] The *Nardin Star* (Nardin, Oklahoma) January 16, 1908, Pg. 1.
[12] *Cushing Independent* (Cushing, Oklahoma) January 16, 1908, Pg. 1.
[13] The *Enid Events* (Enid, Oklahoma) January 16, 1908, Pg. 4.
[14] The *Foraker Tribune* (Foraker, Oklahoma) January 17, 1908, Pg. 1
[15] The *Triangle* (Cleveland, Oklahoma) January 17, 1908, Pg. 4.
[16] The *Republican News Journal* (Newkirk, Oklahoma) January 17, 1908, Pg. 2.

Chapter 2: 1909 — The New Mexico Ride

As the oldest boy is but nine years of age and the youngest only five, the youngsters were alone on the overland trip. It deserves to be classed with the record-breakers, and the little lads to be called baby rough riders.[17]

Anxious to emulate the strenuous life and follow their father's instructions to 'toughen up,' Temple and Louis Abernathy expect to leave late today for a 1,300-mile horseback trip alone.[18]

In the summer of 1909, the Abernathy brothers embarked on their first ride: a 1,200-mile horseback journey from Guthrie, Oklahoma, to Santa Fe, New Mexico. At just 9 and 5 years old, Louis and Temple, captured the public's attention with their youth, courage and independence. This daring expedition was a test of endurance for the boys but also a demonstration of their father's belief in self-reliance and the resilience of youth.

John Abernathy, encouraged his children to embrace challenges head-on. He believed the rugged journey would "toughen them up," as he had taught them the value of perseverance in the face of hardship. This mindset mirrored the ethos of early 20th-century frontier life, where resilience and resolve were held in the highest regard.

---

[17] *Albuquerque Journal*, (Albuquerque, New Mexico) September 13, 1909, Pg. 1.
[18] *Vicksburg Evening Post* (Vicksburg, Mississippi) July 16, 1909, Pg. 7.

The Abernathy boys also reflected a parenting philosophy rooted in the rugged independence and self-reliance of the American frontier.

In an era that celebrated self-reliance, their father's decision to let them ride alone was viewed alternately as daring and reckless. Yet, for John Abernathy, teaching resilience was as natural as catching wolves barehanded.

Each item packed for the journey bore the mark of experience. From their sturdy suits to their lightweight saddles, every detail had been carefully chosen by their father. 'Sam Bass' and 'Geronimo,' and 'Wiley Haines' their trusted ponies, carried not just the boys but a legacy of adventure, having served on wolf hunts and ridden by Theodore Roosevelt himself. Clad in their sturdy ducking suits and hats, and armed with canteens and haversacks, the brothers set off on their journey, drawing curious stares and cheers from the local townsfolk. [19]

> **Abernathy's Boys to New Mexico.**
> Amarillo, Tex., Aug. 24.—Standing the long journey in fine shape Louis and Temple Abernathy, aged 7 and 5, sons of United States Marshall Abernathy, reached Tulia this morning enroute from Guthrie to Santa Fe, New Mexico. The boys were riding their father's famous horses "Sam" and "Geronimo," the former ridden by President Roosevelt in the wolf chase in the big pasture in Oklahoma four years ago.

---

[19] *The Tulsa Tribune* (Tulsa, Oklahoma) August 24, 1909, Pg. 2.

> They go alone, riding grey saddle horses, and clad in summer ducking suits, with a helmet form of head gear. The little fellows will have canteens and haversacks in which to carry water and lunch. As they make each county seat on their journey, they will first make the acquaintance of the sheriffs, that they may not be interferred with and for protection.
>
> A trip of four hundred or five hundred miles is quite an undertaking for grown men, but when boys of nine and five years undertake such a journey, unaided or unaccompanied, they certainly set a new pace, in the realm of youthful adventures, as well as exhibit a new, fine kind of metal and bravery and inheritage courage. After all it is just the kind of fettle one might expect to find in John Abernathy's male offspring. These youthful adventurers will return from Roswell by way of Amarillo and consume about six weeks on their trip.

[20]

Setting Out to New Mexico

The boys' route took them across the sweeping plains and rugged terrain of Oklahoma, the Texas Panhandle, and into New Mexico. They faced the unrelenting summer heat, dust storms, and long days

---

[20] *Daily News-Republican* (Lawton, Oklahoma) July 10, 1909, Pg. 3.

on horseback, but the boys remained unshaken. Newspapers soon caught wind of the boys, and their journey was chronicled in headlines across the country.

The Abernathy brothers were quickly nicknamed "baby rough riders,"[21] a moniker that reflected their connection to Roosevelt's legendary Rough Riders. Their exploits struck a chord with the public, embodying the adventurous spirit of the era

ABERNATHY BOYS' LONG TRIP.

Marshal's Sons, Aged 5 and 8, Start Alone on 1,300-Mile Horseback Ride.

GUTHRIE, Okla., July 10.—Anxious to emulate the strenuous life and carry out their father's instructions to "toughen up," Temple and Louis Abernathy, aged 5 and 8, respectively, sons of United States Marshal John Abernathy, left late to-day for a 1,300-mile horseback trip. They will travel alone through Oklahoma, Texas, and New Mexico, to Roswell, N. M.

Sam, the now famous cow pony mount for Roosevelt during his Oklahoma wolf hunting trip, will carry Louis. Temple will ride Geronimo. Both ponies are trained in "catching wolves alive" expeditions. The boys have been limited by their father to thirty-five miles a day.

[22]

---

[21] *Albuquerque Journal* (Albuquerque, New Mexico) September 13, 1909, Pg. 1.
[22] The *Buffalo Sunday Morning News* (Buffalo, New York) July 25, 1909. Pg. 15.

> **TWO YOUTHS WILL RIDE OVER 1,300 MILES**
>
> Guthrie, Okla., July 9.—United States Marshal Abernathy's boys, Temple, aged 5, and Louie Van, aged 8, leave here Saturday for a thirteen hundred mile horseback ride that promises to surpass President Roosevelt's stunts. They will go alone and will take the hike through Oklahoma, the Texas Panhandle and New Mexico.
>
> "Sam", the famous white horse which served as a mount for President Roosevelt when he hunted coyotes with Abernathy near Frederick, will carry Louie Van and Temple will ride Geronico. Both these horses have been used by Abernathy in catching "Wolves alive."
>
> On the trip out the boys will visit Chris Madsen's place near El Reno, and will then go straight through to Roswell, N. M. On the return they will come by way of Amarillo and through the Panhandle of Texas. The boys have been limited by their father to thirty-five miles a day. [23]

Challenges and Triumphs

Traveling unaccompanied at such a young age was and is unheard of, and the boys faced skepticism from both reporters and bystanders. Questions about their safety and their father's decision to let them travel alone often surfaced. Yet the boys' composure and

---

[23] The *Wichita Eagle* (Wichita, Kansas) July 10, 1909, Pg. 8.

competence often silenced doubters. Reports described how they handled their horses like seasoned cowboys, confidently navigating the long and treacherous trail.

Temple's tiny frame often made him look younger than his five years and one can imagine how big the world seemed to them. The journey was not without its difficulties. The boys endured harsh

---

[24] *Albuquerque Citizen* (Albuquerque, New Mexico) July 10, 1909, Pg. 1.

weather, hunger and fatigue, and there were moments when their resolve was tested. Temple, just 5 years old, sometimes needed encouragement from his older brother, but together they pushed forward.

One night, after riding for hours without finding a place to rest or a meal to eat, they simply staked their horses on the open plain and laid down under the stars. Temple, too restless to sleep, whispered to Louie about the coyotes crying in the distance — a thousand of them, he thought — but the boys reassured each other, drawing strength from their bond even as the frontier stretched endlessly around them. By the next afternoon, starving and exhausted, they finally stumbled upon a ranch house, where the kindness of strangers filled their empty bellies and restored a small piece of their courage.[25] [26]

Along the way, they stopped at ranches and small towns, where they became the center of attention. Their youthful charm and incredible story endeared them to everyone they met. People eagerly offered food, shelter, and supplies, captivated by the boys' adventures. Their father's reputation as a legendary marshal, rough rider and Roosevelt's friend also added to their mystique.

---

[25] *The Daily Oklahoman* (Oklahoma City, Oklahoma) September 23, 1909, Pg 16.
[26] *Daily News-Republican* (Lawton, Oklahoma) September 23, 1909 Pg. 1.

ABERNATHY BOYS REACH ROSWELL ON LONG TRIP

Roswell, N. M., Aug. 26.—The one riding the former hunting mount of Colonel Roosevelt and the other, a one-time steed of Geronimo, Louis and Temple Abernathy, seven and five years old, respectively, sons of United States Marshal J. R. Abernathy, of Guthrie, Okla., arrived here alone yesterday afternoon, having covered seven hundred miles of a trip planned for them by their father to make them hardy. They have been sixteen days on the road, coming by the way of Portales and Estelline, Texas. The mayor of Roswell extended the boys the freedom of the city and wired their parents of their good health and safe arrival.

---

[27] *Las Vegas Optic* (Las Vegas, New Mexico) August 26, 1909, Pg. 1.

Reaching Santa Fe

After weeks on the road, Louis and Temple reached their destination, Santa Fe, New Mexico. Their arrival was met with fanfare, as newspapers documented their journey as a nation began to notice their travels. The boys, however, seemed unfazed by the attention, viewing their trip as just another adventure.

The New Mexico ride established the Abernathy brothers' status as national figures. Their journey symbolized a soon to be bygone era, evoking admiration and nostalgia. They were no longer just the sons of a famous U.S. Marshal—they had become icons of youthful independence and courage.

They have traveled through dust, heat, and storms to reach Santa Fe, earning their place as the youngest adventurers to undertake such a feat. [28]

---

[28] *Albuquerque Journal* (Albuquerque, New Mexico) September *13, 1909*, Pg. 1.

Santa Fe, N.M.; Sept 6 – The Abernathy boys, the 7 and 5 years[29] old sons of United States Marshall John Abernathy of Oklahoma, who arrived here several days ago overland from Guthrie, Oklahoma, by the way of Roswell, N.M., resumed their overland journey this morning over the Old Santa Fe Trail, accompanied to Las Vegas by their father. From there they will travel to Guthrie by the way of Amarillo, Texas. The youngsters are very enthusiastic and feel that Doctor Cook's feat in discovering the north pole was easy. They are in the best of health. They and their father have been the guests for several days of Governor Geo. Curry and have enjoyed themselves immensely during their visit. They made as much as fifty miles a day on their trip here, camping out at night alone. Such a feat undoubtedly breaks the world's records for endurance and bravery.[30]

---

[29] NOTE: you will see many variations in their ages in the various newspaper reports..
[30] The *Dewey World* (Dewey, Oklahoma) September 9, 1909, Pg. 5.

Returning to Oklahoma

The dust of New Mexico had barely settled from their boots when Louie and Temple Abernathy, aged nine and six, embarked on the final stretch of their journey back home to Oklahoma. The brothers, who would become famed for their resilience and youthful nerve, were concluding a round-trip expedition of over 1,000 miles on horseback. The duo's return became a public sensation.

Having left Santa Fe, the boys faced the vast expanse of plains and prairie. Their saddlebags carried the bare essentials—clothes, slickers, and a handful of coins jangling in their pockets. Yet, it was their courage and camaraderie that proved to be their greatest assets. Along the way, they were embraced by ranchers and townsfolk, who marveled at their travels and offered food and stories to lighten the road ahead.

> **Abernathy Boys in Moriarty.**
> The two Abernathy boys aged 8 and 5 years who are riding horseback overland from Guthrie Oklahoma, to Santa Fe, were in Moriarty, Wednesday. The boys have been 18 days on the trip and expect to get to Santa Fe Thursday. They are the sons of U. S. Marshal Abernathy of Guthrie, Oklahoma. Their extreme youth seems to be no disadvantage to them.—Moriarty (N. M.) Messenger.

---

[31] The *Gracemont Graphic* (Gracemont, Oklahoma) September 10, 1909, Pg. 4.

The Abernathy boys mentioned in the News as reaching here last Saturday night en route home from an overland trip horseback from Guthrie, Okla., to Santa Fe and return, spent the day in the city Sunday and took in the ball games, leaving for Amarillo Monday morning. Their father is U.S. Marshal at Gutherie[32] and is the noted Oklahoma wolf hunter with whom Roosevelt made the famous chase, and Abernathy captured a lobo alive. He let his boys undertake this trip to show their endurance in the saddle. They hunt with their father and frequently go with him to Washington. They are bright little fellows and look like migets[33] on horseback but ride like men. They attracted a great deal of attention here and were shown much attention by the people who met them.[34]

---

[32] Original Spelling.
[33] Original Spelling.
[34] The *Tucumcari News & Tucumcari Times* (Tucumcari, NM) September 18, 1909, Pg. 7.

The little sons of Marshall Abernathy who made the record horseback ride from Guthrie, Okla. to Santa Fe are expected to pass

Abernathy Boys In Tucumcari On Their Long Ride Back to Oklahoma.

through Tucumcari this evening on their return ride home. As the oldest boy is but nine years of age and the youngest only five and the youngsters were alone on the overland trip it deserves to be classed with the record-breakers and the little lads to be called baby rough riders.[35]

Abernathy Boys at Memphis.

The two Abernathy boys, aged 5 and 8 years, sons of United States Marshal Abernathy of Guthrie, Oklahoma, registered at the Cobb Hotel at Memphis, Texas, Saturday night and continued their journey this morning, horseback, on their way home from their trip to Albuquerque, N. M.

[36]

"We didn't have no trouble at all comin'" said Louie to his father, as they sat in the executive mansion at Santa Fe, 'cept that we didn't git a bite to eat for more than a day once. We rode and rode and rode, until we got tired, and still, they wusn't any place to stop. Temple, he got so sleepy and tired we just

---
[35] *Albuquerque Journal* (Albuquerque, New Mexico) September 13, 1909, Pg. 1.
[36] The *Tulsa Tribune* (Tulsa, Oklahoma) September 21, 1909, Pg. 2.

staked our horses on the prairie and laid down but Temple couldn't sleep 'Louie,' he said as we lay there lookin' at the Stars and thinkin' how lonesome it was and how far we was away from home, don't you hear the coyotes a-howlin'?

They must be a thousan', I guess, but they ain't going to hurt us for they must be fifty yards away."

Next day at 3 o'clock we come to a big ranch house and we sure was hungry. They fed us and we eat like we was nearly starved to death and then pretty soon we eat some more."[37][38]

The following narrative provides additional details of their arrival in Oklahoma City,

When Louis and Temple — Abernathy aged 8 and 6 years respectively reach Oklahoma City Saturday afternoon they will have completed a journey of 3500 miles alone and accomplished an endurance feat without parallel in the annals of juvenile athletics. As a mark of appreciation Oklahoma City will extend to the youthful riders a reception with features as

---

[37] *The Daily* Oklahoman (Oklahoma City, Oklahoma) September 23, 1909, Pg 16.
[38] *Daily News-Republican* (Lawton, Oklahoma) September 23, 1909 Pg. 1.

unique as the feat the sturdy sons of the United States marshal have completed.[39] [40] [41] [42]

Boys to Speak

Plans for the reception are in the mould[43] and will be announced today. probably from the office of Mayor Scales. Tentatively, they include an outdoor greeting to be given on a Broadway Avenue corner, where a platform will have been erected. On this platform, clad in their riding habits and with the dust of travel yet on their brows, the boys will acknowledge the greeting and in short speeches touch on the 'high places' of their journey. A parade will follow, after which the boys will be permitted to bathe and change clothes in preparation for a dinner at the Threadgill in the evening. At

---

[39] The *Daily Oklahoman* (Oklahoma City, Oklahoma) 23 Sep 1909, Pg. 16.
[40] *Arkansas City Daily Traveler* (Arkansas City, Kansas) 24 Sep 1909, Pg. 3.
[41] The *Guthrie Daily Leader* (Guthrie, Oklahoma) 23 Sep 1909, Pg. 6. NOTE: This instance includes only first two paragraphs.
[42] *Arkansas City Daily Traveler* (Arkansas City, Kansas) 24 Sep 1909, Pg. 3.
[43] Original text.

this dinner speeches will be delivered by Mayor Scales, the Abernathy boys, their father and probably others. Outside the City the boys will be met by a committee who will escort them into town.

Tourists Gone Five Weeks

Five weeks ago Louie and Temple Abernathy set out on their long journey from their father's farm near Frederick, their saddles packed with clothes, slickers, drinking cups and other necessary accoutrements[44], with a few expense nickels jingling in their pockets and their youthful hearts beating with courage. Without mishap, accident, a day of sickness or a single important hindrance they reached Roswell N. M., the destination originally planned and further westward until they reached the portals of the executive mansion at Santa Fe where Governor Curry and other prominent men of the territory became their hosts. Their return journey had been void of accident but replete with incident, and the Abernathy boys are the kind to tell it.

A Hero's Welcome in Oklahoma City – both times

As the boys traversed the plains, their fame grew with each mile. From Guthrie to Santa Fe, the headlines chronicled their journey. In Oklahoma City, they were greeted by a crowd that marveled at their endurance, and by the time they reached New Mexico, the papers were declaring them adventurers and symbols of resolve.

The closer they came to Oklahoma City on the return trip, the louder the buzz of excitement grew. By September 25, 1909, the city

---

[44] Original text.

was ready for a celebration unlike any other. A reception committee comprised of prominent officials, including Mayor Scales and Fire Chief Kesler, orchestrated an elaborate welcome. A squad of mounted police and a procession of automobiles, schoolchildren, and local dignitaries met the boys as they approached Belle Isle. The scene was one of jubilation, with cheers echoing as the procession moved toward Broadway and California avenues.

> **WELCOME ABERNATHY BOYS.**
>
> **Little Sons of Oklahoma Marshal Compelting 2,500-Mile Trip.**
>
> OKLAHOMA CITY, Okla., Sept. 24.—Governor Haskell, former Governor Frantz, former Congressman Flynn, Mayor Scales and others will participate in a reception to be given here tomorrow to the eight and five-year-old sons of United States Marshal Abernathy, who will have completed a 2,500-mile trip to Santa Fe, N. M., and return. Mayor Scales will deliver the welcome address and the boys will respond.
>
> The Abernathy boys reached El Reno this evening. They are riding the horses that Theodore Roosevelt and John Abernathy rode during their coyote hunt in Oklahoma four years ago.

---

[45] The *Commercial Appeal* (Memphis, Tennessee) September 25. 1909, Pg. 2.

Bearing the trail's imprint, the boys climbed to the platform and addressed a crowd of thousands. Louie, confident and composed, expressed gratitude for the reception and reflected on their journey's highlights. Temple, visibly proud, offered a polite bow, allowing his brother to handle the crowd's adoration.

ABOVE: The Threadgill built in 1904 by Dr. John Threadgill, well-known in financial, political and old war veteran circles in Oklahoma, was for years the most prominent hotel in Oklahoma. The Abernathy boys spent the night there on their return from Santa Fe.[46]

---

[46] Oklahoma City, OK, photograph, Date Unknown; (https://gateway.okhistory.org/ark:/67531/metadc1619182/m1/1/?q=threadgill%20hotel: accessed May 28, 2023), The Gateway to Oklahoma History, https://gateway.okhistory.org; crediting Oklahoma Historical Society.

A Night of Festivities

The Abernathy brothers' first long ride culminated with a formal banquet at the historic Threadgill Hotel. Here, a gathering of Oklahoma's elite toasted the boys' success. Mayor Scales and other speakers praised them for their determination and for embodying the pioneer spirit of their homeland. As plates of fine food replaced the trail rations, they had grown accustomed to, the boys reveled in the glow of a community's admiration.

Looking back at the New Mexico Ride

This first major expedition was a precursor to even greater adventures. It demonstrated the boys' fortitude and set the tone for their future feats. Newspapers at the time described the journey in terms of grit, daring, and youthful adventure. It was more than just a horseback ride—it became a national narrative of resilience, self-reliance, and frontier spirit. While headlines of the day celebrated the boys' extraordinary courage, some contemporary voices raised concerns about the wisdom—and safety—of allowing such young children to undertake a journey through the untamed frontier alone. A modern audience might similarly question the risks involved and the parenting choices behind them.

The Abernathy brothers had shown that age was no barrier and that even youngsters could achieve incredible things with courage and determination. Their New Mexico ride captured the essence of an era when the pulse of the frontier still beat strong, and the idea of adventure was a cherished part of the American identity.

For Louis and Temple Abernathy, this was only the beginning. Their next journey would take them even farther and solidify their place in history.

> *"Anxious to emulate the strenuous life and follow their father's instructions to 'toughen up,' Temple and Louis Abernathy expect to leave late today for a 1,300-mile horseback trip alone."*[47]

The Abernathy boys rode at the cusp of change, their journey a swan song for the rugged individualism that defined the American West. As automobiles began replacing horses and cities expanded into the prairies, their New Mexico ride served as a living reminder of the courage and resolve that had carved a country from wilderness.

---

[47] The *Vicksburg Post* (Vicksburg, Mississippi) July 16, 1909, Page 7.

Chapter 3: 1910 — From Oklahoma to New York

Jumping into their big cowboy saddles unassisted and scorning aid offered by those nearby, the two who are aged six and nine years called a hearty goodbye and, with a wave of their hats, were on the road.[48]

Louis and Temple Abernathy arrived at St. Louis today, after an 800-mile ride across the country on their ponies, unaccompanied by any adult.[49]

In the spring of 1910, the Abernathy brothers, Louis, now aged 10, and Temple, aged 6, set off on another journey that folks would be talking about for generations. It would become their most notable adventure and not just because of the distance: a cross-country horseback journey from their home in Oklahoma to New York City. This trip would require them to ride over 2,500 miles to greet former President Theodore Roosevelt upon his return from a year-long safari in Africa. This would be a journey that would cement their place as national icons and prove their mettle to the world.

What began as a wild idea quickly turned into a relentless campaign. The boys' persistence wore down even their father, a man not easily impressed. And so, what might've seemed impossible for most children became the next chapter in the growing legend of the Abernathy boys.

---

[48] *Springfield News-Sun* (Springfield, Ohio) May 12, 1910, Pg. 10.
[49] *Wichita Falls Times* (Wichita Falls, Texas) April 26, 1910, Pg. 8.

Their story begins with a simple question, posed with the earnest boldness only youth can muster:

"Say pop, can me and Temp ride to New York to meet Col. Roosevelt?"

United States Marshal Jack Abernathy looked at his two sons in amazement. The older boy, Louis, a lad of ten years, stood squaring his shoulders and waiting for an answer to his question. Templeton, the younger, a little fellow only six years of age looked hard at his father.

"Say, do let us go, pop," he urged.
Marshall Abernathy found his voice:

"Why sons," he said, "you don't know what you're asking to do. New York is way over two thousand miles from here. It's a long ride and the roads are bad in spots."

"Can't be any worse than the roads we went over going to Mexico, can they, pop?" asked Louis.

"Well, I reckon they can't," replied his father with a smile, "pretty hard to find roads as bad as those anywhere. But it's a long journey and I guess you'd better not think about it."

But that did not stop Louis and Temp. According to Marshal Jack, they pestered him day and night until he said yes.[50]

After this bit of convincing, the boys' father, supported the venture wholeheartedly.

---

[50] *Fall River Globe* (Fall River, Massachusetts) August 23, 1910, Pg. 2.

The Journey Begins

On a brisk April morning, the Abernathy brothers mounted their horses—Louis on Sam and Temple on Geronimo—and waved goodbye to a cheering crowd. Local newspapers reported the boys' confident departure, emphasizing their independence for such young travelers.

Their father gave them a few parting words of advice: be cautious, stay polite, and always keep moving forward. He also provided them with ample funds, knowing that hospitality would be extended to them along the way but ensuring they could pay their way if needed.

The Abernathy brothers quickly made headlines as they traversed Oklahoma and moved into Missouri. They stopped in Oklahoma towns like Pawnee and Cleveland, where they stayed at local hotels or livery stables, and their adventures became the talk of the community.[51][52][53] The *Vinita Daily Chieftain* voiced concern over the young boys traveling alone, questioning whether they should be at home instead of on such a dangerous journey.[54] However, other papers celebrated their courage and determination, noting their enthusiasm and maturity.

---

[51] The *Tulsa Tribune* (Tulsa, Oklahoma) April 19, 1910, Pg. 4.
[52] The M'Alester News-Capital (McAlester, Oklahoma) April 18, 1910, Pg. 4.
[53] The *Springfield News-Leader* (Springfield, Missouri) April 21, 1910, Pg. 5.
[54] The *Vinita Daily Chieftain* (Vinita, Oklahoma) April 19, 1910, Pg.2.

The Pawnee Journal reported,

> Last Friday, two small lads came riding into the city from the west, and arriving in the city put their horses up at the livery barn and then repaired to the hotel for the evening. Upon inquiry they were found to be Louie and Temple Abernathy, sons of the U.S. Marshal John Abernathy, of Guthrie. The boys were on a trip to Hominy and other points in Osage county. The boys ages are six and ten years old, respectively.
>
> These two boys made a 1,500-mile ride to New Mexico last fall during the warm weather.[55]

Abernathy's Boys Here.

Last Friday, two small lads came riding into the city from the west, and arriving in the city put their horses up at the livery barn and then repaired to the hotel for the evening. Upon inquiry they were found to be Louie and Temple Abernathy, sons of U. S. Marshal John Abernathy, of Guthrie. The boys were on a trip to Hominy and other points in Osage county. The boys ages are six and ten years old, respectively.

These two boys made a 1,500 mile ride to New Mexico last fall during the warm weather.

THE JENNINGS NEWS.

Vol. X.   JENNINGS, PAWNEE COUNTY, OKLA., THURSDAY, APRIL 14, 1910.   NO. 44 [56]

A Stop in Cleveland … Oklahoma

---

[55] *Pawnee County Journal*[55] (Pawnee, Oklahoma) April 19, 1910, Pg. 1.

[56] NOTE: Newspaper Mast for the *Pawnee Journal* containing clipping shows the "Jennings News"

Just a day later, the boys rode into Cleveland, Oklahoma, where they stayed with a fellow named Ed Perry. The local paper described them as having a grand old time, riding through the countryside and enjoying every bit of their journey. This was the second of the long horseback rides that were becoming a regular thing for the Abernathy boys. The *Daily Oklahoman* reported,[57]

> **The Abernathy boys, Louie and Temple, the ten and six year old sons of United States Marshal John Abernathy of Oklahoma City, who are making the trip from Oklahoma to New York on horseback to assist in welcoming Colonel Roosevelt on his return from Africa, arrived in Columbus Friday and were the guests of Mayor George E. Marshall of the "Arch City" during their stay.**

The young sons of United States Martial John Abernathy, of Guthrie, passed through this city. Friday, on their way to Pawhuska. The youngsters were on horseback and had come from Guthrie that way. This is only one of their long horseback jaunts which they enjoy making over the country. They seemed to be having a good time. While in Cleveland the boys were the guests of Mr. Ed Perry.[58]

---

[57] The *Daily Oklahoman* (Oklahoma City, Oklahoma) May 15, 1910, Pg. 31.
[58] The *Cleveland Enterprise* (Cleveland, Oklahoma) April 15, 1910, Pg. 5.

> Louis said the reason he and his brother are making the long trip from Frederick, Okla., to St. Louis is because they had never been to a city larger than Guthrie and Oklahoma City. They wanted to see a real big city. He said they pleaded a long time with their father before receiving his consent to make the trip.[59]

The boys often shared their thoughts with the local press in a straightforward manner,

> The boys on reaching here Monday evening took their horses to a local livery stable and saw that the steeds were properly fed and then went to the Metropolitan hotel, where they registered and later ordered supper from the menu card with the ease of experienced travelers. The boys were not fatigued over their long journey and seemed to be enjoying themselves. They visited the post office, where they received a letter from their father, and later they took in a moving picture show.
> Louis, the elder of the two, is spokesman for the riders. He answered The Republican interviewer's questions as readily as do statesmen who make it a business of having themselves interviewed. When asked what he thought of Springfield, the little fellow replied:
> "Springfield is a pretty good town, but I can't say I like it as well as Frederick, Okla. I certainly like Oklahoma. Missouri is a pretty nice country."

---

[59] The *Springfield News-Leader* (Springfield, Missouri) April 21, 1910, Pg. 5.

WANTS TO HITCH ON SQUARE
Young Abernathy thought that the public square was a great thing for the city, but he wanted to know why there wasn't a hitching-post in the middle. The boy was disappointed in the Ozarks. He expected them to be as large as the Rockies and to be covered with snow. He volunteered the information that the Springfield streets were kept much cleaner than those of Joplin, which place he left last Sunday.[60]

It took just a few seconds for Louie and Temple Abernathy—aged ten and six, respectively—to answer the question posed during a stop in St. Louis: *Cowpuncher or President?* Without hesitation, both boys chose the cowboy life.

As the boys rested in St. Louis, their calico ponies recovering on baled hay, preparations were already underway for the second leg of their journey. The boys, meanwhile, took in the "joys of city life," but made it clear they had no plans to trade in the saddle for a politician's chair. They voiced open scorn for governors and mayors "whose knowledge of horsemanship is confined to riding a swivel chair and shooting an occasional manifesto."

> **Abernathy Boys Voice Contempt for Swivel Chairs Mayors Ride.**
>
> Would Rather Be Cowboys Than President and "Busting" Street Cars and Autos Has Them Both Dead Tired.

---

[60] The *Springfield News-Leader* (Springfield, Missouri) April 21, 1910, Pg. 5.

> *It required just two seconds for Louie and Temple Abernathy, 10 and 6 years old, sons of John K. Abernathy, famed as the "catch 'em alive" wolf hunter, and friend of former President Roosevelt, to chorus a preference for the former vocation yesterday. Louie and his brother have been tasting the joys of city life while their trusty calico cayuses are regalling on baled hay and priming for the second lap of their jaunt across the United States to New York, where the youngsters are to meet Bwana Tumbo on his return from the big hunt. They will start east to-day.*

Even the thrill of the trip sometimes proved more exhausting than exhilarating. A single day's itinerary left them, in their own words, "completely fagged out." It had included a trip aboard the tug *Echo* of the steamer *Bald Eagle*, a chauffeured automobile tour with St. Louis Mayor Kreismann through the parks and residential districts, a visit to department stores, and a lively game of "pirates" in the lobby of the Hotel Jefferson. They were accompanied on the tour by city officials and distant relatives, who marveled at the boys' stamina and poise.[61]

---

[61] *St. Louis Globe-Democrat* (St. Louis, Missouri) April 28, 1910, Pg. 7.

> **ABERNATHY BOYS AT RICHLAND MO.**
>
> Richland, Mo, April 23.—The two sons of John Abernathy, U. S. Marshal of the Western District of Oklahoma, passed through here today on their horseback trip from Oklahoma to St. Louis. The two expect to reach St. Louis tomorrow.

The Ride to St. Louis

By April 25, the boys trotted into St. Louis to a mixture of disbelief and admiration from the locals. Temple, riding his trusty Indian pony, and Louis, on a full-sized horse, were greeted with curious onlookers gathering at the livery stable. The local newspaper noted their uncanny confidence:

> *"These young cowboys rode into the city as though born in the saddle, tipping their hats to ladies and greeting gentlemen with a firm handshake."*

---

[62] Oklahoma City Daily Pointer (Oklahoma City, Oklahoma) April 23, 1910, Pg. 1.

> **ABERNATHY BOYS IN ST. LOUIS.**
>
> **One-Third of Their Horseback Journey to Meet Mr. Roosevelt Is Completed.**
>
> St. Louis, April 26.—Louis and Temple Abernathy, 10 and 6 years old, sons of John Abernathy, United States marshal at Guthrie, Ok., rode into St. Louis last night on their horseback trip from Frederick, Ok., across the continent to New York.
>
> Their arrival marked the completion of about one-third of their journey to greet ex-President Roosevelt when he lands at New York June 16. They will leave for Chicago tomorrow. [63]

While in the city, they were invited to a reception at the mayor's office, where Temple famously impressed a group of dignitaries with his straightforward explanation of their method of navigation: *"We inquiah,*[64]*"* he said with a slight grin, drawing laughter from the room. Their method was simple—ask locals for directions and trust the kindness of strangers to guide their way. The mayor's secretary later remarked, "These boys have more poise than most men I've met." Newspapers from Wichita Falls, Texas to Buffalo, New York covered their story, noting their plan to ride all the way to New York to greet former President Roosevelt upon his return from Africa. It was reported,

---

[63] The *Kansas City Star* (Kansas City, Missouri) April 26, 1910, Pg. 4.
[64] Original Text- Probably means "We inquire,"

> *Louis and Temple Abernathy arrived at St. Louis today after an 800-mile ride across the country on their ponies, unaccompanied by any adult.*[65]

Some things were written with sarcasm or even a derogatory tone. Criticism came from many papers including the *Vinita Daily Chieftain*, which stated the boys should be at home with their mother at night,[66] while others commented on either politics and/or Abernathy family business.

> *Those Abernathy boys are having a hard time of it riding over the country breaking records, but the boys from five to ten might as well be at home with mama when night comes on.* [67] [68]

> *The McAlester News-Capital. Republican in politics but unusually sensible and discriminating, is neither enamored of nor closely affiliated with rough rider politics and*

---

[65] *Wichita Falls Times* (Wichita Falls, Texas) April 26, 1910, Pg. 8.
[66] *Vinita Daily Chieftain*, (Vinita, Oklahoma) April 19, 1910, Pg. 2.
[67] The *Vinita Daily Chieftain* (Vinita, Oklahoma) April 19, 1910, Pg. 2.
[68] The Weekly Chieftain (Vinita, Oklahoma) April 22, 1910, Pg. 4.

as an evidence of its objection to cheap rough-rider publicity we reproduce this from its issue of April 18.⁶⁹

The Abernathy boys are making another long trip horseback to draw attention away from the troubles their pa is having with their new ma.⁷⁰ ⁷¹

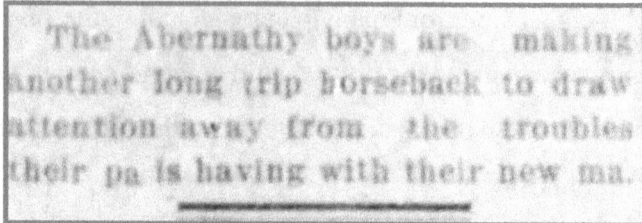

The Nation Begins to Take Notice

By the end of April, the Abernathy boys ride had become national news. Their story was covered by newspapers across the country, from The *St. Joseph Observer* to The *Edina Sentinel.* Their journey inspired admiration and highlighted the distinct contrast between their rugged determination and the more sedate ambitions of other travelers of the era.

---

[69] *Tulsa Daily Democrat* (Tulsa, Oklahoma) April 19, 1910, Pg. 1.
[70] The *M'Alester News-Capital* (McAlester, Oklahoma) April 18, 1910, Pg. 4.
[71] *Tulsa Daily Democrat* (Tulsa, Oklahoma) April 19, 1910, Pg. 1.

> **Abernathy Boys in St. Louis.**
>
> St. Louis, April 25.—The two sons of United States Marshal Abernathy of Oklahoma reached here today after an 800-mile ride across country on their ponies. The boys, aged 9 and 7, were unaccompanied on their long ride.

[72]

As their journey continued, commentary often discussed their courage, resilience, and an unwavering commitment to their goals and the nature of the journey.

Beginning with Mayor Frederick Kreisman of St. Louis, Mr. Abernathy has received letters from nearly every city executive in all the towns visited by the boys on their trip. All are very complimentary and speak of the boys' manliness and courage. Mothers have written him offering the boys a home in after years should circumstances make them homeless.[73]

In St. Louis, their story gained even more traction. The boys were swarmed by reporters and curious onlookers who admired their small frames and determined expressions. In St. Louis, Temple was overwhelmed by kindergarten teachers offering him paper dolls.[74]

---

[72] *Wichita Falls Times* (Wichita Falls, Texas) April 26, 1910, Pg. 8.
[73] The *Daily Oklahoman* (Oklahoma City, Oklahoma) May 15, 1910, Pg. 31.
[74] The *Nebraska State Journal* (Lincoln, Nebraska) April, 27, 1910, Pg. 1.

The boys' journey continually inspired admiration, with one newspaper calling their rides a feat that men of mature years would hesitate to undertake.[75]

YOUTHFUL OKLAHOMANS RIDE FORTH TO MEET ROOSEVELT

St. Louis, April 27.—Temple Abernathy, 6, son of United States Marshal "Catch-'Em-Alive" John K. Abernathy of Oklahoma, who, with his brother, Louie, 10, is riding horseback from their home to New York to be on hand when former President Roosevelt returns home, had the scare of his life today when a swarm of kindergarten teachers swooped down on him in a local hotel and threatened to bring out some paper dolls for him to play with.

The Abernathy boys are making the trip entirely alone. One of the kindergarteners asked Temple how they found their way, and he replied: "We inquiah." Temple is riding an Indian pony, but his brother rides a full-sized horse. They expect to reach Cincinnati within a few days.

The boys' father counts Roosevelt as one of his best friends and acted as a guide to the former president on his last western hunting trip.

---

[76] [77]

Meeting Civic Leaders Along the Way

By May, the Abernathy boys had reached Cincinnati, where they were warmly received by local dignitaries. Mayor Schwab personally greeted them and arranged for their stay at the Sinton Hotel, where the

---

[75] *Press Herald*, (Pine Grove Pennsylvania) May 27 1910, Pg. 1.
[76] The *Nebraska State Journal* (Lincoln, Nebraska) April 27, 1910, Pg. 1.
[77] The *Omaha Daily News* (Omaha, Nebraska) April 28, 1910, Pg. 3.

boys marveled at the luxury and the attention they received. Local papers described their polite demeanor and sense of purpose, which impressed everyone they met.

> **TO GREET ROOSEVELT.**
>
> Special to The Beacon.
>
> Guthrie, Ok., May 9.—Dispatches received here state that Louis and Temple Abernathy aged ten and six respectively, sons of United States Marshal John Abernathy of Oklahoma, have reached Cincinnati on their journey from Guthrie horseback to New York to greet President Roosevelt upon his return to America. The boys expect to reach New York by June 16. The Abernathy boys recently made a trip on horseback from Guthrie to New Mexico and return.

[78]

---

[78] The *Wichita Beacon* (Wichita, Kansas) May 9, 1910, Pg.1.

ABERNATHY BOYS ARE GOING TO MEET TEDDY

Cincinnati May 7 — Louis and Temple Abernathy aged ten and six years, respectively, sons of United States Marshal Abernathy of Oklahoma reached Cincinnati today on their journey horseback to greet Col. Roosevelt upon his return to America They say that just as soon as they see the former president they will go back to Oklahoma.

Both boys were met this afternoon at the outskirts of the city by Police Lieutenant Branagan and conducted to the office of Mayor Schwab, where they told the official that they are having a great time on their trip and are making it according to their schedule. Both lads went later to Charles P. Taft's Sinton hotel and registered. They said this evening that they expect to get into New York by June 16 and that they will start on the trip back home about the first of July.

Both boys were well equipped with money Their father, the particular favorite of Roosevelt among the Rough Riders, is said to have told his boys to get out into the world for a little airing, and to have provided them with their means of travel.[79]

Mayor Schwab reached City Hall before 9 o'clock Monday to bid farewell to the Abernathy boys, Louie and Temple, who are riding

---

[79] *Morning Examiner* (Bartlesville, Oklahoma) May 8, 1910, Pg. 1.

horseback from Guthrie, Okla., to New York City, to greet Col. Roosevelt. A police escort took them to the eastern boundary of the city. Their route will be along the line of the B. & O.S.W. Railroad.

The boys expect to reach New York City June 16. They will be joined by their father.

They went to Sunday School with Mayor's Secretary Evans and later were taken for rides in Dick Witt's fast motor boat, and on the ponies at the Zoo. What they enjoyed most were rides on the inclined planes.[80]

BOY TRAVELERS END CIN'TI VISIT

Mayor Schwab reached City Hall before 9 o'clock Monday to bid farewell to the Abernathy boys, Louie and Temple, who are riding horseback from Guthrie, Okla., to New York City, to greet Col. Roosevelt. A police escort took them to the eastern boundary of the city. Their route will be along the line of the B. & O. S. W. Railroad.

The boys expect to reach New York City June 16. They will be joined by their father.

They went to Sunday School with Mayor's Secretary Evans and later were taken for rides in Dick Witt's fast motor boat, and on the ponies at the Zoo. What they enjoyed most were rides on the inclined planes.

---

[80] The *Kentucky Post and Times-Star* (Covington, Kentucky) May 9, 1910, Pg. 1.

Cincinnati, Ohio, May 7. — *(Special)* United States Marshal Abernathy of Oklahoma today wired his two little boys, who are here on their way by horseback to Washington, to greet the president and then go to New York to greet Col. Theodore Roosevelt upon his return to this country, a unique message. Louis Abernathy received the message this morning at the Sinton hotel and after a long "conference" with Temple, aged 6, gave it out for publication. It reads:

"You are great boys. I am proud of you. Do not leave until Monday; it is not right to ride on Sunday. Be good boys as I know you will. Do not ride too hard. Write every day. Wire often."

"Father sends us a message every day telling us that he thinks we're making a great record," said Louis this afternoon. "We want to do so, if we can, so as to make him feel that we're trying to do right. We expect to see Colonel Roosevelt in New York and tell him that our papa still thinks he's one of the greatest men who ever lived. Then we'll go back to Oklahoma."[81] [82]

---

[81] The *Daily Oklahoman* (Oklahoma City, Oklahoma) May 8, 1910, Pg. 2.
[82] T*ulsa World* (Tulsa, Oklahoma) May 11, 1910, Pg. 1.

> The two Abernathy boys of Guthrie, aged respectively 10 and 6 years, are on their way horseback to greet Col. Roosevelt at New York. They are now at Cincinnatti. Pretty plucky boys. Last summer they rode to El Paso and return.

[83]

---

[83] The *Daily Midget* (Kingfisher, Oklahoma) May 7, 1910, Pg. 3.

Oklahoma Boys on 2,000 Mile Ride to Greet Colonel Roosevelt

Louis and Temple Abernathy, sons of United States Marshal Abernathy of Oklahoma. Picture was taken in Cincinnati during their trip.

Cincinnati, May 19.—The two small sons of United States Marshal John Abernathy, who are making a 2,000 mile horseback journey from Guthrie, Oklahoma, to New York to meet Colonel Roosevelt, are now several days out of this city. Despite bad weather they are making rapid progress, and expect to reach New York long before the ex-president arrives.

The boys are Temple, aged six, and Louis, ten. They have journeyed over the whole south alone and are the pride of the southwest. They left Oklahoma City April 15, arriving in St. Louis 10 days later. They passed through here in a happy mood. They had no maps and trust to people along the way to direct them properly.

Marshal Abernathy and Colonel Roosevelt are close friends. Abernathy won fame as a wolf catcher by "catching them alive." He has no fear of them, but they soon began to avoid him.

Abernathy intended going abroad with Roosevelt.

The boys have been receiving royal welcome at all points along the route. There will be a celebration of a large part of Oklahoma when they return to Guthrie. It is expected that the return trip will also be made on horseback.

Youthful Travelers, who are en route from Oklahoma to New York to greet ex-President Roosevelt.

---

[84] *Ottumwa Semi-Weekly Courier* (Ottumwa, Iowa) May 21, 1910, Pg. 6.
[85] The *Journal-Press* (Lawrenceburg, Indiana) May 19, 1910, Pg. 5.

At Dayton, they were met by Mayor and Mrs. Edward F. Burkhart, and entertained at the Atlas hotel. After an automobile tour, they were taken on a "joy ride in the air" on the aeroplanes of the Wright brothers at Wright Aviation Field, by Wilbur Wright.

"They're not as big as 17 cents," was the remark of Mayor Schwab of Cincinnati when he first saw them. The mayor wired their father after the boys' departure, "You certainly have a pair of boys

you can be proud of." A big article in the *Cincinnati Enquirer* by Rudolph Benson was headed by a big picture of the boys taken on Vine Street on their horses and a great crowd of spectators about them.

In Columbus Ohio, Mayor and Mrs. Marshall took the boys to call on Gov. Judson Harmon, followed by an auto ride. The boys stated they were much impressed with the High Arches on High Street. Among other things of interest to the boys was a review of the Columbus High School Cadets on the State House lawn Friday night. They saw Indianola Saturday.[86]

Mr. Abernathy, father of the boys, had a lengthy telegram from his sons stating extensive preparations had been made by Mayor Marshall and the members of the executive committee of the new club for their entertainment, and that they would be the guests of the Mayor Friday night and Saturday, when they expected to push eastward, arriving in Zanesville, Ohio, Sunday morning.[87]

Challenges on the Trail

The journey was not without hardships. The boys encountered severe weather, including a snowstorm in Sullivan, Missouri, which tested their endurance. The storm forced the boys to huddle beneath their blankets under the shelter of a large oak tree. The local paper reported.

With the temperature plummeting, they huddled together under a thin blanket. The wind howled, and frost formed on their saddles.

---

[86] The *Daily Oklahoman* (Oklahoma City, Oklahoma) May 15, 1910, Pg. 31.
[87] The *Daily Oklahoman* (Oklahoma City, Oklahoma) May 15, 1910, Pg. 31.

'We'll make it, Temp,' Louis assured his brother, though his own hands were numb and his voice shook. By morning, they emerged from their makeshift camp, cold but determined to continue.

> *The Abernathy boys, aged 6 and 10 years, spent last Saturday night in Sullivan and left Sunday morning in the snowstorm. "We're not cold; we're just toughening up," Louis reportedly quipped to a passerby who expressed concern.*[88]

> Last year these small boys rode over half a dozen states, in the southwest. Such an occurrence as a rainstorm or a big wind does not perturb them in the least. They are true sons of the out-of-door theory, and show their birthright by ability to take care of themselves al-, though hundreds of miles from home and on their own resources excepting the remittances which they receive by drawing on their father by bank drafts.—Cincinnati Enquirer, May 2.[89]

The sheer physicality of their journeys was a challenge in itself. Riding 40 to 50 miles a day, the boys grew weary, their small hands gripping the reins and their bodies aching from hours in the saddle. But Louis and Temple were toughened up in the saddle, had been taught to persevere, and each day they mounted their horses with renewed resolve, eager to conquer another stretch of the trail.

---

[88] *Sullivan Sentinel,* (Sullivan, MO) April 29, 1910, Pg. 5.
[89] The Daily Oklahoman (Oklahoma City, Oklahoma) May 11, 1910, Pg. 16.

"Since leaving their home in Oklahoma the little fellows have been traveling unaccompanied and averaged about fifty miles per day."[90]

> **Abernathy Boys Ride 128 Miles.**
> Oklahoma City, May 21.—United States Marshal John Abernathy today received a message from the elder of his two boys in Wheeling, W. Va., which indicates that the boys rode 128 miles, the distance between Newark, Ohio, and Wheeling, yesterday. This is a record-breaking journey and probably required most of the night.

[91]

Wheeling, W. Va., May 18 — (Special) — Louis and Temple Abernathy arrived at Wheeling Tuesday evening, both in good condition with the exception of a slight cold contracted by the younger boy. They covered sixty miles Tuesday, leaving Cambridge, Ohio, in the morning. They made one stop for dinner.

---

[90] The *Tulsa Tribune* (Tulsa, Oklahoma) June 6, 1910, Pg. 1.
[91] *Tulsa Weekly Democrat* (Tulsa, Oklahoma) May 21, 1910, Pg. 7.

The boys were royally received by the proprietor of the Hotel McLure, Mayor Schmidt and other prominent citizens. A curious crowd assembled in the lobby. The boys were given a hearty meal and later were sent to bed.

Wednesday they were shown about town and both proved bright and interesting talkers, being acquainted with the ways of the people and the geographical outlay of the section. They have made quite an impression here and are the talk of the town.

Their clothes were wet and soiled, owing to travel in the rain, and new garments were secured for them here and both were made comfortable. An automobile trip through the surrounding territory in the morning helped out on the plan of entertainment. They will receive the attention of both the Elks order and Masonic order while in the city.

They will remain here until Thursday, when they start for Washington, going by way of Washington, Pa., over the national road to Cumberland, and through to the capital, where they will meet President Taft, thence they go to New York to greet Roosevelt upon his return.[92]

ABERNATHY BOYS NEAR WASHINGTON

Cumberland, Md., May 23.—(Special.)—Louis and Temple Abernathy arrived here this evening after a thirty mile ride during the day. The boys made a thirty-six mile trip Saturday, and a forty mile trip Friday. It is expected they will arrive in Washington, D. C., some time Wednesday. Thence after a short stay and a visit to the president they will go to New York to meet Col. Roosevelt upon his return.[93]

---

[92] The *Daily Oklahoman* (Oklahoma City, Oklahoma) May 19, 1910, Pg 1.
[93] The *Daily Oklahoman* (Oklahoma City, Oklahoma) May 24, 1910, Pg. 13.

> The front page of several leading dailes bore last week an important special, announcing the fact that the Abernathy boys, in their cross country jaunt, had stopped long enough to wash their faces and change shirts. Wouldn't it have been horrible had not that thrilling event been duly chronicled![94]

> The Abernathy boys, who are on their way horseback from Oklahoma City to New York, are being given warm receptions all thro the east. The fact of their being 10 and 6 years and travelling alone is winning the admiration of all easterners. This is only a sample of the metal Oklahoma boys are made of. Hardy and unafraid, they plunge into the world to battle, fighting and overcoming all obstacles.[95]

---

[94] The *Purcell Register* (Purcell, Oklahoma) May 27, 1910, Pg. 27.
[95] The *Butler News* (Butler, Oklahoma) May 20, 1910, Pg. 2.

> **ABERNATHY BOYS' LONG RIDE.**
>
> **They Travel From Oklahoma to New York City Alone.**
>
> New York City.—Wearing grins as broad as their hats, Louis and Temple Abernathy, the young sons of "Jack" Abernathy, finished the last lap of their horseback ride alone from Oklahoma City, Okla., when they dismounted from their broncos at the door of the Hotel Breslin amid the applause of several thousand persons.
>
> The two boys, ten and six years old, started from their Oklahoma home on April 16, and have ridden across the continent, a feat that men of mature years would hesitate to undertake. They are here with their father to welcome former President Roosevelt. [96]

As Louis and Temple Abernathy traversed the country, their story spread like wildfire. From the plains of Oklahoma to the bustling avenues of Washington D.C., their adventure captivated a nation eager for tales of daring and youthful exuberance. With each hoofbeat, their fame galloped ahead of them, carried on the backs of thousands of newspapers across the country.

Over seventy newspapers from New York to Arkansas featured stories about the Abernathy boys' ride into the nation's capital. Headlines screamed their feats, such as 'Abernathy Boys Ride Into History'

---

[96] *Pine Grove Herald* (Pine Grove, Pennsylvania) May 27, 1910, Pg. 6.

and 'Young Cowboys Meet the President.' Each paper added its own flair to the tale, ensuring that readers across the nation followed every twist and turn of their journey.

In an era before radio waves and television screens, newsprint was the lifeline of the American news. Local papers, from the bustling metropolises to the quietest hamlets, chronicled the boys' journey with enthusiasm that bordered on reverence. From the *Potosi Journal*[97] in Missouri to the *Muskogee County Republican*[98], their story leapt from one front page to another. The Abernathy boys weren't just crossing miles—they were weaving their legend into the very fabric of the nation.

The boys' journey became a beacon of possibility, uniting readers in awe and debate. Was it sheer pluck, naivete, or something else? Letters to editors and opinion columns offered a cacophony of praise, critique, and speculation. Their exploits were often recorded in a fashion which reminded people of a rugged, adventurous spirit that resonated deeply in the collective American psyche.

The 2000-mile journey culminated with a stop in Washington, D.C. before continuing on to New York. While in the nation's capital where the boys would be granted an audience with President William Howard Taft and speak before congress. The president, captivated by

---

[97] *Potosi Journal* (Potosi, Missouri) Jun 1, 1910, Pg. 2.
[98] *Muskogee County Republican* and *Fort Gibson Post* (Fort Gibson, Oklahoma), Jul 7, 1910, Pg. 4.

their story, was reportedly so impressed with their determination that he cleared his schedule to meet them.

> **The solemn interest with which a horseback ride of 110 miles in three days is contemplated must seem something of a joke to those Abernathy kids.** [99]

A Nation's Fascination

The Abernathy brothers' ride from Oklahoma to New York with a visit to Washington sparked nationwide fascination. Newspapers across the country chronicled their every move, marveling at their courage and independence. In an era when tales of travel and exploration were becoming increasingly rare, the boys' journey served as a nostalgic reminder of the pioneer spirit that had once defined America.

The press played a pivotal role in the Abernathy brothers' rise to fame. Newspapers from coast to coast chronicled their journey in breathless detail, with headlines like 'America's Youngest Adventurers' grabbing the headlines. Reporters eagerly sought interviews, and the boys' father received letters from admirers offering homes and scholarships for the brothers should they ever need them.

The 1910 ride remains one of the most unique youthful feats in the history of our nation. The Abernathy brothers' journey became a media sensation, resonating deeply in a nation hungry for tales of

---

[99] *Evening star* (Washington, District of Columbia) May 31, 1910, Pg. 1.

youthful adventure and resilience. As the boys galloped their way into Washington, D.C., their story unfolded in the headlines of countless newspapers across America. For a brief moment, they were the stars of an American epic, proving that even the smallest among us could capture the largest audiences.

Chapter 4: 1910 — Visiting the Nation's Capital

President Taft shook hands today with the two little Oklahoma horsemen who have ridden all the way from the west to be in New York in time to greet ex-President Roosevelt upon his return from abroad. [100]

Temple and I want to see some of the animals Mr. Roosevelt sent from Africa, and tomorrow we will go over to the Smithsonian to see if we can have a look at them. [101] [102] [103]

Arriving in Washington, D.C

After weeks on the road, enduring snowstorms and bad or nonexistent roads, the boys found themselves at the epicenter of American political power. Their determination and charm had already captured the hearts of townsfolk and newspaper readers across the nation, and now it was time to impress the President of the United States, William Howard Taft.

Newspaper coverage of their arrival in Washington continued to expand and included publications such as *The Kirksville Graphic*[104] (Kirksville, Missouri), *The Prescott Daily News*[105] (Prescott, Arkansas), *and The Payne County Farmer*[106] (Yale, Oklahoma), among others. This was one of the more numerous announcements about

---

[100] *Evening Star,* (Washington D.C.) May 31, 1910, Pg. 1.
[101] The Daily Oklahoman (Oklahoma City, Oklahoma) May 28, 1910, Pg. 1.
[102] *Detroit Free Press* (Detroit, Michigan) May 28, 1910, Pg. 2.
[103] *Morning Examiner* (Bartlesville, Oklahoma) May 29, 1910, Pg. 1.
[104] The *Kirksville Graphic* (Kirksville, Missouri) May 27, 1910, Pg. 9.
[105] The *Prescott Daily News* (Prescott, Arkansas) May 30, 1910, Pg 1.
[106] *Payne County Farmer* (Yale, Oklahoma) June 1, 1910 Pg. 5.

their travels. For a full list of newspapers announcing their arrival in Washington, see Appendix 2.

> **Abernathy Boys in Washington**
>
> Washington.—After riding on horseback most of the way across the continent to meet Col. Roosevelt on his arrival at New York, Louie and Temple Abernathy, aged 9 and 6 respectively, sons of "Jack" Abernathy of Oklahoma, the wolf catcher and friend of the former president, arrived in the national capital Friday.

The Bartlesville, Oklahoma *Morning Examiner*[107] noted,

> "After riding on horseback most of the way across the continent to meet Colonel Roosevelt... Louie and Temple Abernathy... arrived in the national capital tonight. They rode in from Frederick, Maryland, today, a distance of 57 miles." While Temple was fast asleep under the crisp, white hotel covers, Louis regaled reporters with tales of their adventure. "Temple and I want to see some of the animals Mr. Roosevelt sent from Africa," Louis remarked. "Tomorrow we will go over to the Smithsonian to see if we can have a look at some of them."

---

[107] *Morning Examiner* (Bartlesville, Oklahoma) May 29, 1910, Pg. 1.

As they trotted down Pennsylvania Avenue, the boys caught the attention of bustling city crowds. The clatter of their ponies' hooves against the cobblestones was a sharp contrast to the polished automobiles and streetcars that filled the capital's streets. News of their arrival had reached the city long before they did. Onlookers paused to marvel at the young cowboys, their dusty attire a stark juxtaposition to the formal suits and dresses of Washington's elite.

On a crisp May morning, Louis and Temple Abernathy, dressed in their finest travel clothes and sporting Shriner buttons in their coat lapels, waited eagerly outside the White House. They had no formal appointment, but as their story had preceded them, President Taft himself requested to meet the young travelers. When the President finally greeted them, he bent down to shake their hands and laughed heartily as Temple confidently declared,

> ***"We've ridden all this way to see you and Mr. Roosevelt. What else were we supposed to do?"***

The meeting lasted only a short time, but the boys left an impression. Taft later commented to his aides, "They're proof of what this country's youth can accomplish—courage and determination in the saddle of an untamed land."[108]

The boys rode up Pennsylvania Avenue, their ponies trotting confidently toward the White House gates. Onlookers were both amused and amazed at the sight of the two diminutive cowboys navigating the

---

[108] *Evening Star,* (Washington D.C.) May 31, 1910, Pg. 1.

bustling streets of the capital. Here is one account of their arrival in Washington:

After riding on Horseback most of the way across the continent to meet Colonel Roosevelt and his arrival at New York, Louie and Temple Abernathy aged 9 and 6, respectively, Sons of "Jack" Abernathy of Oklahoma, the wolf catcher and friend of the former president, arrived in the national capital tonight. They rode in from Frederick Maryland today a distance of 57 miles. Temple dropped off to sleep the minute his head touched the pillow. Well, the little fellow was curled up restfully under the white cover while Louie talked of their trip.

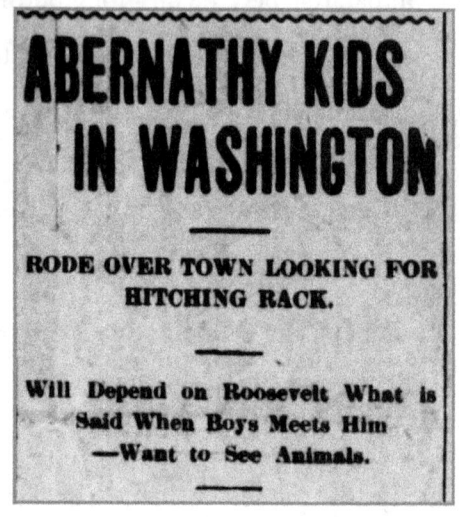

"*Temple and I.*" *he said, "want to see some of the animals Mr. Roosevelt sent from Africa and tomorrow we will go over to the Smithsonian Institution to see if we can have a look at some of them."*

When he asked what he intended to say to Mr. Roosevelt when he met him in New York, Louie replied, it would depend on what Mr.

Roosevelt said to them and that he could not cross that fence until he came to it. President Taft will receive the two little travelers.

When the boys arrived in Washington they rode up and down Pennsylvania Avenue for some time looking for a "wagon yard" where they might tie up horses. Not finding such a convenience in the national capital they finally stopped at one of the best hotels and their horses were taken to a nearby livery. The boys will remain here several days.[109] [110]

Announcing their intention of staying several days longer in Washington to see all the sights, the Abernathy boys, Louis, aged nine, and Temple, aged six, who are traveling on horseback from their home in Oklahoma to New York to meet Col. Theodore Roosevelt when he reaches this country, are preparing to thoroughly

---

[109] *Detroit Free Press* (Detroit, Michigan) May 28, 1910, Pg. 2.
[110] *Morning Examiner* (Bartlesville, Oklahoma) May 29, 1910, Pg. 1.

enjoy themselves. Yesterday they received new suits of clothes from their father, Marshal John Abernathy, and immediately got into their "new rags." The boys announced their intention of going to see President Taft.

"I'll call him Bill." said Louie. "We always called Roosevelt 'Teddy,' and I guess we can call Taft 'Bill.[111]

"We've had a bully day," said 9-year-old Louis Abernathy, who with his 6-year-old brother Temple is traveling on horseback from Oklahoma to New York. "Washington is a dandy place. We are going to stay here a few more days. It goes without saying the youngsters are having the time of their lives. Early yesterday, both of the boys received new suits of brown clothing and light blue waistcoats from their father, Marshal John Abernathy, who is prominently known in this city, and the new 'rags,' as they called them, created a favorable impression. Attired in their 'Sunday' clothing, the boys left the Raleigh Hotel right after breakfast to 'do' town, and though they were weary lads last night, they had enough energy left to pay a visit to the Congressional Library in the evening.

They'll See All the Sights

It is the intention of the boys from the 'wild and woolly' to see everything worth seeing in Washington before taking their departure. And there isn't the least doubt that the youngsters will cuddle up to the President just the same as if they had known him for years. When

---

[111] *Evening Star* (Washington, District of Columbia) May 30, 1910, Pg.16.

up yesterday, the lads enjoyed themselves somewhat to the discomfiture of others, engaging in a pillow fight in their room on the eighth floor of the Raleigh. Late in the afternoon, they wrestled with each other in a friendly way, and at 5 o'clock hurried to the dinner table. They are never late for meals. Rosy-cheeked and healthy, the boys are ever on the move. The morning was spent in sightseeing from a 'rubberneck' wagon, and the afternoon in looking at moving picture shows.

Old Friend Calls on Them

Central Office Detective O'Brien paid a visit to the boys yesterday. He was recognized by the younger of the two as soon as he entered the room. Three years ago, the detective accompanied the lads from this city to Oklahoma. The youngsters will continue their journey to New York about the middle of the week, stopping in Baltimore, Wilmington, Philadelphia, Trenton, New Brunswick, and Newark on the way. "We only stop at the best hotels," said Louie. "Dad foots the bills." L.H. Winkler, a special writer for a New York morning paper, arrived last evening and will make the balance of the trip to New York with them.[112] [113]

---

[112] The *Washington Post* (Washington, District of Columbia) May 30, 1910, Pg. 11.
[113] The *Shawnee Daily Herald* (Shawnee, Oklahoma) May 28, 1910, Pg. 1.

ABERNATHY BOYS, HUNTED WASHINGTON, FOR A WAGON YARD TO STABLE THEIR PONIES

Louis and Temple Abernathy, eight and six years old, and their horses, on which they have nearly completed a 2,000 mile ride from Frederick, Okla., to New York, where they are coming to greet Col. Roosevelt on his arrival from Europe. The two boys have made the entire trip alone. Their father is a United States Marshal and a personal friend of Col. Roosevelt.

---

[114] *Morning Examiner* (Bartlesville, Oklahoma) May 29, 1910, Pg. 1.

Abernathy Boys In Washington Look For Place to Tie Horses

WASHINGTON, D. C., May 27.— After riding on horseback most of the way across the continent to meet Colonel Roosevelt on his arrival at New York, Louie and Temple Abernathy, aged nine and six respectively, sons of "Jack" Abernathy of Oklahoma, the wolf catcher and friend of former president, arrived in the national capital tonight.

They rode in from Frederick, Md., today, a distance of 57 miles. Temple dropped off to sleep the minute his head touched the pillow. While the little fellow was curled up restfully under the white covers, Louie talked of their trip.

Want to See Teddy Lions.

"Temple and I," he said, "want to see some of the animals Mr. Roosevelt sent from Africa, and tomorrow we will go over to the Smithsonian institution to see if we can have a look at some of them."

When asked what he intended to say to Mr. Roosevelt when he met him in New York, Louie replied that it would depend on what Mr. Roosevelt said to them and that he "could not cross that fence until he came to it."

Taft to Receive Them.

President Taft will receive the travelers.

When the boys arrived in Washington they rode up and down Pennsylvania avenue for some time looking for a "wagon yard" where they might "tie up the horses."

Not finding such a convenience, they finally stopped at one of the best hotels and thir horses were taken to a nearby livery. The boys will remain here several days.

---

[115] *Muskogee Daily Phoenix & Times-Democrat* (Muskogee, OK) May 28, 1910, Pg 1.

[116] The *Washington Times* (Washington, D.C.) May 28, 1910, Pg. 1.

Ensconced behind a plate of strawberries and ice-cream that looked positively huge in comparison to his diminutive size, Temple Abernathy, aged six, today said that he and his brother Louie would start on the last lap of their trip from Oklahoma to New York on horseback "sometime within the next few days." Louie, aged nine, is usually the one who does the talking. At the breakfast table, however, he gave way to his younger brother that he might not be interrupted in the pleasant task of getting on the outside of a breakfast that covered almost the complete top of a small table at the Raleigh Hotel.

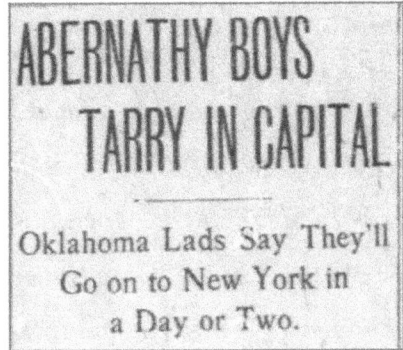

He had arisen a few moments later than Temple and was making up for lost time. Temple stopped long enough with a large spoonful poised dexterously midway between the ice cream plate and his mouth to say:

> *"We don't know just when we'll get started. We like Washington, and may stay over for another and perhaps two days."* [117]

---

[117] The *Washington Times* (Washington, District of Columbia) June 1, 1910, Pg. 2.

President Sees Abernathy Boys.

President Taft shook hands today with the two little Oklahoma horsemen who have ridden all the way from the west to be in New York in time to greet ex-President Roosevelt upon his return from abroad. These youngsters, Louis and Temple Abernathy, nine and six years old sons of "Jack" Abernathy, the wolf killer and United States marshal, called at the White House just before the cabinet meeting. They had no appointment, but when the President found they were waiting he admitted them without delay and cordially greeted them.

Both boys wore long trousers, more befitting youngsters of twelve or fourteen, and in their coat lapels were Shriner buttons, their father being a high Mason. The President "jollied" the little fellows by asking if big horses were not required to hold them. He also wished them good luck in the continuation of their *journey to New York, which they will resume in a few days.*

The two boys had been in the White House before, having taken luncheon with ex-President Roosevelt. They had been thoroughly coached as to observing as confidential whatever took place between them and the President, and they would not discuss their conversation with the chief executive.[118]

Inside the White House: Is Bill in?

The White House had long been a symbol of the nation's hopes and power, but when the Abernathy brothers arrived—unannounced and undeterred—it became the stage for an extraordinary moment. The unplanned visit underscored their journey's significance. Being received by the President without an appointment spoke volumes—not just about their determination, but about their rising prominence as youthful figures in the public eye.

> ### 'Is Bill In?' Queried the Two Abernathy Boys, Who Calmly Passed Whitehouse Doorkeeper

[119]

---

[118] *Evening star* (Washington, District of Columbia) May 31, 1910, Pg. 1.
[119] The *Kansas City Post* (Kansas City, Missouri) Jun 1, 1910, Pg. 7.

As Louis and Temple Abernathy approached the gates of the White House, their bold and yet innocent attitude preceded them. Dressed in high-topped riding boots, black serge coats, and broad-brimmed sombreros, the boys embodied the rugged charm of the Oklahoma frontier. *"Is Bill in?"*[120] Louis asked a bewildered doorman, whose bemusement only deepened when the boys brushed past him with the unshakable confidence of cowboys who had tamed the trails.

> **THEY SEE "BILL"**
> WASHINGTON, June 1.—(Spl.)— "Is Bill in?" asked the Abernathy boys, who are riding from Oklahoma to New York to greet Roosevelt, as they appeared at the White House Tuesday afternoon. The youngsters saw Taft, a Cabinet meeting stopping business while they were being received.

The boys were eager to make the most of their time in Washington. The *Washington Post* described the following, *"Washington is proving attractive to the Abernathy boys… They had planned to see President Taft yesterday, but the absence of the President in New York broke up their program."*
The boys visited Union Station, the Capitol, and Fort Myer, marveling at the soldiers' drills and the grandeur of the capital. Louis, ever pragmatic, joked, *"We only stop at the best hotels. Dad foots the bills,"*—a line that, even if already quoted, further fueled public fascination with

---

[120] The *Kentucky Post and Times-Star* (Covington, Kentucky) June 1, 1910,` Pg. 7.

their journey. It showed up in headlines across the country, reinforcing the perception of the Abernathy boys as both adorable and a bit absurd: wide-eyed innocents with the swagger of pint-sized elites.

YOUNG "COWBOYS" TO SEE TAFT

Louie and Temple Abernathy Will Visit President Today.

The boys were ushered into the White House, where they were warmly greeted by Taft himself.

President Taft, a man known for his geniality, greeted the boys with a booming laugh. *'So, you two rode all the way here without losing a boot or a hat?'* he asked, a twinkle in his eye. Temple, undaunted, replied, *'We lost a few biscuits along the way, but not our hats!'* The President roared with laughter, clapping the younger boy on the shoulder.

The President, intrigued by their story, asked them questions about their journey. Temple, the more talkative of the two, described their adventures with his characteristic wit, while Louis chimed in with occasional details.

The visit was not just ceremonial. The President took a personal interest in the boys, asking about their father, and praising them for their grit and determination. Taft even arranged for a tour of the

White House and its grounds, where the boys explored the historic residence with wide-eyed wonder.

Walking through the grand corridors of the White House, the boys could barely contain their excitement. Temple whispered to Louis, 'Do you think they'll let us stay for supper?' Louis, always the more composed, nudged his brother to focus. Standing before President Taft, the brothers felt a mix of pride and nervousness, their dusty boots and cowboy hats a reminder of how far they'd come.

The *Kentucky Post and Times-Star* reported that Louis candidly told reporters, "Bill's a good feller, but we knew Teddy better." When asked about the difference, Temple offered his own brand of wisdom: "*He's too fat ter sit on the floor,*" comparing Taft's more formal demeanor to Roosevelt's playful familiarity.[121] [122]

Sitting at the table, the boys recounted tales of snowstorms and grueling days on horseback. Temple asked Taft how much he weighed, eliciting a chuckle from the President and an amused cabinet.

The boys' candid observations only endeared them further to the public, with newspapers across the nation marveling at their precociousness.

They eagerly explored the Smithsonian Institution, where they marveled at the exotic animals Roosevelt had sent from Africa. Temple pressed his face against the glass of a lion exhibit, exclaiming, '*I*

---

[121] *The Washington Post*, (Washington, D.C.) May 30, 1910, Pg. 11.
[122] *The Kentucky Post and Times-Star*, (Covington, Kentucky) June 1, 1910, Pg. 1.

bet Pa could catch one of these barehanded!' Louis, examined the tags on Roosevelt's trophies, quietly imagining the stories they carried from distant lands. [123]

The White House visit solidified their status as national icons. Newspapers from coast to coast captured the boys' White House visit with headlines like 'Young Cowboys Meet the President.' Reporters described the Abernathy's' dusty outfits juxtaposed against the opulence of the Executive Mansion, framing the event as a meeting of rugged frontier spirit and refined political power. Reporters documented every detail of their interaction with the President, turning the event into front-page news across the country.

The boys' reception in Washington attracted congratulatory messages from all over. Interestingly for this author, it also drew connections to J.D.F. Jennings, a U.S. District Attorney from Oklahoma whose earlier exploits had been chronicled in my book *Old Boston: As Wild as They Come*. Jennings, in a congratulatory telegram, remarked on the boys' endurance, noting their feat had outdone anything their father had achieved.[124] This discovered link between

---

[123] *Morning Examiner* (Bartlesville, Oklahoma) May 29, 1910, Pg. 1.
[124] *The Washington Post* (Washington, D.C.), May 31, 1910, Pg. 5.

Jennings and the Abernathy family proved a certain smallness and interconnectedness of adventurous spirit that tied together the themes of boldness and unyielding determination across generations.

By the time they left Washington, the Abernathy boys had become full-fledged national icons. As the *Washington Post* described, the boys spent their downtime "playing with choo-choo cars" and purchasing nearly $50 worth of toys. Their rooms at the Raleigh Hotel were strewn with the paraphernalia of boys who, despite their fame and adult interactions, were still very much children.

"We've had a bully day,"

Louis said, echoing the Rooseveltian exuberance that had captured the hearts of the nation.[125][126]

Louie and Temple Abernathy's White House visit became one of many stories of their journey. Multiple papers chronicled their encounter, capturing every humorous and bold moment. From their unabashed query—"Is Bill in?"—to their easy banter with Taft's Cabinet, the boys charmed all they encountered. Here's how one reporter described their meeting:

Washington, June 1. — Two queerly dressed little figures approached the White House entrance shortly before 10 o'clock Tuesday morning. They wore high-topped riding boots, long trousers, black

---

[125] *The Washington Post*, (Washington, D.C.) May 31, 1910, Pg. 5.
[126] *The Kentucky Post and Times-Star*, (Covington, Kentucky) June 1, 1910, Pg. 1.

serge coats and broad-brimmed sombreros, beneath which peeped sturdy little features tinted with sun bronze.

"Is Bill in?" the elder inquired of the doorkeeper.

"Bill who?"

"Why, Bill Taft, o' course. We've came ter see him."

"Sure, the President's in," said the attendant, recovering from his surprise, "but you can't see him."

"Yer bet your life we kin see him. Yer see, I'm Louis Abernathy, an' this here's my brother. Ain't you, Temple?"

"Uh-huh," grunted the smaller boy.

Senators? Nuthin' Doin'!

"But haven't you a letter from a Senator or Congressman or some one?" asked the doorkeeper.

"Why don't we care 'bout Senators an' such things. All we come fer is ter see Bill. But we gotter letter from Dad." Louie flashed an envelope that had once been white from the bosom of his outing shirt. "See, it says here 'To Hon. William Howard Taft.'"

"That'll be all right, then," said the White House Cerberus, reaching for the envelope. "You give me the letter and I'll give it to Secretary Carpenter. Then you may be able to arrange an audience."

"Naw yer don't," said Louie firmly. "We'll give it ter him ourselves. Come on, Temple," and the youthful Oklahomans pushed past the keeper of the gate and pattered down the hallway toward the executive offices.

"Maybe Bill's in here," said Louie, indicating a massive oaken door which stood before them. The youngsters pushed open the door and beheld a bevy of distinguished looking men who sat about a long table in earnest conversation.

"Know Where Bill Is?"

"We're lookin' for Bill," explained Louie. "Know where he is?"

"And who might you be, sonny?" asked one of the men.

"We're th' Abernathys from Oklahoma, sir."

A broad grin ran around the circle.

"Oh, I see; and you're looking for Bill, eh? Well, we're expecting Bill here pretty soon."

"You see, they call us the Cabinet, not a piece of furniture, but a sort of board, you understand. Bill talks things over with us."

"I guess we'll jus' wait here for Bill, if you don't mind," said Louie, sinking into an easy chair.

"Sure," said the distinguished-looking man, politely. "Make yourselves at home."

ABERNATHY KIDS SEE BILL

Fifteen minutes later, when "Bill" arrived, he found the members of his Cabinet grouped about the "Cowboy Kids" and eagerly listening to the tale of their adventures on the road.

After gravely shaking hands with the little travelers, "Bill" perused the letter from Marshal Abernathy and then insisted that the boys repeat the story of their adventures to him.

"Bill" Hears Their Story.

"It was marvelous, boys, marvelous. I don't see how you did it," he remarked. "And young men (taking in their slender lines). There's another thing I can't understand about your feat. I don't understand how you got horses big enough to carry you."

Everybody laughed but little Temple.

"Oh, it was easy," he lisped. "I only weigh forty-six pounds. How much do you weigh?"

The President only smiled and asked the little lad where he got the huge special policeman's badge which was pinned to his sombrero.

Temple explained that it was a gift from the chief of police of Dayton, O. Each lad wore also a Masonic button in his lapel.

"You have performed a feat that I thought impossible for boys of your age," said the President, as the little Westerners made their exit.

The youngsters absolutely ignored the rapid fire of questions put to them by newspapermen and White House attaches, and it was only late this afternoon, as they were playing marbles in their room at the Raleigh, that they consented to tell the reporter all about the visit to "Bill."

"Bill's a Good Feller."

"He's a good feller, Bill is," said Louie. "He's all I thought he'd be, an' I think he's great. But, of course, you know, we knew Teddy 'er lot better; and, besides, he got dad a job. This President seems kinder dignified, too. Teddy, he used 'ter sit on th' floor an' play with us. But this President didn't do that."

"He's too fat ter sit on th' floor," said Temple shortly, answering the implied criticism of "Bill." "I like fat mans."

> **Say He's Good Fellow, but Is Too Fat to Play Marbles.**
>
> Special to The Star-Telegram.

The boys are enjoying themselves so much in the national capital that they may not start on the last lap of their 2,000-mile horseback hike until Friday or Saturday. They are not missing anything in the sight-seeing line here. They have become particularly fond of shows, and are beginning to be taken to the vaudeville and moving picture houses.[127] [128] [129] [130]

---

[127] *Press and Sun-Bulletin* (Binghamton, New York) June 2,1910, Pg. 12.
[128] *Fort Worth Star-Telegram* (Fort Worth, Texas) June 2. 1910, Pg. 8.
[129] *Guthrie Daily Leader* (Guthrie, Oklahoma) June 4, 1910, Pg. 8.
[130] The *Press-Democrat* (Hennessey, Oklahoma) June 10, 1910, Pg. 10.

The boys' ability to seamlessly transition from rugged frontiersmen to engaging storytellers fit perfectly into the narrative of Rooseveltian vigor and the pioneering spirit of early 20th-century America. Even President Taft, often seen as a more reserved leader, found himself captivated by the cowboy kids' youthful nerve and charm.

> THE "Cowboy Kids," Louis and Temple Abernathy, nine and six years old, who made a 2000-mile horseback ride to meet Col. Roosevelt upon his arrival home, have been in Washington having a good time. They are the sons of the famous Jack Abernathy, who showed Mr. Roosevelt how to catch a wolf with his naked hands. Mr. Abernathy is U. S. marshal out in Oklahoma.
> WASHINGTON, June 6.—On their long horseback journey from Oklahoma to New York, whither they are riding to meet Col. Roosevelt, Louie and Temple Abernathy left the national capital early today. Since leaving their home in Oklahoma, the little fellows, who are traveling unaccompanied, have averaged about 50 miles a day. They spent about a week taking in the sights of Washington. While here they called on President Taft and also met Speaker Cannon. They ride as far as Baltimore today. [131]

[132]

---

[131] The *Buffalo News* (Buffalo, New York) June 6, 1910, Pg. 20.
[132] *Press and Sun-Bulletin* (Binghamton, New York) June 2, 1910, Pg. 12.

A Visit to Congress

The Abernathy boys' stop at the United States Capitol was another milestone in their journey, placing them squarely in the halls of American democracy. Their youthful curiousness and rugged charm made them an immediate sensation among the lawmakers who encountered them. Dressed in their dusty riding boots, black coats, and

---

[133] *Fort Worth Star-Telegram* (Fort Worth, Texas) June 3, 1910, Pg. 8.

wide-brimmed hats, the nine and six-year-old adventurers stood out sharply from the polished figures of Washington.

WEE GUESTS OF CONGRESS

Abernathy Boys Take the House by Storm.

WASHINGTON, June 3.—The two young Abernathy boys, sons of the rough rider, United States marshal and friend of Roosevelt, who have ridden 2,000 miles from Oklahoma to meet former President Roosevelt upon his arrival in New York, threw the House of Representatives into confusion today when they were brought upon the floor, upon the suggestion of Speaker Cannon.

"You own as much of this city as Rockefeller or Carnegie," said Mr. Cannon, addressing them. The Speaker suggested that the boys be taken into the House, where they were the center of interest. Members crowded about and questioned them about their long horseback ride. They remained half an hour, when they were taken on a tour of the city.

---

[134] *Pittsburgh Post-Gazette (Pittsburgh,* Pennsylvania) June 4, 1910, Pg. 6.
[135] *Salt Lake Telegram* (Salt Lake City, Utah) June 4, 1910, Pg. 19.
[136] *Quad-City Times* (Davenport, Iowa) June 5, 1910, Pg. 1.
[137] The *Morning Press* (Santa Barbara, California) June 5, 1910, Pg. 1.

By the time Louis and Temple Abernathy arrived in Washington, D.C. in late May 1910, they had already become national sensations. Newspaper headlines declared they were "Having 'Bully Time'" and noted that the boys were "Rooseveltian in their expressions." The *Washington Post* quoted Louis, then just nine years old, saying, "We've had a bully day," before adding, "Washington is a dandy place. We are going to stay here a few more days."[138]

Their energy seemed boundless. That morning, dressed in new brown suits and light blue waistcoats their father had sent ahead—"new 'rags,' as they called them," according to the *Post*—the boys set out from the Raleigh Hotel to explore the capital. They spent the morning sightseeing from a "rubberneck" wagon and the afternoon watching moving pictures. Despite the full schedule, they still found time and stamina for a visit to the Congressional Library that evening.

---

[138] *The Kentucky Post and Times-Star* (Covington, Kentucky) June 1, 1910, Pg. 7.

The boys had charmed every city on their route, but Washington brought with it a special kind of reverence. You can imagine Louis saying something like, "Temple, this place is taller than anything we've seen yet," as they approached the Capitol steps. Temple, squinting against the sun, might've replied with wide-eyed curiosity, "Do you think this is where they make all the rules, Louis?"

Though no reporter documented the exact exchange, the tone echoes countless articles that described the brothers' unfiltered wonder and natural charm. A friendly Capitol clerk, amused by their earnestness, might well have leaned in and said, "Come along, boys—I'll show you where the magic happens."

Their polished manners and youthful curiosity, combined with the toughness of their trip, left a strong impression. Applause filled the chamber, and many lawmakers stood to get a better look at the young cowboys. You might imagine Temple leaning toward Louis, whispering, "Do you think they'd clap if we told them about that time we outran a storm?" Louis smirked but said nothing, letting the moment sink in.

One news report provided the following: *Louis and Temple Abernathy, sons of United States Marshal Jack Abernathy of Oklahoma, who have ridden 2,000 miles from Oklahoma to meet ex-President Roosevelt upon his arrival in New York, threw the House into confusion today when they were brought upon the floor at the suggestion of Speaker Cannon. Members crowded about and asked them about their long horseback ride.*

ABERNATHY BOYS GET GLIMPSE OF CONGRESS

Uncle Joe Cannon Acts as Host—Boys Think Washington is a "Bully" Place.

"How do you like Washington?" the Speaker asked of the boys.

"Bully," said Louis.

"Well," said the Speaker, "the city belongs to ninety million people. You own just as much of it as Carnegie or Rockefeller. How much do you ride?"

"Oh, forty or fifty miles a day," answered Temple.

"You mean a week, don't you?" said the Speaker.

"No," said Louis, "we make fifty miles a day easy."

The boys probably will leave here tomorrow.

As part of their visit, the boys were taken to the Library of Congress. The grandeur of the rotunda and the endless shelves of books left them wide-eyed with wonder. Temple, always curious, asked their guide, "Are these the books that tell the President what to do?" The guide laughed, explaining that the Library of Congress was a resource for all branches of government. Louis, always pragmatic, responded, "I bet Pa's library wouldn't even fill one shelf in this place."[139]

YOUTHFUL HORSEMEN INVADE HOUSE OF REPRESENTATIVES

Washington, June 3.—The two young Abernathy boys, sons of the Rough Rider United States Marshal and friend of Roosevelt, who have ridden 2,000 miles from Oklahoma to meet former President Roosevelt upon his arrival in New York, threw the House of Representatives in o confusion to-day when they were brought upon the floor upon the suggestion of Speaker Cannon.

[140]

---

[139] *Washington Post* (Washington, D.C.), May 31, 1910, Pg. 5.
[140] The *Courier-Journal* (Louisville, Kentucky) June 4, 1910, Pg. 3.

---

[141] *Press and Sun-Bulletin* (Binghamton, New York) June 2, 1910, Pg. 7.
[142] NOTE: This photo appears again later in the chapter with a different caption. Although this version is higher quality, both images offer distinct perspectives on the boys' journey.

The following provides additional details about their time in the nation's capital.[143]

In the handshaking that will come when Colonel Roosevelt steps ashore in New York on June 18 two Oklahoma youngsters will get a hearty grip from the ex-president. They are Louis and Temple Abernathy, aged ten and six respec-

GUTHRIE TO GOTHAM.

Remarkable Ride of Marshal Abernathy's Boys to Greet Roosevelt.

tively, the sons of John Abernathy, United States marshal of Guthrie. The boys, as well as their father, are warm friends and admirers of Mr. Roosevelt, and to be among the first to welcome him home; they started in April to ride on horseback from Guthrie to New York, a distance of 2,000 miles. At all points along the route they have been receiving a royal welcome.

This country has no better or more daring boy riders than the Abernathy youngsters, and they have inherited their father's courage and self-reliance. They have made many overland journeys alone, the first notable being horseback from Guthrie to Roswell, N. M., a journey of 720 miles. The boys are proud not only to perform this, their longest ride and to meet Roosevelt, but also to do it without proper assistance.

---

[143] NOTE: And finally, you see where the title of this book came from!

Marshal Abernathy is a close friend of Mr. Roosevelt—who went hunting with him in Oklahoma in the spring of 1905. On this occasion Abernathy showed Mr. Roosevelt how to catch wolves alive with his bare hands, a feat that has brought him much fame. Since then Mr. Wolf has given the husky Oklahoman a wide berth.

After greeting Colonel Roosevelt, the boys plan to return home on horseback, and a large part of Oklahoma is planning a celebration in their honor when they arrive.[144]

LOUIS AND TEMPLE ABERNATHY.

---

[144] *Hiawatha Daily World* (Hiawatha, Kansas) June 4, 1910, Pg. 6.

WASHINGTON, June 4. — Bright and early Monday morning the "cowboy kids" will hit the trail on the last lap of their 2,000-mile horseback ride. They will travel at a "very moderate pace" — only fifty miles a day. On Monday the lads will content themselves with reaching Baltimore — forty-five miles from Washington, by the route they will travel. They also will make stops at Wilmington, Philadelphia, and Trenton.

Today the boys received a letter from their "dad," the well-known "Catch 'Em Alive Jack" Abernathy, saying that "Jack" will be in New York on Wednesday and will meet them on Friday at the Breslin Hotel. They are eagerly

ABERNATHY BOYS TO HIT THEIR LAST LAP

looking forward to seeing their father again after being away from him for almost two months.

Today the youngsters received an invitation from C.F. Troupe, a millionaire furniture manufacturer at Baltimore, to stop en route at his country home, "Poplar Grove," ten miles this side of Baltimore. Against his wishes the boys had to decline to accept the invitations from admirers, but they have undertaken to follow a fixed schedule and are determined to adhere to it.

An acquaintance of Speaker Cannon asked the lads if they would like to call on the Speaker and Vice-President Sherman.

"Who is them men?" asked the "Cowboy Kids" indifferently.

"Uh, he ain't never heard o' Sherman nor nothin' 'bout Cannon," they remarked when they went out.

"Anyways," they added, "we ain't bother 'bout no little fellers in Washington. We'd ruther see the big fellers, if there is such men up there, which we ain't seen. We'd ruther see us some more little fellers after we've seen them in the White House. It 'ud kinder look like we wasn't thinkin' much of Bill. An' we wouldn't have Bill think that fer anythin'.

There has been only one fly in the boys' ointment in their entire stay in Washington. This was caused by a trick pony being exhibited at a vaudeville house, and which has vanquished every man it has been pitted against.

The little Oklahomans are confident that they can ride the pony. But there's an obstacle in the way of their making the attempt.

'You see, it's this way,' said Louie tonight. 'We promised Dad we wouldn't take part in no tomfoolery while we was on th' way ter New York. An' so I can't ride that measly little pony.'

'But still,' added Louie, sighing wistfully, 'say, that pony 'ud be the easiest thing in th' world fer me ter ride. It 'ud be easier than er three-months-old colt. I'd be a leadpipe cinch ter ride him.'

For two hours this morning Louis and Temple were 'at home' to young Washington, and dozens of the boys and girls of the Capital City took advantage of the opportunity to meet them. The little Westerners who have performed such a remarkable feat, were heroes, especially in the eyes of the little boys of Washington. The ranch-bred boys have been a little shy of the fair sex in their stay in Washington, but this morning they showed themselves to the girls, whom they taught how to tie a lasso and rope a steer. Captain Jack Herbert, of the high police patrol at Fort Myer, Va., was working at the herd.

The boys have traveled a dozen states and have traversed a dozen states on horseback. Their mounts are full bred horses. Louie's mount, Sam, is a magnificent horse of high breed, and Temple's mount is Sam's equal. Both horses are well groomed, their suits broad-brimmed sombreros and high-topped boots. They are much surprised at the notice and attention they have received, however, and they elude the crowds as much as possible.

The little Westerners have a high opinion of Washington and have expressed their gratitude, and have already spent a considerable part of their trip money in purchasing maps of the city to guide them.

They find their way through the maze by making inquiries of passersby.[145]

BOYS TO LEAVE ON MONDAY.

Father's Telegram Fixes Time of Departure of Abernathys.

The Abernathy boys will leave Washington Monday. They received word from their father, "Jack" Abernathy, United States marshal at Frederick, Okla., yesterday, informing them that he would arrive in New York on Wednesday of next week, and directing them to leave the Capital on Monday.

Yesterday the little fellows received an invitation from Charles F. Troupe to spend an evening at his country place, Poplar Grove, at Relay, Md., outside of Baltimore.

At the invitation of the Oklahoma representaives in the House and Senate, the boys visited Congress yesterday morning. They were introduced to Speaker Cannon.

[146]

ABERNATHY BOYS VISIT WASHINGTON. Washington, June 6. — Bright and early this morning the "Cowboy Kids" will hit the

---
[145] The *St. Louis Star and Times* (St. Louis, Missouri) June 5, 1910, Pg.1.
[146] The *Washington Post* (Washington, District of Columbia) June 4, 1910. Pg. 16.

trail on the last lap of their 2,000-mile horseback ride. They will travel at a "very moderate rate" — only fifty miles a day.

Today the lads will content themselves with reaching Baltimore — 45 miles from Washington, by the route they will travel. They will also make stops at Wilmington, Philadelphia, and Trenton.

Yesterday the boys received a letter from their dad, "Catch-'em-alive Jack" Abernathy, saying that "Jack" will be in New York on Wednesday and will meet them on Friday at the Breslin hotel. They are eagerly looking forward to seeing their father again after being away from him almost two months.

The youngsters received an invitation from E. Troup, a millionaire furniture manufacturer of Baltimore, to stop en route at his country home, "Poplar Grove," ten miles this side of Baltimore.

Nothing would please the boys better than to accept the invitation and be entertained there, but they have undertaken a task and are determined to adhere to it. They are determined to adhere to schedule.

For the most part early this morning Louis and Temple were "at home" to girls and scores of schoolboys and girls of the capital city took advantage of the opportunity to meet them. The little westerners have performed such a remarkable feat, were heroes — especially in the eyes of the little misses of Washington. The ranch-bred boys have been a little shy of the fair sex in their stay in Washington, but this morning they devoted themselves exclusively to the girls, whom they taught how to lasso and rope a steer Oklahoma fashion.

Here are some interesting facts about the young equestrians' long hike:

They left Frederick, Okla., on April 18 and have since been continuously on horseback. They have traversed a dozen states and have traveled, though unaccompanied, 1,775 miles. Their mounts, Sam, a full-blood horse, and Geronimo, both horses of high breed, are in splendid condition. The boys' outfit consists of khaki suits, broad-brimmed sombreros, and high-topped boots.

They have a little check book, however, and have entered

therein, signed by their little leather hands, "Keepin' with Lou's signature and Temple's mark, for whatever they purchase."

They have received nothing extraordinary as yet, but already spent almost $1,000 of their trip money.

The little riders have a map of Washington with a leather key to guide them. They find their way from place to place by inquiring of passers-by.[147]

For the first time since the two Abernathy boys started on their long horseback ride across the continent, sickness has overtaken them. Nothing serious, however; Temple, 6 years old, is just a little 'knocked out.' Louis, 9 years old, is as cheeky as a pippin, and as chipper as a lark.

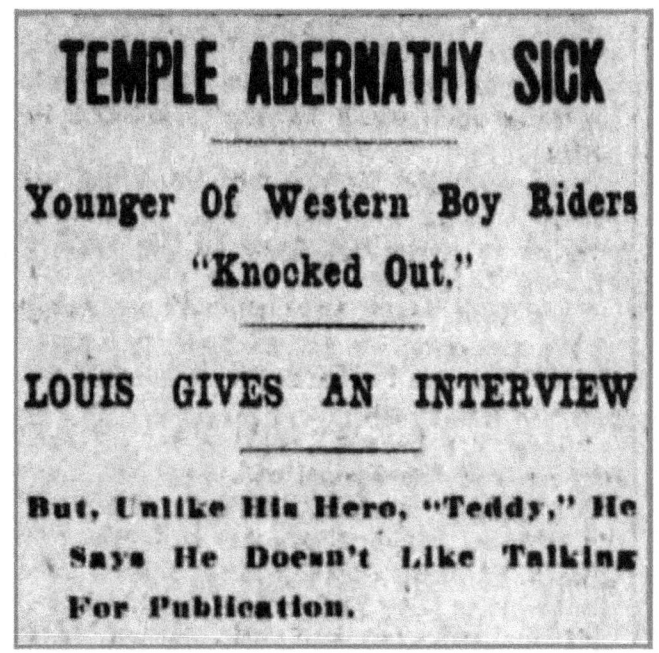

They are not caring a rap what Baltimore looks like. Bernheimer Bros. turned them loose in their toy department this morning, and

---

[147] The *Chickasha Daily Express* (Chickasha, Oklahoma) June 6, 1910, Pg. 1.

that is as much of the city as they are worrying about. A red velocipede is all that Louis can see.

There is hardly a 'kid' in this town but who would go through fire and water to ride a pony. And here is that Abernathy youngster who will hardly take time to eat because it will take him out of the sight of the big toy. That home of delights for children is proving a paradise for the little Westerners. The intense interest displayed by the boys in toys and trifles impressed upon the minds of onlookers what a brave undertaking it is for them to travel from Oklahoma to New York on horseback and alone.

Pursued By Inquiring Women.

When a reporter for The Evening Sun went on a hunt for the horsemen, he found Louis astride that velocipede. Temple, it was learned, was down in the office asleep. His stomach was a little out of order, and he was tired. It was amusing to watch the people try to question Louis. He led inquisitive women a chase. He was willing to talk, all right, if one was willing to run along behind the tricycle. Finally, the reporter got him in a corner.

'Want to talk to you,' said the reporter.

'Haven't time. Whoop, look out!' and he tried to pedal past.

A Two-Minute Interview.

"Want to write about you in the paper,' was sent over next.

'All right, give you two minutes,' said Mr. Louis, with the patronizing air of one who is frequently interviewed. He whipped out a watch, and two minutes to a tick was all the reporter got. Louis is a *polite little chap, but he doesn't waste any time over words.*

'How are you feeling?' was the opener.

'Fine.'

'Where is your brother?'

'Sick.'

'What is the matter with him?'

'Don't know; I'm not a doctor.'

'How do you like riding across the country?

'Great.'

'What do you think of all these toys?'

'Great.'

'Your opinion of Roosevelt.'

'Going to see Roosevelt?'

'Yep.'

'Do you like him?'

This question brought forth a long answer. 'You bet I do. He is a fine man, a great man, and I like him—but I like him.'

'How do you like being interviewed?'

'Rotten.'

Louis told in his monosyllable way that he was going to meet his father in New York. He and his brother have enjoyed the ride. 'They have no map, but depend solely upon inquiry as to the route. Louis pays all of the bills by check.'

The boys have been patted, praised, and questioned all along their ride until they are heartily sick of it. Clad in knickerbocker suits, leather boots and broad-brimmed slouch hats, they are a picturesque pair. Each time that Louis shook hands this morning he would cap off the shake with a backward fling that bespoke a man of the plains. They will leave for Wilmington, Del., tomorrow morning."[148]

THE ABERNATHY BOYS, WHO ARE ON THE LAST LEG OF THEIR JOURNEY. [149]

---

[148] The *Evening Sun (*Baltimore, Maryland) June 7, 1910, Pg. 5.
[149] The *Kansas City Star* (Kansas City, Missouri) June 7, 1910, Pg 2.

ABOVE: WASHINGTON, June 6. — On a long horseback journey from Oklahoma to New York, whither they are riding to meet Colonel Roosevelt, Louie and Temple Abernathy, 9 and 6 years old, sons of United States Marshal Abernathy, wolf hunter and friend of Roosevelt's, left here early today. Since leaving Oklahoma the little fellows, unaccompanied, have averaged twenty miles a day.[150]

---

[150] The *Fort Worth Record & Register* (Fort Worth, Texas) Jun 7, 1910, Pg. 2.

This is a photograph of the Abernathy boys who have been enjoying themselves in Washington before starting out on the last lap of their long journey to New York to greet ex-President Roosevelt. The boys had a great time in the Capital and were loathe to leave.

ABOVE: ENJOY EASTERN LIFE. This is a photograph of the Abernathy boys who have been enjoying themselves in Washington before starting out on the last lap of their long journey to New York to greet ex-President Roosevelt. The boys had a great time in the Capital and were loathe to leave.[151]

---

[151] *Press and Sun-Bulletin* (Binghamton, New York) June 7, 1910, Pg. 3.

COWBOY KIDS GOING TO WELCOME COLONEL ROOSEVELT NEARING LAST LEG OF LONG JOURNEY ON HORSEBACK

NEW YORK, June 8. — Jack Abernathy of Oklahoma City, who showed Theodore Roosevelt how to capture and kill a wolf with his bare hands, has reached New York and will remain to welcome the colonel later in the month.

Father of Two Boys Already in New York Arranging for the Meeting

Abernathy is the father of the "cowboy kids," Louis and Temple, who are making the trip from Oklahoma on horseback and who passed through Washington, where they saw President Taft. Charles E. Hunter, president of the Roosevelt Rough Riders association, is another recent arrival in New York. He will proceed at once to make arrangements for the welcome to the returning colonel by the survivors of his band. He expects to muster about 150 of the 400 Rough Riders who are at present in this country. They will wear khaki uniforms in the parade.[152]

---

[152] *Billings Evening Journal* (Billings, Montana) June 8, 1910, Pg. 8.

ABOVE — THE Abernathy boys, Louie, aged 9, and Temple, aged 6, who are on the last stage of their 2,000 mile horseback ride from their home in Oklahoma to New York, where they are going to greet Colonel Roosevelt. Recently the boys invaded the White House, walked into a cabinet meeting and introduced themselves to President Taft. He received them kindly and spent several minutes in conversation with them. They are making the long trip entirely alone.[153]

---

[153] *Billings Evening Journal* (Billings, Montana) June 8, 1910, Pg. 8.

Trenton, N. J., June 10. — Louis and Temple Abernathy, the two boys who are riding from Frederick, Okla., to New York to greet former President Roosevelt on his arrival from Europe, reached here tonight. They will leave for New York early tomorrow. [154] [155] [156] [157]

NEW YORK, June 10. — John R. Abernathy, United States Marshal from Oklahoma, is in town. He has come here to meet Theodore Roosevelt on his return from abroad and to be with the boys when they whoop 'er up on June 18. Marshal Jack is the man who catches the elusive wolf with his bare hands and he is the advance guard of the rough-riding cowboy cohorts who are coming to join in the big show.

---

[154] The *Topeka Daily Capital* (Topeka, Kansas) June 11, 1910, Pg. 1.
[155] The *Daily Oklahoman* (Oklahoma City, Oklahoma) June 11, 1910, Pg. 4.
[156] *Muskogee Daily Phoenix & Times-Democrat* (Muskogee, OK) June 11, 1910, Pg. 1.
[157] The *News Journal* (Wilmington, Delaware) June 11, 1910, Pg. 5.

"Eat 'Em Alive Jack[158]" was at the Hotel Breslin yesterday when a Post-Dispatch reporter called to see him to ask him about his two boys, who are on the last stretch of their remarkable horseback ride from Oklahoma to this city. The papers recently have been filled with accounts of the exploits of the Abernathy boys, Louis, who is 10, and Temple, 6, and Marshal Jack shines just now in the reflected glory of his offspring. His eyes lit up with the fatherly pride at the thought of them.

"I am waiting for a message now," he said, "which will tell me of their

"EAT 'EM ALIVE JACK" AND HIS BOYS ON WAY EAST ON HORSEBACK

---

[158] NOTE: While U.S. Marshal Jack Abernathy was famously known as "Catch 'Em Alive Jack" for capturing wolves with his bare hands, some newspaper accounts erroneously referred to him as "Eat 'Em Alive Jack." This may have been sensationalized, a typographical slip or editorial oversight, not necessarily an intentional distortion. Such variations were not uncommon in early wire service reporting, where rapid reproduction and reprinting across publications often introduced errors.

progress from Baltimore. A Baltimore paper promised to communicate with me by telephone and I am a little bit anxious".

"This isn't the first ride they have taken, for they went to Mexico, a 2300-mile trip, some time ago, and they had all sorts of experiences. This time I hesitated about letting them go. I wasn't afraid about their not finding their way, but I feared they might catch cold. Had I said 'no' they would have given up the plan right away, but their hearts were set on it, they had been talking it over for months, and it was a chance for them to learn something they could not get out of their school books, so I said they might set out. But when we go home we are going in a Pullman and we are all three going to sleep in the same berth, too."

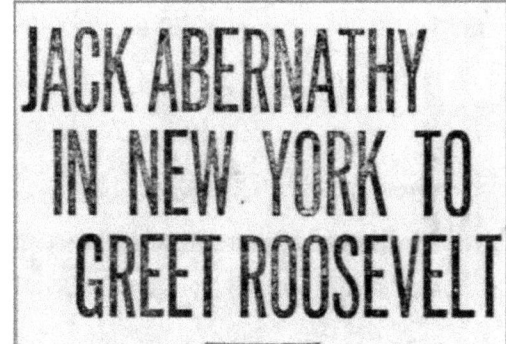

"I don't think that another man as fine as he ever lived on this earth or ever will live on it again," was the way he expressed himself in talking of his hero. "I would have thought just as much of Mr. Roosevelt if he had never made me Marshal. I want to tell you that the State of Oklahoma feels the same way about him as I do."[159]

---

[159] *St. Louis Post-Dispatch* (St. Louis, Missouri) June 11, 1910, Pg. 3.

The Abernathy boys arrived in Trenton, N. J., late yesterday afternoon, where they were met by their father who rode horseback from New York to the New Jersey Capital to greet them.

They stayed in Trenton all night and left early this morning for New York. They will remain in that city until after Colonel Roosevelt arrives from abroad.[160]

POLICE ESCORT FOR BOYS.

New York, June 11. — "Jack" Abernathy, United States Marshal in Oklahoma, called at the City Hall yesterday to see Mayor Gaynor. The Mayor was attending a session of the Board of Estimates at the time.

After the meeting was over the Mayor received Abernathy in his office and gave him a letter to Police Commissioner Baker regarding arrangement for necessary police escort for Louis and Temple Abernathy, the marshal's sons, when they arrive in this city today on their horseback ride from Oklahoma.[161]

---

[160] The *News Journal* (Wilmington, Delaware) June 11, 1910, Pg. 5.
[161] *Muskogee Daily Phoenix & Times-Democrat* (Muskogee, OK) June 11, 1910. Pg. 1.

ABERNATHY BOYS SPEND THE NIGHT IN TRENTON.

TRENTON, June 11. — Louis and Temple Abernathy, the two boys who are riding from Frederick, Oklahoma, to New York to greet former President Roosevelt on his arrival from Europe, reached here last night.[162]

The boys traveled from Wilmington, Del. They left for New York early this morning.

Jack Abernathy's boys, who are waiting at the Breslin until Col. Roosevelt comes home, went out to see as much of New York as was visible today through the rain. They went to Mr. Rockefeller's church in the morning with their father and a friend whom Marshal Jack had met overnight at the Breslin. Mr. Rockefeller wasn't at the Fifth Avenue Baptist church today at all, but the boys had a good time nevertheless.[163]

---

[162] *Newark Star-Ledger* (Newark, New Jersey) June 11, 1910, Pg. 16.
[163] *Detroit Free Press* (Detroit, Michigan) June 13, 1910, Pg. 1.

TINY ROUGH RIDERS WHO TAKE 2,000-MILE RIDE TO MEET ROOSEVELT.

(Louis Abernathy, 9 years old, and his brother Temple, aged 6, traveled all the way from Oklahoma alone on horseback without mishap. They reached this city last night, after meeting their father, United States Marshal "Jack" Abernathy, one of Roosevelt's Rough Riders. They spent the night at the Trenton House, and proceeded this morning to New York to meet Roosevelt upon his arrival there next Saturday.)[164]

ABOVE: *TINY ROUGH RIDERS WHO TAKE 2,000-MILE RIDE TO MEET ROOSEVELT.* Louis Abernathy, 9 years old, and his brother Temple, aged 6, traveled all the way from Oklahoma alone on horseback without mishap. They reached this city last night, after meeting their father, United States Marshal "Jack" Abernathy, one of Roosevelt's Rough Riders. They spent the night at the Trenton House, and proceeded this morning to New York to meet Roosevelt upon his arrival there next Saturday.[165]

---

[164] *Trenton Evening Times* (Trenton, New Jersey) June 11, 1910. Pg. 11.
[165] *Trenton Evening Times* (Trenton, New Jersey) June 11, 1910. Pg. 11.

Chapter 5: 1910 —Triumph in New York City

Wearing grins as broad as their hats, Louis and Temple Abernathy finished the last lap of their horseback ride alone from Oklahoma City, Okla., when they dismounted from their broncos at the door of the Hotel Breslin amid the applause of several thousand persons.[166]

From Washington, D.C

From Washington, D.C., the Abernathy brothers set out on the final leg of their journey to New York City. The anticipation grew with each mile, as newspapers and telegraphs continued to report their progress. By the time the boys reached the outskirts of Manhattan, they were national celebrities, with crowds gathering to catch a glimpse of the young adventurers. The became so much of a spectacle that at one point they were given a police escort to help them through the crowds.

With each passing mile, the buzz surrounding the Abernathy brothers grew louder. Newspapers published daily updates on their progress, and telegraph wires carried their latest sighting. Crowds gathered along the route, hoping to catch a glimpse of the brothers.

[166] The *Press Herald* (Pine Grove, Pennsylvania) May 27, 1910, Pg. 6.

ABERNATHY BOYS NEARING GOTHAM [167]

A Hero's Welcome

The brothers arrived in New York to thunderous applause. Thousands lined the streets as the boys rode into the city, their ponies carrying them past cheering onlookers. The spectacle was unlike anything the boys had experienced before.

As the Abernathy boys crossed into Manhattan, the sound of their ponies' hooves was nearly drowned out by the cheers of the crowd. Banners fluttered from windows, children waved American flags, and newsboys darted through the throng shouting headlines. Temple tipped his hat to the onlookers, grinning broadly, while Louis, ever composed, gave a subtle nod of acknowledgment. The sheer size of the crowd—thousands of New Yorkers lining the streets—left the boys in awe.

The highlight of their time in New York was their invitation to board the cutter that would meet former President Theodore Roosevelt's ship as it arrived in the harbor. The boys eagerly awaited this moment, which had been the ultimate goal of their journey.

New York, June 11. — Between cheering lines, Louis and Temple Abernathy rode up Broadway tonight on the last stage of their

---

[167] The *Dayton Herald* (Dayton, Ohio) June 10, 1910, Pg. 10.

2,000-mile journey from Oklahoma. As their bronchos halted in front of the Hotel Breslin, 1,000 persons joined in the final cheer. "Jack" Abernathy, United States marshal of Oklahoma and proud father of the lads, hustled them to their rooms to prepare for dinner.

From the moment they reached the city the little rough riders were the center of a continuous reception. They rode off a ferry boat that brought them from Jersey City into a reception that took all of the mounted police on guard to keep in line. The purpose of the boys in making the trip was to be in New York to join the welcome to Theodore Roosevelt on his return next Saturday. Louis, the older of the lads, is 9 years of age, while Temple is only 5. They began their long trip on April 16. [168]

New York, June 11. — The two small sons of "Eat 'Em Alive Jack" Abernathy, friend of Col. Roosevelt and United States marshal of Guthrie, Okla., arrived in this city at 6:20 tonight, the final stretch of their 2,300-mile jaunt on a pair of Oklahoma bronchos being a 60-

---

[168] The *Arkansas City Daily News* (Arkansas City, Kansas) June 13, 1910, Pg. 1.

mile ride from Trenton through the rain. An hour after their arrival they were tucked into their bed at the Hotel Breslin, after an enthusiastic reception all along the line.

The two boys, Louis, who is 10, and Temple, who is 6, left their father's ranch on March 8 on horseback. The distance is about 2,000 miles, but the side trips they took made the journey total up to 2,300 miles. On the entire trip they pushed on as they chose, making their own arrangements, receiving no money aid either at home or en route, and handling themselves in every way as mature travelers.

CHILDREN FINISH 2,300 MILE RIDE

Abernathy Boys Enter New York on the Horses That Carried Them From Alabama.

THEY ARE IMPRESSED AND SO IS NEW YORK

Big Crowd Celebrates Their Feat of Traveling Half Across Continent Alone.

Thirty-Seven Miles at Noon.

They reached New Brunswick, 37 miles from Trenton, at noon. Little Temple wanted to push right on to New York without stopping for luncheon, but Louis, the masterful, felt hungry.

"You go on now; you get off that horse and eat."

"Naw," said Temple

Without a word Lous jumped off his pinto, grabbed the bridle of Temple's horse and struck his brother with the whip. Temple got off.

For two boys that

have been lionized for 2,300 miles, both are modest. They don't talk much and are extremely polite to their elders. It was this deference to age that Louie was instilling in his little brother. After luncheon they kept on their way to Newark, reaching there at 4 o'clock. Their father met them there in Princeton, and took them to a little runabout. He followed it to New Brunswick and returned to New York with it, while he himself was driven in an automobile and came upon them two miles this side of Newtown.

They were still plodding through the mud. Louis scored Temple out and ran along at a break-a-way run. The little one took his scolding. Once in a while Louis went back to the line among travelers' shops. There was a portion of the rush in the hopes of its Western life. Both needed riding boots with sharp spurs on them. A battered sombrero crowned his head.

Temple in a Rubber Coat.

Temple, who is small for his age, was enwrapped in a black rubber coat, which was so long it tangled in his spurs when he walked. Jersey mud had left its impression his chubby face, but the rain had washed out clean patches. Old Sam the broncho the smaller boy was riding, was the horse used by the father when he coursed wolves with Colonel Roosevelt.

At the Pennsylvania ferry house in Jersey City several hundred persons gathered around the boys to see them off on their final lap. The two pressed close to the edge, both anxious to shake hands with them.

All through it the boys kept up their indifference. They were tired, just like other people, all but said that. Anything at last. They smiled and nodded, but it was nearly midnight when they were in the saddle and off on their arrival in New York. Through the ferry halfway across a bunch of roses, Temple plucked a leaf and said:

"There's nothing like a cowboy in the saddle."

"They'll get to London," added a man. He is like Jack.

The two smiled, laughed. "That's the stuff!" said Louis, as his eyes met Temple's. The elder brother's smile was suddenly effaced as he turned to his horse.

"How do you like New York, Louis?" he was asked.

Which is New York.

"Ah! Which is New York?" was the answer. And he nodded as he looked hard into the East River at Brooklyn. "If the boys knock him till they win the fight, the black horse will knock that hollow."

The procession through New York was triumphant. An escort of four mounted policemen met the boys, and there was a string of waiting automobiles two blocks long. The procession moved through Twenty-fourth street to Seventh avenue and then up to Twenty-ninth street and across to the Breslin.

All along the route they were cheered as they came into the streets. Hands of all the posts on the pranks and women smiled and exclaimed, "How cute!"

When they stopped in front of the hotel the street was jammed with a swarming mass of spectators. The women shrieked and waved handkerchiefs, and the boys were literally forced into the hotel through the crowd.

One young woman in blue managed to secure exclusive possession of Temple for a moment. She kissed him once and then repeatedly, to his somewhat modest air. She kissed him, kissed him nearly every minute. He didn't seem happy.

The two of them were taken upstairs by their father. There was an air of quiet in the crowd while the man shut out of the room until the marshal washed and dressed them in clean suits for city wear.

Impressed by Their City Togs.

In blue coats, long trousers properly creased, they looked like city slickers. They removed the silk ties with ties that were taken off, even if that was packed, and the back of Temple's head and every few minutes he would leave the dinner and look at himself in a tall mirror.

They were too impressed to talk and looked awkwardly solemn, sitting on top of things, "like city men from Texas." "You know how," was how Louis and I don't know. A thick piece of roast and a mouthful of steak and a glass of milk, and they were both packed for bed.

The young Americans are seeing as much of New York as the boys want tomorrow, except on Broadway. There will be no more of the city until they go home. "Col. Roosevelt will visit us," said the marshal. He will call on us, see Judge Cogan, Mayes, and Hunter, C.J., and see what is to be done with the boys about the 28th of the month.

The boys will be shipped home by train. "But guess they'll earn a place on the pension roll," said the marshal.[169] [170]

Meeting Roosevelt

When Roosevelt's ship docked, the boys were among the first to greet him. Roosevelt, a close friend of their father, was both amused and impressed by their achievement. He clasped their hands warmly and congratulated them on completing such a daring feat. Roosevelt exclaimed, 'Well, if it isn't the two finest young cowboys I've ever seen!' He clasped their hands firmly, leaning down to meet them at

---

[169] *Detroit Free Press* (Detroit, Michigan) June 12, 1910, Pg. 2
[170] *The Sun* (New York, New York) June 12, 1910, Pg 6.

eye level. 'Your father taught you well,' he said, his voice filled with admiration. Temple, eager to impress, recounted tales of their journey. Roosevelt chuckled heartily and said, 'Never lose that spirit of adventure, boys. It's what built this country.' The boys regaled the former President with tales from their journey, and he, in turn, encouraged them to continue embracing adventure.

The meeting with Roosevelt was a dream fulfilled for the brothers when setting out on the ride. Temple later remarked that he would always remember the moment Roosevelt shook his hand and laughed at his stories.

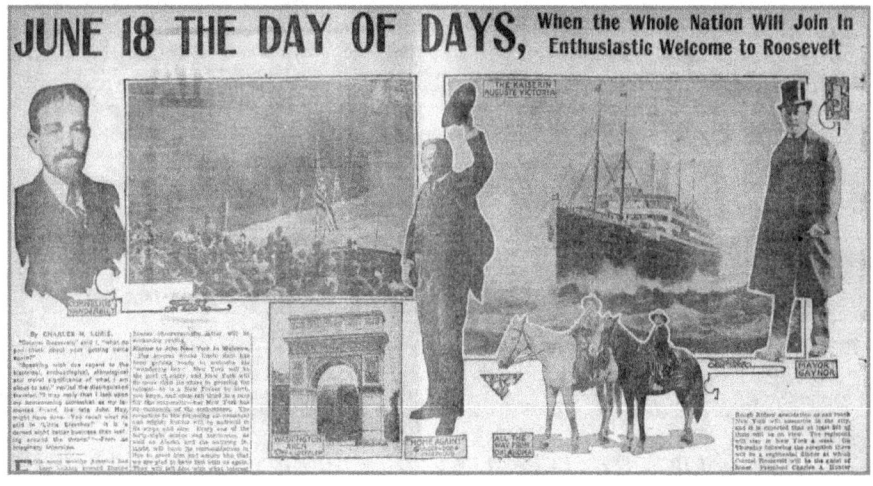

"Colonel Roosevelt," said I, "what do you think about your getting home again?"

"Speaking with due regard to the historical, archaeological, ethnological and moral significance of what I am about to say," replied the distinguished traveler, *"I may reply that I look upon my homecoming somewhat as my lamented friend, the late John Hay, might have done. You recall what he said in 'Little Breeches'? It is a darned sight better business than loafing around the throne."—From an Imaginary Interview.*

For some months America has been looking toward Europe with eyes that had an unutterable yearn behind the irises. We have seen as children after a rest of a parent, and scholars without an accustomed kindly mentor, as men without a wise counselor. The African hunt was past; the ports of civilization had been reached; steamers were making regular sailings to the United States. Why couldn't our own Roosevelt, our only living ex-president, hurry home at once instead of making a scientifically interested but slightly bored looking board of European constitutional authorities as he did, our own man, his due dessert? They had seen their diplomas and degrees and presents by mail, good and early.

But it's all over now; the period of waiting is almost past, and Miss Columbia won't have to display Penelope for her wandering Ulysses much longer. For June 18 the Kaiserling Auguste Victoria will steam into New York harbor with Roosevelt on the bridge, giving the kind of a hasty and glad return that brought all Europe to the deck of that ship, after reading the dispatches that same date and the papers assuring us that that ship was safe. The news of the arrival will bring joy to the throat specialists and the favored opinion of the former will be counting the fat fees received for treating hoarse cheerers; the latter will be reckoning profits.

Nation to Join New York in Welcome.

For several weeks Uncle Sam has been getting ready to welcome his "wandering boy." New York will be the port of entry, and it is with as much interest as the state in greeting its colonel—he is a New Yorker by birth, we know, and once had considerable to say in the mayoralty—but New York has no monopoly of the enthusiasm. The whole United States will be roused and mighty men under all the national flags will be likewise. Every one of the forty-eight states and territories, as well as Alaska and the outlying islands, will have its representatives on the scene to greet him and assure him that they are glad to have him with them again.

And we all shall believe what he tells us about his fellow citizens who followed his hunter caravan everywhere he went, or they have ever lived by telling how he hobnobbed with princes and potentates, and these same New Yorkers, all except the Germans, will be exceedingly in the great reception that never accorded any two thousand men.

The reception in New York to Colonel Roosevelt is expected to be more earnest, sincere enthusiasm that given to him in Europe. In some states and places he is honored as a king; in America and is proud of it, and he understands what his Americanism means. Perhaps he has had an occasion now and then in Europe that the reception will be wildly, madly, enthusiastically, warmly insane. The Chinese, the Japanese, the German-American, the Scandinavian, the Italian-American, the Mexican-American, every man who is here and knows what it is to know of what old Yankees have said, they said, he could be here to greet their own.

The reception in New York to Colonel Roosevelt is expected to be more earnest, sincere enthusiasm than given to him in Europe. In some states and places, he is honored as a king; in America and is proud of it, and he understands what his Americanism means. From one viewpoint it may be looked upon as a private affair, since the national, state, and city governments have no official part in it. It is to be a spontaneous outpouring of the feelings of the populace toward a man who has earned by years of service the right to be considered the representative American. He will be welcomed at the Battery in New York City by Mayor William J. Gaynor, but the city's head will extend him a welcome, not as a great body of American citizens eager to extend the hand of one to themselves. That hand is one of the reception committee appointed by Mayor Gaynor is Cornelius Vanderbilt, the hardest working member of the famous wealthy family.

Water Parade on the Program.

The program of the Roosevelt reception includes a great parade similar to that witnessed at the Hudson-Fulton celebration, but not so long. The vessel on which the welcome party will be transferred if necessary so as to have to reach quarantine exactly at 9 o'clock next morning. The citizens' committee of the 350 has chartered the Hudson River steamer Albany, and it will come down the bay to greet the incoming liner. A great fleet of ships of every size and description will accompany the Albany, every available vessel having been chartered by organizations anxious to be among the first to welcome the homecomer.

Those persons gifted with strong imaginations may now put their hands behind their ears and try to imagine the noise of the myriad whistles and sirens that will greet the first glimpse of the Kaiserin. A little later the colonel and his party will leave the steamer and embark on the revenue cutter that will take them to the Battery. Colonel Roosevelt's demands that the reception committee will disband at the Battery, where Mayor Gaynor, despite the presence of a crowd, will receive him officially, and the reception platform especially erected for the purpose have been *listened to and the received appropriate replies the party will board up Broadway in the following order:*

First, mounted police; second, the riders themselves, a corps of rough riders; then will be red rough riders (the men who accompanied Roosevelt through the African jungles in his celebrated hunt); fourth, Colonel Roosevelt in a carriage; fifth, carriages of the reception committee. The procession will then turn from Broadway into Washington square and through Washington arch up Fifth avenue to a point above Fifty ninth street, where paraders will break ranks. Lined up on both sides of Fifth avenue will be the organizations which will welcome the colonel home. The proposed parade has been abandoned.

Even Tody Hamilton, champion circus press agent, would find himself at a loss for words to describe the welcome. It will be national in character. Weeks and weeks before the date it was decided upon it became known in the land that a great assemblage was planned to greet Roosevelt when he first touched American soil again, requests and appeals for places in the line began to pour in on Captain Arthur P. Cosby, a former rough rider and regular army man, who is secretary of the reception committee. The problem early became one of selection, limitation, and rejection. New York, characteristically American, took the opportunity to pay honor to its great citizen by going the limit for strictness and ease, and permission to turn out no less than

20,000 sent out. Of course, it could not be granted, but they will be liberally represented.

Syrians and Others in Costume.

There will be many others of foreign extraction in line. The Syrians of the city will turn out in their national headgear, the fez, and there will be hundred Hungarians in national costume. The ranks will be extremely rich in character, with the exception of the rough riders, in western costume, and the Spanish war veterans. It is estimated that there will be from 15,000 to 20,000 in line. Some members of the reception committee will wear distinctive dress. The Hamilton club of Chicago, from which he ran out to get early request for a place, will be garbed in high silk hats and frock coats, as will many of the members of state clubs and organizations from many cities, as well as cowboys and others in the West, who will be liberally decorated, it is expected, with flags and bunting. The owners and occupants of houses to make such visible manifestations of their joy over Roosevelt's return.

Probably the feature of the reception that will attract the greatest number of popular attention will be the rough riders, former and still, who will be paraders on the central figure at the affair. At the coming celebration New York will have its first opportunity since the Spanish-American war to see the famous body of men. As many of the 500 members of the Roosevelt Rough Riders' association as can reach New York will assemble in the city, and it is expected that at least 300 of them will be on view. The regiment will stay in New York a week. On Thursday following the reception there will be a regimental dinner at which Colonel Roosevelt will be the guest of honor. President Charles A. Hunter of the association, who is clerk of the United States court at Guthrie, Okla., recently issued a call to all rough riders to assemble in New York before June 16. President Hunter will have personal charge of the regiment and will answer for its good behavior in the metropolis.

Two Thousand Miles to Greet Him.

An interesting little feature of the parade will be the presence of the two Abernathy boys, Louis and Temple, aged ten and six, who undertook a 2,000 mile ride on horseback from Frederick, Okla., to New York, in order to be on hand to greet Colonel Roosevelt, their father's friend. The father of the two boys is John R. Abernathy, United States marshal at Guthrie, who went hunting with President Roosevelt in the spring of 1905 and showed him how to catch wolves alive with his bare hands. Soon afterward the president sent to Abernathy his commission as marshal. The boys have inherited their father's pluck and endurance.

Oyster Bay will have its own welcome for its famous fellow citizen. Soon after his return Colonel Roosevelt will visit various cities to which he has been invited. In August he will speak in Kansas and will attend the annual frontier celebration at Cheyenne, Wyo.[171] [172]

---

[171] *Deseret News* (Salt Lake City, Utah) June 13, 1910, Pg. 8.
[172] The *Coffeyville Weekly Journal* (Coffeyville, Kansas) June 17, 1910, Pg. 6.

The Abernathy embodied the spirit of adventure that Roosevelt so admired and thus were not just spectators. Their journey not only paid tribute to their father's bond with the former president but also embodied the pioneering values that shaped early 20th-century America and which Roosevelt loved.

Exploring New York

Their time in New York wasn't all business. The city's elite took an interest in the boys, inviting them to various events and showing them the wonders of the bustling metropolis. The boys visited the iconic Hotel Breslin, where they stayed as guests of honor. They were given a tour of Central Park, dined with local dignitaries, and even attended performances on Broadway.

The Hotel Breslin was even more grand than anything the boys seen on their trip thus far. Crystal chandeliers cast shimmering light across the marble floors, and the scent of polished wood and fresh flowers filled the air. Temple, wide-eyed, whispered to Louis, 'This sure beat sleeping under the stars.' Their rooms, complete with plush bedding and steaming hot baths, were a far cry from the dusty trails they had traveled. Yet, despite the grandeur, the brothers maintained their down-to-earth charm, delighting the hotel staff with their politeness and wit.

One afternoon, the boys rode their ponies through Central Park, drawing a curious crowd. Children ran alongside them, asking questions about their journey, while adults snapped photographs. Later that evening, they attended a Broadway performance, their first glimpse of the theater's dazzling lights and lively energy. Temple whispered to Louis during the show, 'Do you think Pa would like this?' Louis, grinning, replied, 'Only if it had horses in it.'

> "Both lads went later to Charles P. Taft's Sinton Hotel and registered. They said this evening that they expect to get into New York by June 16, and that they will start on the trip back home about the first of July."[174]

---

[173] The *Los Angeles Times (*Los Angeles, California) June 14, 1910, Pg. 9.
[174] *Tulsa World* (Tulsa, Oklahoma) May 8, 1910, Pg. 1.

BOY RIDERS SEE NEW YORK

Spend Half Hour at City Hall, Talking With High Officials.

ABERNATHY BOYS ENDING THEIR LONG RIDE.
This Photograph of Louis and Temple Abernathy, Sons of U S Marshal Jack Abernathy, Was Taken at Trenton, N J, When the Lads Were on the Last Lap of Their Horseback Ride from Frederic, Okla, to New York to Meet Roosevelt. Louis Abernathy is 10 Years Old and His Brother Only 6.

[175]

The press marveled at their adaptability. Though they were cowboys at heart, the boys seemed equally at ease in the refined settings

---

[175] The *Boston Globe* (Boston, Massachusetts) June 14, 1910, Pg. 11.

of New York City. Temple's precocious humor and Louis's quiet strength won over even the most skeptical New Yorkers.

The Abernathy boys "did" Coney Island yesterday. They saw everything that was to be seen and took rides on slides innumerable. At Steeplechase Park they had a whirl on the roulette wheel, descended the Niagara steps and ascended the golden stairs to their heart's content. The only thing that seemed to be familiar to them was the shooting galleries on Surf avenue, and they didn't seem to think much of them as a fun-producing proposition.[176]

---

[176] The *Brooklyn Daily Eagle* (Brooklyn, New York) June 15, 1910, Pg. 21.

> The Abernathy boys will be T. R.'s only rival in the spotlight next Saturday.

[177]

The Abernathy Boys leading the Roosevelt Parade Down Broadway.
(All photographs by the American Press Association.)

[178]

---

[177] *Birmingham Post-Herald* (Birmingham, Alabama) June 15, 1910, Pg. 4.
[178] *Poughkeepsie Eagle-News* (Poughkeepsie, New York) June 20, 1910 Pg. 1.

ABERNATHY BOYS MARCHING IN ROOSEVELT PARADE IN NEW YORK

One of the features of the parade welcoming the former President home was the young sons of United States Marshal Jack Abernathy of Oklahoma. Louis, 9, and Temple, 6, rode horseback to New York from Oklahoma to welcome their daddy's friend, Roosevelt.

Despite the Abernathy boys' heroic arrival in New York, not everyone was eager to share the spotlight. On June 13, 1910, a surprising tension surfaced: the Rough Riders—Roosevelt's famed cavalry veterans from the Spanish-American War—objected to the boys' participation in the parade honoring the former President's return. At a special meeting of the Roosevelt Reception Committee, it was decided that the Abernathy brothers, who had just completed their arduous horseback journey from Oklahoma, would not ride

---

[179] The *Kansas City Post* (Kansas City, Missouri) June 21, 1910, Pg. 4.

alongside the Rough Riders, nor even among the Spanish-American War veterans.

Rough Riders Would Bar from Parade Boys Who Rode Across the Continent on Horseback

New York, June 13. — It developed today that the Rough Riders are unwilling to have the Abernathy boys, who rode on horseback from Oklahoma to New York, take part in the Roosevelt parade — at least, in that portion of it in which the Rough Riders hope to shine unrivaled. A special meeting of the Reception Committee, held to-day, decided that the Rough Riders are unwilling that the boys should ride with the Spanish war veterans instead.[180]

The decision, though cloaked in formality, hinted at an undercurrent of competition. The Rough Riders, proud of their hard-won heroism, were unwilling to risk being upstaged by two small boys who had captured national headlines. Though the Abernathy brothers had traveled thousands of miles, showing true toughness and heart, they would now find themselves, at least officially, less prominent than other honorees in the grand celebration they had worked so hard to reach.

---

[180] *Democrat and Chronicle* (Rochester, New York) June 14, 1910, Pg. 2.

Louis and Temple Abernathy, sons of "Catch-em-Alive Jack" Abernathy of Oklahoma, who recently arrived in New York on horseback, completing the 2,500 mile trip from Oklahoma City to New York, according to their father, in forty four days. This is an average of almost sixty miles a day. The boys made the trip in order that they might be in New York City to greet former President Roosevelt upon his arrival in New York.

ABOVE Louis and Temple Abernathy, sons of "Catch-em-Alive Jack" Abernathy of Oklahoma, who recently arrived in New York on horseback, completing the 2,500-mile trip from Oklahoma City to New York, according to their father, in forty-four days. This is an average of almost sixty miles a day. The boys made the trip in order that they might be in New York City to greet former President Roosevelt upon his arrival in New York.[181][182][183][184]

---

[181] *Midland Empire News* (Billings, Montana) July 5, 1910, Pg. 6.
[182] The *Billings Gazette* (Billings, Montana) July 2, 1910, Pg. 7.
[183] *Williamsport Sun-Gazette* (Williamsport, Pennsylvania) June 16, 1910, Pg. 2.
[184] The *Post-Standard* (Syracuse, New York) June 15, 1910, Pg. 1.

> Abernathy Boys End Trip.
> New York.—Between cheering files, Louis and Temple Abernathy rode up Broadway Saturday night on the last stage of their 2,000 mile journey from Oklahoma. As their bronchos halted in front of the Hotel Breslin, 1,000 persons joined in the final cheer.

Abernathy Boys End Trip. New York—Between cheering files, Louis and Temple Abernathy rode up Broadway Saturday night on the last stage of their 2,000 mile journey from Oklahoma. As their bronchos halted in front of the Hotel Breslin, 1,000 persons joined in the final cheer.[185] [186] [187] [188] [189] [190]

Reflecting on Their Accomplishment

Their journey had ended in New York City, but its impact would reverberate for years. The boys had achieved what few adults would even attempt. Their visit to the White House and their triumphant arrival in New York symbolized the adventurous spirit of a bygone era.

For Louis and Temple Abernathy, the journey was about reaching Roosevelt, but also it was about testing their limits, embracing the unknown, and inspiring a nation hungry for heroes. Their courage,

---

[185] The Crete Democrat (Crete, Nebraska) June 15, 1910, Pg. 1.
[186] *Blue Valley Blade* (Seward, Nebraska) June 15, 1910, Pg. 2.
[187] The *Stromsburg News* (Stromsburg, Nebraska) June 16, 1910, Pg. 3.
[188] *DeWitt Times-News* (De Witt, Nebraska) June 16, 1910, Pg. 3.
[189] The *Banner-Press* (David City, Nebraska) June 16, 1910, Pg. 2.
[190] The *Bradshaw Monitor* (Bradshaw, Nebraska) June 16,1910, Pg. 7.

resourcefulness, and charm made them more than just average travelers—they became American legends.

Washington, May 27.—After riding on horseback most of the way across the continent to meet Mr. Roosevelt on his arrival at New York, Louie and Temple Abernathy, 9 and 6 years old respectively, sons of "Jack" Abernathy of Oklahoma the wolf catcher and friend of the ex-president, arrived in the capital tonight. They rode in from Frederick, Md., a distance of fifty-seven miles. Temple dropped off to sleep the minute his head touched the pillow. While the little fellow was curled up restfully under the white covers, Louie talked of their trip.[191]

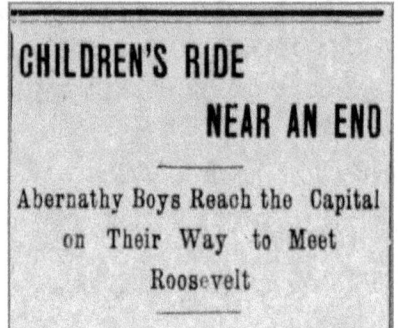

Newspapers couldn't get enough of the Abernathy brothers. The *New York Times* called them 'modern pioneers,' while The *Buffalo News* dubbed them 'fearless symbols of the American spirit.' Reporters followed their every move, from their entrance into the city to their meeting with Roosevelt. Editorials praised their courage, and photographs of the boys in their cowboy hats and dusty boots graced

---

[191] The *Southwest Mail* (Nevada, Missouri) June 3, 1910, Pg. 25.

the front pages of papers across the country with compliments printed over and over such as the following:

"They're not as big as 17 cents," was the remark of Mayor Schwab of Cincinnati when he first saw them., "You certainly have a pair of boys you can be proud of." A big article in the Cincinnati Enquirer by Rudolph Benson was headed by a big picture of the boys taken on Vine street on their horses and a great crowd of spectators about them.

Beginning with Mayor Frederick Kreisman of St. Louis, Mr. Abernathy has received letters from nearly every city executive in all the towns visited by the boys on their trip. All are very complimentary and speak of the boys' manliness and courage.[192]

The Abernathy boys' horseback journey from Oklahoma to New York transcended mere distance—it embodied youthful determination and the bold drive that characterized America's formative years.

---

[192] The *Daily Oklahoman* (Oklahoma City, Oklahoma) May 15, 1910, Pg. 31.

Editor Herald: Mr. Roosevelt seems to have been the favorite topic of discussion in the Letter Box for some time, but none of the writers has struck the keynote to that gentleman's character so well as his son Kermit.

When the Abernathy boys rode from Oklahoma to New York to greet the ex-president upon his return from Africa, they made the acquaintance of Kermit Roosevelt, and in conversation with him asked: "What kind of a man is your father?" Kermit replied: "Father is the kind of a man who wants to be the bride at a wedding or the corpse at a funeral." E. PAYNE Los Angeles, September 28.[193]

---

[193] *Los Angeles Herald* (Los Angeles, California) October 1, 1910, Sat Pg. 14.

Chapter 6: 1910 — Books, Film & Lectures

These little Western children were very much impressed by the great sky-scrapers and crowds of people. In fact, Louie remarked that it looked as though every day was a holiday at New York.[194]

When Louis and Temple Abernathy returned to Oklahoma after their headline-making horseback ride to New York City and their modern return by automobile, they didn't just ride into history—they galloped into the public conscience.

The public's fascination with the young adventurers extended well beyond newspaper clippings and local receptions. Early film makers wasted no time in capturing it for a broader audience.

A Silver Screen Sensation

By August 1910, just weeks after completing their journey, theaters were already advertising a dramatized film titled "The Abernathy Kids to the Rescue." The *Pensacola News Journal* featured the following headline:

> ***"The Abernathy Kids to the Rescue" to Play at the Elite Theatre Today! A western picture that has created a sensation everywhere... the two famous Abernathy boys play the principal parts***[195]

---

[194] The *Central New Jersey Home News* (New Brunswick, NJ) May 15, 1911, Pg. 6.
[195] *Pensacola News Journal* (Pensacola, Florida) August 24, 1910, Pg. 2.

> **ELITE THEATRE**
> **SPECIAL TO-DAY**
>
> "Abernathy Kids to the Rescue," a story of the west in which the famous Abernathy boys play the principle parts.
>
> Illustrated Song by Mr. Rayfield.
>
> Prof. Seel's full orchestra.

The film dramatized their real-life adventures and starred the boys themselves, turning the Abernathys into early child celebrities of silent cinema. The theater added flair with Mr. Rayfield singing under a spotlight and Prof. Seel's Orchestra providing live musical accompaniment.

Shown at venues across the country, this Western-themed motion picture featured the real-life Abernathy boys themselves as the

> **AMUSEMENTS.**
>
> **The Abernathy Kids.**
> A western picture that has created a sensation everywhere will be shown at the Elite Theatre. It's title is "The Abernathy Kids to the Rescue," and the two famous Abernathy boys, who made the daring ride on horseback from Oklahoma City to New York to greet Colonel Roosevelt on his return from Africa play the principal parts. The boys were the "hit" of the parade following Roosevelt's arrival in New York.
> Mr. Rayfield will sing one of his best songs in spot light and Prof. Seel's Orchestra will play some good selections.

stars. Audiences were captivated not just by the novelty of child adventurers on screen, but also by the authenticity—they weren't actors playing parts; they were reenacting their own real-life feats.

These early silent films were often accompanied by live musical performances. In a nation hungry for heroes, especially young and daring ones, the Abernathys fit the bill perfectly.[196]

"Abernathy Kids to the Rescue." You have undoubtedly heard of the Abernathy boys, Louis, nine years of age, and Temple, six years, who made that daring ride on horseback from Oklahoma City, Okla., to New York to take part in the great reception given in honor of the homecoming of Theodore Roosevelt. They traveled no less than 2500 miles on horseback, a feat which old men have not been able to excel. They are wonders in feats of horsemanship that will make you grab your seat handles and open your mouth. This picture is the greatest tale of western daring that you ever gazed upon. The picture finishes by showing Col. Roosevelt, Louis, and Temple with their mammoth Teddy Bear which was presented to them by Roosevelt's Rough Riders at their reception. This is the picture that every little boy and girl in the city should see.

Besides the above feature picture we have:

---

[196] *Pensacola News Journal* (Pensacola, Florida) August 24, 1910, Pg. 8.

"Delightful Dolly." A tale of a doll who isn't a doll at all, but in her efforts to be doll-like, makes you laugh till the tears come to your eyes. We mean it, the tot is actually so funny in her imitations of the doll that you'll yell every time she fools the child opposite with the still, jerky movement of the limbs that usually belong to toy children.

Two of the best pictures you ever saw...

Spotlight and illustrated song by Myrtle and Zelma.

Best program in the city for 5c. To beat the above program, you will have to leave the city.[197]

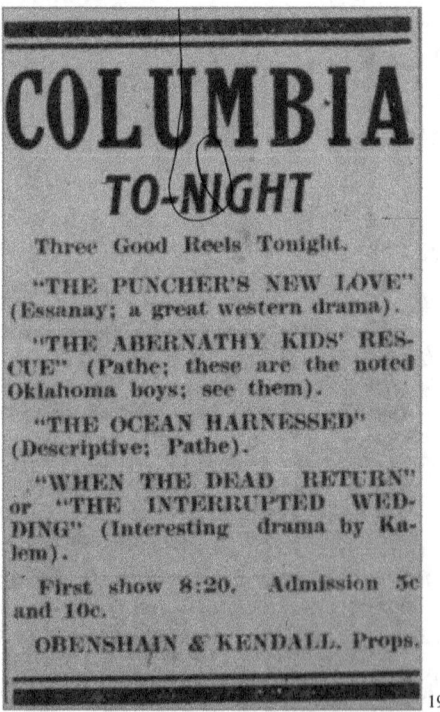

[198]

---

[197] The *Morning News* (Coffeyville, Kansas) October 24, 1910, Pg. 1.
[198] The *Courier-Gazette* (McKinney, Texas) August 12, 1911, Pg. 4.

Soon after their return, the boys' image was also being used to market the very car that brought them home. The *Benson Times* in Nebraska reported:

> **WM. McKEOWN SELLING CAR MADE FAMOUS BY ABERNATHY BOYS.**
> Wm. McKeown is selling the Brush automobile in Benson.
> This is the car made famous by the Abernathy boys in their long run from Oklahoma City to New York and return.
> On this trip the efficacy of the machine was demonstrated. That the Brush can travel any road, can climb any hill and has the strength to stand any strain was proven without a doubt.

"Wm. McKeown Selling Car Made Famous by Abernathy Boys"

The messages received today included one from the Abernathy boys, Louise and Temple, dated Guthrie, Okla., reading: 'Just returned from our run... are sorry...hope you will as well.'[199] Even their telegrams were worthy of press coverage.

---

[199] The *Benson Times* (Benson, Nebraska) 15 October 15, 1910, Pg. 1.

The Book "They" Wrote

At the same time the boys were being cheered on by moviegoers, they were also preparing to share their story in a more lasting medium: a book. In the fall of 1910, it was announced that the boys, with the help of Rev. J.R. Abernathy, a cousin of their father, were writing a book recounting their travels.

Rev. Abernathy had taken the boys on a camping trip to help gather their stories, capturing the adventures in their own words—the excitement, the hardships, the people they met, and the sheer scale of their undertaking. Their journey on horseback to New York and the return trip by Brush automobile would all be included. A New York publisher was already lined up to bring the story to print. [200] [201] [202] [203]

The book promised more than just a travelogue. It offered a rare, unfiltered look at American childhood, resilience, and the pioneering

---

[200] The *Waco Times-Herald* (Waco, Texas) September 22, 1910, Pg. 3.
[201] The *Shawnee Daily Herald* (Shawnee, Oklahoma) September 25, 1910, Pg. 7.
[202] The *Tulsa Tribune* (Tulsa, Oklahoma) September 29, 1910, Pg. 7.
[203] The *Frederick Leader* (Frederick, Oklahoma) September 30, 1910, Pg. 2.

spirit at the dawn of the 20th century. With the boys' natural charm and candor, the book was poised to become a national hit, much like the boys themselves.

Horseback riding isn't the only thing the Abernathy Kids can do. —Just now both Louie and Temple are engaged in the scholarly pursuit of correcting the proofs of their book, "The Ride of the Abernathy Boys," soon to be published by Doubleday, Page & Co.[204]

ANNOUNCEMENT. — "The Ride of the Abernathy Boys," whose father caught 'em alive, is to be one of the new summer books. The Abernathy boys are going to ride over about 200 pages of nice print paper and occasionally jump an illustration. Doubleday, Page & Company will furnish the oats, and any money found rolling up hill in a wagon track between the beginning and the end will be divided between the boys and Doubleday-Page.[205]

---

[204]The B*rooklyn Daily Eagle* (Brooklyn, New York) June 18, 1911, Pg. 53.
[205] *St. Louis Post-Dispatch* (St. Louis, Missouri) June 17, 1911, Pg. 4.

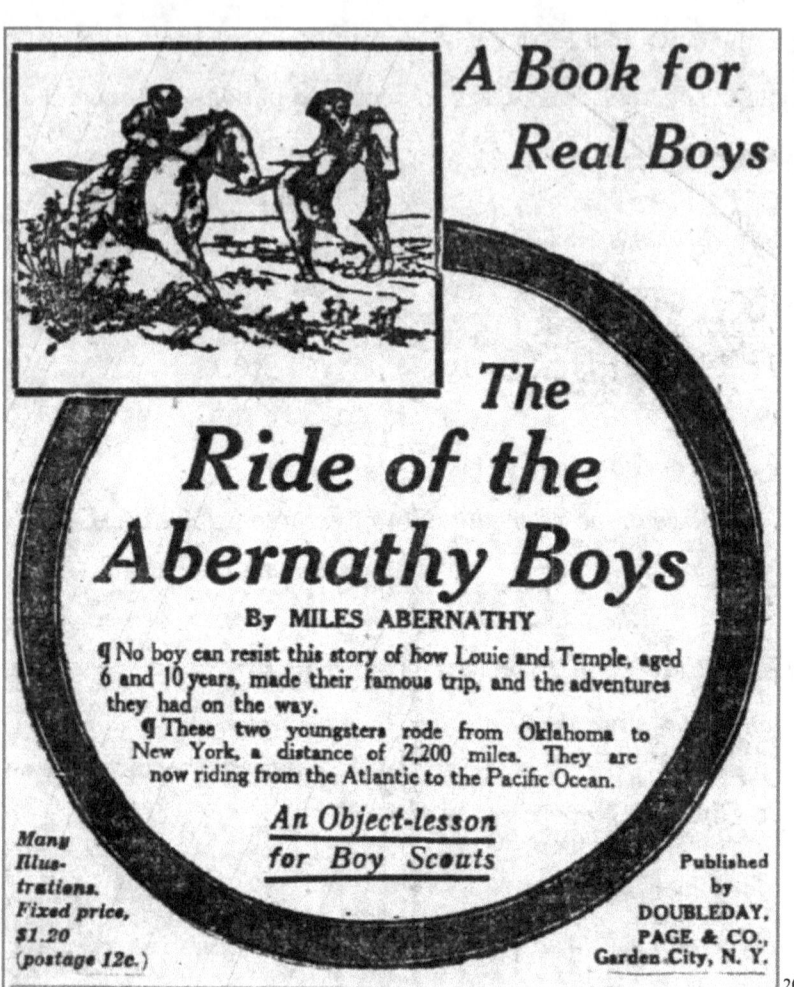

[206] The *New York Times* (New York, New York) August 5, 1911, Pg. 53.
[207] The *New York Times* (New York, New York) August 6, 1911, Pg. 4.

Abernathy Book Published.

"My froat is stopped up and I can't get my breaf good," is the way little Temple Abernathy described his feelings last summer following a siege of cold rainy weather while the boys were riding through Ohio on their horseback trip from Oklahoma to New York, according to their book, "The Ride of the Abernathy Boys," just from the presses of Doubleday, Page & Co. It was true, for the 6-year-old child, with an attack of bronchitis, rode until he lurched from his saddle into the arms of his brother, a man of 10. Nowhere is the book describing their great feat of riding more touching than when telling of Temple's sickness. It only delayed him a couple of days.

"My tummy hurts," wept little Temple Abernathy on the night of July 21, the eve of the start of their ride from the Atlantic to the Pacific. Weeping bitterly, not only because the strawberry pop and the ice cream cones were making trouble for him, but because he couldn't ride, Temple saw his brother and father start on the transcontinental trip. A day later this child of 7 joined them in Poughkeepsie and began the ride, having caught up by rail.

How many boys at the age of 6 or 7 could carry through such feats of riding with such manly disregard of boyish ills?

❖ ❖ ❖

---

[208] *Austin American-Statesman* (Austin, Texas) Aug 27, 1911, Pg. 11.

THE RIDE OF THE ABERNATHY BOYS

How Temple and Louis, 6 and 10, rode 2218 miles, from Oklahoma to New York.

The same boys are the heroes of the even more sensational ride from the Atlantic to the Pacific.

No boy living can resist this true tale of their adventures.

For every Boy Scout it's a direct object lesson.

Illustrated. The price $1.20.

George A. Mullin Co.

BOOKS REVIEWED

"*Along the Andes and Down the Amazon*," by H. J. Mozaus.
"*The Harvester*," by Gene Stratton Porter.
"*Virginia of the Rhodesian*," by Cynthia Stockley.
"*Day Unto Day*," by Louis Howland.
"*Back Home*," by Charles Phillips.
"*The Ride of the Abernathy Boys*," by Miles Abernathy.
"*The Winning of Barbara Worth*," by Harold Bell Wright.

---

[209] The Gazette (Cedar Rapids, Iowa) August 31, 1911, Pg. 2
[210] The *San Francisco Call and Post* (San Francisco, CA) September 3, 1911, Pg. 29.

"Ride of the Abernathy Boys"

This is a true story of the rides and adventures of the two Abernathy boys, who were in Omaha this week. The book is full of life, and is just the thing for your boy. $1.20 the copy.

"Ride of the Abernathy Boys" — $1.20 the Copy

This is a true story of the rides and adventures of the two Abernathy boys who were in Omaha this week. The book is full of life and is just the thing for your boy. $1.20 the copy.

The little Abernathy boys, having published a book on their first cross-country ride, show plainly that they appreciate their opportunities.

---

[211] *Omaha World-Herald* (Omaha, Nebraska) September 8, 1911, Pg. 7.
[212] *Omaha Daily Bee* (Omaha, Nebraska) September 8, 1911, Pg. 9.
[213] *Omaha Daily Bee* (Omaha, Nebraska) September 10, 1911, Pg. 12.

THE RIDE OF THE ABERNATHY BOYS. By Miles Abernathy. Illustrated. New York: Doubleday, Page & Co. Washington: Woodward & Lothrop.

To accept this book first aid to credulity is required for those who did not see these children on the trail, or who have forgotten the newspaper stir over their adventure. Temple Abernathy, six years old, and Louis, ten, rode by themselves from Oklahoma to New York, from the Atlantic to the Pacific. One looks about to measure the capabilities of other boys of corresponding age. But he is driven back to the veracity of the writer of the story, for boys are babies at six and not alarmingly daring at ten. The father of these Abernathy boys makes a plain story of the matter, fully aware that the bare facts of this adventure discredit embellishment of any sort. It is a completely irresistible story of two sturdy heroes—one six, the other ten. It is the sort of thing that everybody in the world should have a chance to read.

[214]

---

[214] *Evening star* (Washington, District of Columbia) September 9, 1911, Pg. 9.

| Always the largest stock of books and the finest stationery and engraving. | **McCLURG'S** | Always the most exclusive importations for wedding, holiday and other gifts. |

Xmas Books for the Children

WHY wait until December to pick them out? We have them all now—the beautiful, elaborate ones—the inexpensive, useful ones—the lively, amusing ones—the exciting school stories—everything. Just bring the children up to our Second Floor today and see how fascinated they'll be.

All the conditions for looking at the books in comfort are at their best right now. Our Juvenile Book Department has just been moved to the Second Floor (near the games), so that a large part of this floor is now devoted to the interests of young people.

You may want suggestions, so we give the names of some of the newest and most promising children's books:

One of the finest things we have is the new illustrated edition of "Treasure Island"—full of really wonderful pictures by N. C. Wyeth. Then there is "Peter and Wendy," in which Mr. Barrie tells more about Peter Pan; and for smaller children "The Glittering Festival," a fairy book with delightful pictures, by Mrs. Carter Harrison.

Boys between ten and sixteen years old will be glad to have any of these: "Team Mates" by R. H. Barbour, "Rolf in the Woods" by Ernest Thompson Seton, "The Second Boys' Book of Model Aeroplanes," "Handicraft for Handy Boys," "The Scout of Pea Ridge," "The Adventures of Bobby Orde," and "The Night Riders of Cave Knob."

For girls especially there are "The Four Corners at College," "Dorothy Dainty at the Mountains," "Patty's Motor Car"—all of which are the latest volumes in three very popular series.

Nor should you fail to see these new ones: "Further Adventures of Nils," "The Land We Live In" (the boy's book of conservation), "The Ride of the Abernathy Boys" (the newspapers have been full of this), "Home Fun" (conjuring, experiments, etc.), Lillian Bell's "Runaway Equator," "Child's Book of Stories" (a splendid collection).

As to BOY SCOUT BOOKS, we are headquarters for this literature and have everything that could possibly be wanted.

(5)

| 218-224 South Wabash Avenue | **A. C. McClurg & Co.** | Between Jackson Blvd. and Adams St. |

"The Ride of the Abernathy Boys," by Miles Abernathy. Doubleday, Page & Co., Garden City, Long Island, New York. $1.20.

There is nothing better for boys than stirring truth and wholesome adventure, and both of these good things are to be found in good measure, flowing over, in this book. Here is told the story of how two real boys, just now entering school in their home town in Oklahoma, rode from Oklahoma to Santa Fe, New Mexico, on the good nags, Sam and Geronimo, and home again. And then the more exciting story of their ride from Oklahoma to New York to see Mr. Roosevelt on his return from the African hunts. Temple was but 6 years old and Louie but 10 when their father trusted them upon the long adventurous journey. Well might he trust two boys brought up, as Temple put it, not "to do just three things—not to drink whisky, nor tell lies, nor tuss." These were two little boys who remembered to say their prayers, too, even when they spent the night with makers of "moonshine," or out in the open with but a fire to frighten away the wolves whose eyes could be seen shining in the dark outside the ring of firelight.

A great book that every boy will be the better, the wiser and the happier for reading.

[216] *Birmingham Post-Herald* (Birmingham, Alabama) September 10, 1911, Pg. 4.

> "Of making books there is no end," remarked the ancient wise man. In one of the latest contributions to the literature of the land, Oklahoma figures conspicuously through the achievements of a pair of her juvenile citizens. "The Ride of the Abernathy Boys," is the title of a volume issued by the Doubleday-Page company. It describes the horseback trip of Miles and Temple Abernathy, ages ten and six years, respectively, from Oklahoma to New York and its authorship is attributed to the older boy [217]

The Abernathy Boys Take the Stage

By the spring of 1911, Louis and Temple Abernathy were no longer just names in the headlines—they had become a national fixation. With two cross-country horseback rides behind them, including

---

[217] The *Chickasha Daily Express* (Chickasha, OK) September 21, 1911, Pg. 4.

their celebrated journey to New York to greet Colonel Roosevelt, the boys were now retracing their path not by trail or rail, but from behind a podium.

The brothers took to the stage in cities across New Jersey to share their story—this time not from the saddle, but through moving pictures and their own voices. With confidence far beyond their years, they recounted tales of terrible roads, political receptions, and nights spent under the stars. Audiences came to see the boys and those who did were rarely disappointed.

In Trenton, New Jersey, the boys delivered what the *Trenton Evening Times* called an "illustrated lecture" at the Masonic Temple. The newspaper noted the crowd was captivated, not just by the tale of their ride to meet Roosevelt, but by the fact that it was being told by boys "only 9 and 12 years old." [218] [219] Their age added a layer of wonder that no adult speaker could match.

---

[218] *Trenton Evening Times* (Trenton, New Jersey) May 13, 1911, Pg. 1.
[219] *NOTE:* There are various reports of their age that aren't consistent. The novelty of their rides is certainly their young age. We know that the first of these trips was planned when Temple was a little more than six and Louie was scarcely more than ten.

THE CELEBRATED

ABERNATHY BOYS

Louis and Temple

and their father, Marshal Abernathy, of Oklahoma, will be in Trenton, Friday, May 12, in a fascinating entertainment. These are the boys who rode horseback from Oklahoma to New York to meet Colonel Roosevelt on his return from Africa. They have ridden over 4,500 miles on horseback alone. They will tell their own stories, which will be illustrated by still and moving pictures.

A wholesome, educational entertainment of great interest to old and young.

At Masonic Temple, Friday, May 12

AFTERNOON AND EVENING.

ADMISSION 25c. and 35c.

[220]

4,500 MILES ON HORSEBACK.

ABERNATHY BOYS

Still and Moving Pictures.

MASONIC TEMPLE
FRIDAY, MAY 12th, 1911

Afternoon and Evening

[221]

---

[220] *Trenton Evening Times* (Trenton, New Jersey), May 9, 1911, Pg. 8.
[221] *Trenton Evening Times* (Trenton, New Jersey) May 10, 1911, Pg. 8.

Just days later in New Brunswick, the Central New Jersey Home News offered more detail: *"These children, Louie and Temple… carried on the entertainment entirely by themselves, no one else appearing on the stage."* Their lecture was accompanied by several reels of moving pictures, a novelty in 1911, giving visual life to the tales they told. Temple, somewhat shy but undaunted, gave a short talk about the U.S. government buildings in Washington. "While very small he spoke out bravely and firmly," the paper reported, "and helped to make the lecture interesting."[222]

ABERNATHY BOYS AT OPERA HOUSE

The crowd learned not just about their ride to New York, but about their earlier journey to Santa Fe—another 2,000-mile expedition, taken when Temple was barely six. The boys shared stories of surviving on mountain ledges, going hungry when shelter was scarce, and being welcomed by mayors and townsfolk alike. They described meeting President Taft in Washington, "Uncle Joe" Cannon, and of course, their audience with Theodore Roosevelt himself in Oyster

---

[222] The *Central New Jersey Home News* (New Brunswick, NJ) May 15, 1911, Pg. 6.

Bay. As Louie put it, "it looked as though every day was a holiday in New York."[223]

But not every lecture went according to plan. In Newark, the *Star-Ledger* reported that the boys did not speak at the New Auditorium as scheduled. Their father, had fallen ill, and his absence meant the show could not go on. Still, the very mention of the boys drew attention. Even when they didn't speak, they were stars.[224]

> **BOYS DID NOT SPEAK.**
>
> The illness of "Ketch 'em Alive Jack" Abernathy, father of the Abernathy boys, Louie and Temple, prevented the youngsters from making addresses at the New Auditorium last night. The youngsters, who are 7 and 11 years of age, respectively, rode all the way from their home in Oklahoma to New York city on horseback to greet Theodore Roosevelt on his return from Africa last year.

[225]

These lectures marked a new chapter in the Abernathy boy's story — one where the boys became not just participants in history,

---

[223] The *Central New Jersey Home News* (New Brunswick, NJ) May 15, 1911, Pg. 6.
[224] The *Star-Ledger* (Newark, New Jersey) May 17, 1911, Pg. 8.
[225] The *Star-Ledger* (Newark, New Jersey) May 17, 1911, Pg 8.

but storytellers of their own adventures. They weren't simply known for what they had done; they were admired for how they told it. And with every stop on their speaking tour, their legend grew

The Spotlight Dims

By December of 1910, the Abernathy boys had ridden into American folklore. However, their names, once printed in bold type across front pages from New York to San Francisco day after day, had begun to fade from the national spotlight. The whirlwind of headlines, crowds, and camera flashes gave way to quieter days. The Abernathy boys, who just months earlier had been greeted by presidents, mayors, and adoring crowds, had finally done the unthinkable: they went home.

The *Tampa Tribune*, ever the bearer of warmth and grace, noted:

> **"The Abernathy boys having passed out of the lime light, their father is trying to keep the name in the papers."**[226]

After a year of newspaper columns practically foaming at the typewriter about two boys riding ponies to New York, the national tone had shifted to something more familiar: indifference tinged with smugness. According to *The Dothan Eagle*:

---

[226] The *Tampa Tribune* (Tampa, Florida) December 11, 1910, Pg. 6.

> *"Jack Abernathy, who is chiefly known as being the father of the two Abernathy boys... has given over the job that the president had given him... Jack says the job is an expensive one and cost more to run than he planned."*[227]

So ended the Abernathy boys' most sensational ride. More was to come on their way home and in 1911, but nothing compared to the initial media storm of 1910.

For the moment, the boys were heading back to where they began, just two little adventurers with big hats, bigger dreams, and no idea they'd just lived one of the most amazing stories the country had ever seen.

---

[227] The *Dothan Eagle* (Dothan, Alabama) December 13, 1910, Pg. 2.

Chapter 7: 1911 — From Saddles to Steering Wheels

Did you little boys really cross the country in a small machine like that?" asked one matron. 'Yes'm, Bud drove the car all the way, but I steered part of the time,' answered Temple, the six-year-old.[228]

The Abernathy boys, dressed in their traveling attire, explained the workings of their automobiles to curious onlookers, showing once again their remarkable adaptability and charm.[229]

I don't remember when I began to ride. I must have been a baby. Any boy could take that trip

— Louis Abernathy[230].

Having completed their daring horseback journey to New York City and met their ultimate goal of greeting former President Theodore Roosevelt, Louis and Temple Abernathy faced a new challenge: returning home. But this time, the adventure would take a different form. Instead of retracing their steps on horseback, the boys opted for a modern twist. It was reported that they purchased a Brush Runabout automobile to drive back to Oklahoma. However, some skepticism is warranted as to whether the Abernathy boys actually purchased the Brush Runabout themselves; it's quite possible the car was provided by Brush Motor Company, especially given that it prominently flew

---

[228] *Brooklyn Eagle*, (Brooklyn, New York) January 11, 1911, Pg. 27.
[229] *The Morning Union*, (Springfield, Massachusetts) January 15, 1911, Pg. 19.
[230] *Fall River Globe* (Fall River, Massachusetts) August 23,1910, Pg. 2.

Brush banners from flagpoles mounted on the vehicle throughout their journey. Their return journey would once again captivate the nation.

The Decision to Drive

The decision to swap saddles for steering wheels was not entirely unexpected. The Abernathy boys, always eager for a new challenge, had become fascinated by the burgeoning automobile industry during their time in New York. Temple, the younger of the two, reportedly took particular delight in testing the vehicles, despite his legs barely reaching the pedals.

> A good many people are wondering if those Abernathy boys intend to ride back to Oklahoma horseback, or sell out and take the cars. [231]

---

[231] The *Vinita Daily Chieftain* (Vinita, Oklahoma) June 4, 1910 Pg. 2.

The two Abernathy boys, Louis and Temple, who came to town to see Colonel Roseveit las june when he arrived in New York, riding horseback, have returned to Gotham and will be a feature of the Brush machine exhibit at the Licensed Automobile Manufacturers' show which opens at Madison Square Garden January 6. The famous kids will probably remain in the east for some time, as it is said they have developed a healthy liking for metropolitan life.

---

[232] *East Oregonian* (Pendleton, Oregon) January 5, 1911, Pg. 6.
[233] The *Dispatch-Republican* (Clay Center, Kansas) January 6, 1911, Pg. 3

Brooklyn Eagle (Brooklyn, New York) January 8, 1911, Pg. 54.

"Yes'm, Bud drove the car all the way, but I steered part of the time," Temple proudly told a reporter during a demonstration of his driving skills at a Brush exhibit in Madison Square Garden.[235]

> The lowest priced car in the show is the Brush runabout, and a special feature of the exhibit is the car in which the Abernathy boys made their return trip when they came from Oklahoma City to New York on the bronchos to assist in welcoming Colonel Roosevelt on his return from his African expedition. The boys are six and nine years old, respectively, and they are usually to be found around the Brush exhibit. Besides the Abernathy boys' car there are in the space a chassis, a runabout with a rumble seat, another with gas tank in the rear and a coupe. In the Brush space is also shown the New Sampson car, which has a four cylinder en bloc motor. The chassis and a fore-door tourer make up the exhibit.[236]

Their father, supported their decision, seeing the adventure as an opportunity for his sons to learn a new skill while navigating the rapidly modernizing world.

---

[235] *Brooklyn Eagle,* (Brooklyn, New York) January 11, 1911, Pg. 27.
[236] The *Columbia Record* (Columbia, South Carolina) January 16, 1911, Pg. 5.

Brush Cars at the Show with Abernathy Kid's Car on Right

The Brush runabout is one of the smallest cars in the show, but it well illustrates that old saying about the "best things being done up in the smallest packages." When the quiet-mannered attendant remarks to the visitor who is unacquainted with the history of this car that this one-cylinder, 10 horse-power car climbed Pike's Peak three years ago and also that it averaged as high as twenty miles a day in a Munsey tour, the visitor opens his eyes with astonishment and marvels at the progress in the

---

[237] *Boston Evening Transcript (*Boston, Massachusetts) March 8, 1911, Pg. 6.

169

motor world. It was in this car that the now famous Abernathy boys returned to Oklahoma after their trip to New York, on horseback, to see Colonel Roosevelt, and a little booklet issued by the Brush Runabout Company gives an exceedingly interesting account of what these two youngsters did.[238]

Learning to Drive

The transition from horseback to the motorized Brush automobile wasn't as seamless as one might think. Before departing New York, Louis and Temple received a crash course in operating their new automobile. Driving in the early 1900s was no small feat; cars required manual cranking to start, constant adjustments to the throttle and spark, and a firm grip on the steering wheel. For the Abernathy boys, who had just mastered horseback navigation, the transition to motor vehicles was an exciting challenge.

The journey quickly proved to be a blend of excitement and frustration.

Temple's small stature presented a unique problem. Too small to see over the dashboard, Temple steered by looking through the spokes of the wheel. Still, his skill and steady hand amazed onlookers as they watched a six-year-old handle a car with ease.

---

[238] *Boston Evening Transcript (*Boston, Massachusetts) March 8, 1911, Pg. 6.

Temple crawled into a Brush roadster, advanced the spark and throttle, and gave a complete and noiseless pantomime of the way to run the car. The youngest salesman at the show had the crowd in awe.[239]

Their ability to adjust to the car's quirks highlighted their adaptability. By the time they reached St. Louis, they had not only mastered the Brush's mechanics but also learned to navigate the early, often unpredictable roads of America.

> It is alleged that the Abernathy boys have learned the workings of an automobile to their entire satisfaction. This means that the little cow punchers have discovered some means of hobbling the critter at night and spurring it in the neck to make it buck.[240]

Challenges on the Road

As the boys began their motorized journey home, they encountered an entirely new set of challenges. The unpaved roads of the early 20th century were rough and unpredictable, often little more

---

[239] *Brooklyn Daily Eagle*, (Brooklyn, New York) January 11, 1911. Pg. 27.
[240] The *Topeka State Journal* (Topeka, Kansas) July 8, 1910, Pg. 4.

than dirt paths riddled with potholes and rocks. Mechanical breakdowns were common, requiring the boys to rely on their wits and the kindness of strangers to keep moving forward.

In one town, Temple reportedly charmed a resident into helping fix a flat tire, promising him a ride in exchange for his assistance. Meanwhile, Louis quickly learned to diagnose engine troubles, earning respect for his practical knowledge and steady demeanor.

Despite these difficulties, the boys maintained a steady pace, covering dozens of miles each day. Newspapers reported on their progress, noting that their transition from horseback to automobile had not dampened their adventurous spirit.

The Abernathy boys arriving at the Wichita Eagle office. Louis is standing up and Temple, the younger lad, is seated n the extra automobile tire.

Louis and Temple Abernathy and their father, John R. Abernathy, browned by exposure since last June, reached Wichita yesterday afternoon at 3 o'clock, visited an hour and started for the last lap of their round trip from Oklahoma to New York, where they were among the thousands who waved a greeting to Colonel Theodore Roosevelt when he landed after a year and a half spent in the jungles of Africa and at the palaces of Europe.

The party, consisting of the two boys, the central figures, and four men, arrived from Emporia and proceeded on toward the goal, expecting to stop at Caldwell last night. The journey will come to an end some time this afternoon, when the dust-smeared men and machine pull up on the streets of Oklahoma City.

The two boys are bright little youngsters, one aged 9, the other but 6. Both are a picture of health, plump and spry. Louis, the elder, drives one machine, and Temple, the baby, rides with his father in a touring car.

Rode Horseback to New York.

The boys left Oklahoma last June on horses and made the long ride of nearly 2,000 miles to New York in time to be with their father at the reception given to Colonel Roosevelt. This trip was made by the boys alone. Through every city they passed demonstrations greeted them. When the lads reached New York it was necessary to send out squads of policemen to keep the boys from being run down by the crowds.

Colonel Roosevelt greeted the boys personally, and they spent several hours with him during their stay in the metropolis. At one time the ex-president placed his arms about the little chaps and praised them for their pluck and manliness.

Marshal Abernathy directed the automobile drivers to head for the Eagle office, and although a reception had been planned for them they arrived unaccompanied, owing to having made better time than anticipated.

"Gee, but this is hot work!" exclaimed Marshal Abernathy, as he shook hands with a representative of the Eagle. "But we are having a fine time and the boys are enjoying it greatly."

What He Thinks of the Colonel.

"Temple who do you think of Colonel Roosevelt?" was asked of the lad of 6.[241]

> **What He Thinks of the Colonel.**
> "Temple who do you think of Colonel Roosevelt?" was asked of the lad of 6.

"Why, I think he is all right," exclaimed the little man, and he forthwith stood on his head in the rear seat of the big Maxwell touring car, then tumbled over his dad and squirmed about until he got a fair chance to kick the hat off the driver, who retaliated by picking up the little tot and standing him on his head, this time on the steering wheel.

---

[241] NOTE; Although "who" doesn't seem contextually correct. I have provided the clipping to show the original text.

All during the conversation the little chap played with his father and the men in the car with him. He was thirsty, too, and after being taken down to Paul Eaton's concrete corner he showed that he had a good taste by drinking a big glass of soda water, using five straws during the process. The lad drank at the expense of the Eagle's representative, and when he had finished he turned his chubby face up to the man at his side and said, "Thank you."

Louis Is Tired.

Louis is the silent one of the two. He seemed to be weary with the strenuous days that have fallen to his lot since he started East astride one of his father's big horses.

"I think that Colonel Roosevelt is the greatest man I ever saw," he said in reply to a question and then wearily "scrooched" down in his seat and closed his eyes.

The two boys were lined up by their new Brush automobile and a picture was taken of them for the Eagle. When the camera snapped Temple turned to his father and said: "That is enough, let's go."

Both lads have been plied with questions until they answer in a sort of random manner. Temple, the younger, has happily struck upon a phrase that baffles his questioners and proves a very good preventative. To the multitude of queries flung at him yesterday invariably he said: "I don't know sir."

In speaking of the boys' trip to New York astride horses, Marshal Abernathy said:

Marshal Abernathy Delighted.

"My sons did better than I expected. They proved that a Western lad is as good as any army officer. They were given the best of treatment wherever they went and I never had the least bit of apprehension concerning their safety.

"Do you know that they left Oklahoma without a cent of money. I provided them with check books and not once was one of their checks turned down. I have heard from two of their checks. The men who hold them say that I shall never be called upon to pay them. Very few of the checks they wrote have turned up and I don't expect many.

"If they could go through the world this way it would suit me all right. Their trip will cost just about half as much as I anticipated.

"The horses they rode east have been shipped back to Oklahoma City and I expect to keep them as long as they are able to eat.

"A world of news and comment has been printed about the lads. I even have clippings from Europe, some in foreign language. The press of Europe made nearly as much of the trip of the boys as did the American papers.

Marshal Abernathy had little to say concerning Colonel Roosevelt. He is one of the ex-president's closest friends and probably could throw light on many things that the public is anxious to know.

Says Roosevelt Is Unchanged.

"I believe that Colonel Roosevelt is the greatest man in the world today. His trip made no change in him. He has all the honor a man could desire and is wealthy. There is but one thing that would *cause him to run for president again and that is the demand of the American people.*

"I know that Roosevelt does not wish to run for president again, but I know that he would get in the race if the nation should need such as he."

While it is too far ahead to anticipate another hunting trip by the ex-president, it is highly probable that when he goes again Marshal Abernathy will accompany him. Mr. Abernathy has asked if Colonel Roosevelt was coming west soon for a hunt and his only reply was, "Well, I cannot say just yet," and then he smiled.

The friendship between Colonel Roosevelt and Mr. Abernathy is one of the lasting kind. Abernathy became a marshal for Oklahoma because of his bravery in catching wolves bare-handed while the president was on his western wolf hunt. This feat secured his appointment.

Marshal Abernathy lives at Oklahoma City. He sold his Guthrie property a few months before the capital election and moved away. He said he was unacquainted with the merits of the capital fight, and did not care to discuss it.

Mrs. Abernathy, mother of the boys, is dead, and they look to their father to fill the place of both father and mother, and from the tenderness shown by the big, dare-devil Oklahoman, he is right well filling the place.

The party consisted of John R. Abernathy, Louie, aged 9, and Temple, aged 6; William Tuesday, agent for the Maxwell car; Harvey

Lincoln, agent for the Brush runabout, and F. M. W. Hall, a New York journalist.

As soon as the party reaches Oklahoma City the last three named will return directly to New York, traveling by rail. They have had enough experience with long distance auto trips, and they show it not only in actions but in looks.[242]

THE ABERNATHY BOYS LEAVING NEW YORK [243]

---

[242] The *Wichita Eagle* (Wichita, Kansas) Jul 27, 1910, Pg. 1.
[243] *St. Louis Post-Dispatch* (St. Louis, Missouri) July 10, 1910 Pg. 28.

Reception Along the Way

Much like their horseback journey to New York, the return trip in their Brush Runabouts continued the boys traveling celebrity. Newspapers continued recording the rowds gathered in small towns and cities along their route, eager to see the young adventurers and their newfangled machines. The boys, ever polite and composed, greeted their admirers with enthusiasm, posing for photographs and answering questions about their journey.

> *The Abernathy boys, dressed in their traveling attire, explained the workings of their automobiles to curious onlookers, showing once again their remarkable adaptability and charm.* [244]

Their story captured the public's attention as a symbol of the nation's transition from traditional ways of life to the modern age. They had shown what persistence could accomplish on horseback—and now, they were channeling that same drive into mastering the tools of a new age.

Reaching Home

After weeks on the road, Louis and Temple rolled into Oklahoma, greeted by a jubilant crowd. Their journey had showcased their ability to adapt and highlighted the potential of the automobile as a

---

[244] *The Morning Union*, (Springfield, Massachusetts) January 15, 1911, Pg. 1.

transformative technology. The boys' return marked the end of another adventure, but it was clear that their legend was only growing.

Their father beamed with pride as he welcomed his sons back. The Brush Runabout, now dusty and well-worn, stood as symbol of the transition to the modern age of transportation. For the Abernathy brothers, this homecoming was another chapter in their unfolding legacy.

A Ride Worth Selling

As if making national headlines wasn't enough, the Abernathy boys added another notch to their fame in 1910: they became unofficial spokes kids for the automotive revolution.

After their return to Oklahoma in the sturdy little Brush Runabout, newspapers and car dealers across the country didn't just report on their journey—they capitalized on it. The Brush Motor Car Company, recognizing marketing gold when they saw it, turned the Abernathy adventure into one of the most memorable automotive endorsements of the era.

> *"Think for a moment about the 2,500 mile trip of the Abernathy kids!"*

proclaimed newspapers from *The Boston Globe* to *The Daily Oklahoman* and many spots in between.[245] [246] [247]

---

[245] The *Boston Globe* (Boston, Massachusetts) August 28, 1910, Pg. 53.
[246] The *Daily Oklahoman* (Oklahoma City, Oklahoma) August 28, 1910, Pg. 11.
[247] The *Herington Times* (Herington, Kansas) August 25, 1910, Pg. 4.

The ad went on to call Louie's drive home "proof that even a 9-year-old boy could handle the Brush as well as a professional driver." It was hard to argue. In just nineteen days, he covered more than 2,400 miles—averaging nearly 140 miles per day. He manned the crank himself, bundled up in blankets at night when needed, and pulled into the driveway claiming he felt better than when he'd left New York.

In Louie Abernathy, the Brush company found the perfect mix of American boyhood and mechanical dependability. If a kid could do it, what excuse did grown-ups have?

> *"Thousands greeted them... the sight of seeing this youngster easily starting, driving and stopping his car was such proof of BRUSH simplicity that even the most skeptical could doubt no longer."*

And it wasn't just talk. Brush dealerships used the Abernathy's' name to boost sales from Boston to Benson, Nebraska. Ads such as the one to the right appeared in the New York Times.[248] One dealer advertised:

> *"This is the car made famous by the Abernathy boys..."*

---

[248] The *New York Times* (New York, New York) January 10, 1911 Pg. 12.

So, while the boys were already riding into the history books, they also drove themselves straight into American advertising lore—earning endorsement deals by way of their travels and youthful charm.[249]

---

[249] Note the text presented from the advertisement is almost the same in all the ads. The full ad text is provided in Appendix 3.

9-Year-Old Boy Drives Brush 2,500 Miles

Abernathy Kids, having welcomed "Uncle" Teddy, return by automobile instead of on horse back

The Abernathy Kids, famous because of their horseback ride from Oklahoma City to New York to meet Colonel Roosevelt on his return from jungle and Court, returned to their home in the far Southwest in their own Brush Runabout, with Louie, aged 9, at the wheel. They left New York July 6th and reached Oklahoma City July 29th.

The boys chose a Brush Runabout because it is the only car they could start and handle without help, and so simple mechanically they could understand everything about it. Their car was a standard stock model, an exact duplicate of the car you may for $485. Louie did all the driving, his brother Temple being too small to properly manipulate the foot pedal.

Driving the car with one hand, while blowing the horn with the other, this 9-year-old boy threaded his way through the traffic and between lanes of cheering people out of New York City and into the open country, with the seeming indifference and freedom from worry that a racing driver would display under the same conditions.

Louie Abernathy is a wonderful boy, but no other car, except the Brush, could he have so successfully mastered in such a short time, and successfully managed under 30% trying conditions.

Any good automobile made today can be driven from New York to Oklahoma City, but the Brush is the only automobile built which a 9-year-old boy could drive and handle for 500 miles.

The trip of the Abernathy Kids attracted the attention of the whole country. It demonstrated beyond argument the features of the Brush which we have been emphasizing in our advertising—features responsible for the thousands of Brush cars giving such complete satisfaction.

These features are—simplicity, easy riding qualities, freedom from mechanical worries, low tire expense, power to travel any road and strength to stand every strain.

We have been consistently telling you about these features for years. We have been trying to prove to you what an investment the Brush would be for you, both from the standpoint of pleasure and utility. But it is sometimes hard to prove, by the evidence of someone you don't know, probably hundreds of miles away, just how reliable the Brush is. Here is a test made out in the open, with the eyes of the whole United States watching.

The Abernathy Kids are famous the world over.

This feat of their driving a Brush car 2,500 miles has been watched carefully along every mile of the road. Thousands have seen this 9-year-old boy at the wheel. They have seen him start the motor and stop it. They have seen him drive up steep hills, and over the roughest roads. They have talked to him—have had him tell them how much fun he and his younger brother had and how easily he handled his Brush car.

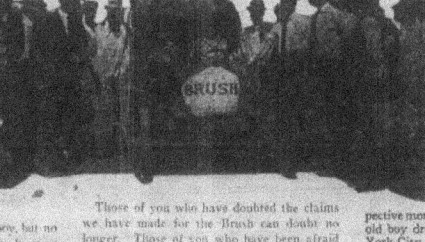

Those of you who have doubted the claims we have made for the Brush can doubt no longer. Those of you who have been afraid that an automobile was something that only an expert could handle and that only a mechanic could understand, must look at the Brush in a new light.

There is a lesson in this Abernathy "stunt" which you should take home to yourself. Think what it means to you to be able to buy an automobile for $485, which you, or any one of your family can drive, which can be operated either for business or pleasure at an expense of less than one cent a mile.

You may be at the mercy of inconvenient transportation facilities. The Brush will not only make you independent, but it will cost you less than car fare to operate. You may be using horses. The Brush has proven beyond any shadow of doubt that the horse-drawn vehicle cannot compete with it, either in cost or upkeep, or in efficiency. Your income may depend on how much ground you can cover in a day, and how many people you can see in a day. If so, the Brush will pay for itself and make you money besides. You may be a contractor having several building jobs to oversee at one time. It is worth money to you to be able to make the rounds quickly and economically. For this work the Brush has no equal. You may be a physician. The ease with which the Brush can be started appeals to the physician, because he has to stop and start his car perhaps oftener than any other user, and so on down the list—merchant, manufacturer, city or country salesmen, R.F.D. Carrier, farmer—all are using the Brush and are finding it the best investment they ever made.

The longer you delay investigating it, the longer you may be doing yourself an injustice, the longer you may be postponing the opportunity to increase your income and decrease your expenses.

We have not said a word about the pleasure side of the Brush. The Abernathy Kids have demonstrated that feature so well that we need say little about it. No car offers more as a pleasure car, except size and carrying capacity. No car offers as much, when you take into consideration the lack of tire trouble and the ease and economy with which it can be operated—all of which go to make automobiling for pleasure worth while.

No tour—no endurance run—no race ever answered so many questions important to the prospective motor car buyer as this feat of a 9-year-old boy driving a Brush runabout from New York City to Oklahoma City.

Our Minneapolis salesroom and Brush dealers everywhere have Brush cars at your disposal for demonstration purposes. They are kept in readiness to prove just how valuable the Brush would be to you. Decide right now to examine the Brush, ride in it, drive it, to see for yourself just how it can be adapted to some particular use or uses, either in your working or playing time, or both.

Brush Runabout Company
Detroit, Michigan

Kemp Brothers Automobile Company
1514 Hennepin Avenue, Northwestern Distributors

Ask Yourself This Question

"Would an Automobile that I Could Buy for $485.00 and Operate for Less than One Cent a Mile, be a Good Investment for Me?"

The way to arrive at a sensible conclusion as to whether or not you should buy an automobile, is to talk it over with yourself. You know all about your own business. You know how you make your money. If you have much getting around to do, you know how much time it takes and what it costs you to do it. So you are the best judge of whether or not you could increase your own efficiency or that of some of your employees by the use of an automobile.

If time is worth anything to you, the chances are you would save a great deal of it by the use of any automobile. But its first cost would have to be so low and the up-keep of it so small that the result would show a net profit. The BRUSH RUNABOUT, because of its first low cost, because of the very small amount of money necessary to operate and maintain it, is the logical car for you to use as a basis for making your investigation. If the BRUSH will not do the things that you want an automobile to do and show a profit, then no motor car built will. If you have much getting about to do, a BRUSH will do it for you cheaper than carfare. If you are now using a horse or horses, a BRUSH will enable you to cover twice the ground, and your gasoline and oil bills will be much less than you are now paying for feed and blacksmith's bills. This may sound to you like a strong statement. The proof is found in the testimony of thousands of BRUSH owners who are proving it to their satisfaction every day. It is a simple matter for you to prove it for yourself.

Think for a moment about the 2,500 mile trip of the Abernathy kids! After riding from Oklahoma City to New York on horseback to pay their respects to Colonel Roosevelt, these youngsters decided to make the return journey by automobile. Louie, the older of the two (and he is only nine years old,) chose a Brush Runabout to make the long drive, because it is the only car which is so simple mechanically and so easy to handle that a boy of his age could run it as well as a professional driver operates a large machine. Louie Abernathy drove the BRUSH all the way himself. They "honked" up the main street of Oklahoma City just twenty-three days after they left New York. They stopped a day each in four of the larger cities to see the sights. So they were on the road nineteen days, averaging almost 140 miles a day.

Louie Abernathy demonstrated in a way that admits of no argument that the BRUSH features which we have been telling you about in our advertising are real features. He demonstrated that the BRUSH is simple to operate and easy to handle. He demonstrated its easy-riding qualities, both the boys arriving home feeling better than when they left New York. He demonstrated that a 9-year-old boy could crank it and that the motor starts without fuss and trouble. He demonstrated that the BRUSH driver is practically free from mechanical worries. He demonstrated that the BRUSH can travel any road, can climb any hill, has the strength to stand any strain.

These are the things which should go a long way toward helping you solve the automobile question for yourself. The Abernathy boys attracted the attention of the whole country. Thousands greeted them and cheered them along the roads. The sight of seeing this youngster actually starting, driving and stopping his car was such proof of BRUSH simplicity that even the most skeptical could doubt no longer.

For every effect there must be a cause. We can make claims for the BRUSH that no other automobile manufacturer can make for his product—because no other automobile is like the BRUSH either in its mechanical or important construction features. The motor in the BRUSH is simplicity itself. You can learn all about it in five minutes. The BRUSH has a spiral-spring suspension, the like of which is found on no other motor car built. You can drive a BRUSH over rough, rutty roads at a speed impossible for any other automobile. It is so light you can lift one wheel and prop it up to make a tire repair without the aid of a jack. Weight, more than anything else, is responsible for tire trouble. The easiest car on tires is the lightest car. The lightest car, by wide margin, is the BRUSH.

We could go on enumerating BRUSH features which make the car loom up so big purely as an investment. The best we can do, however, in any piece of advertising, is to arouse your curiosity to the point of making a personal investigation of the BRUSH. The way to find out all about the BRUSH RUNABOUT, the way to prove to yourself that the things we say about it are true, the way to know just what it will do for you—is to examine it, ride in it, drive it. It will not take you long to go to the dealer nearest you who handles the BRUSH. He is more than willing to give you an actual BRUSH demonstration. And remember, the car that you can buy for $485 is an exact duplicate of the BRUSH car which the Abernathy boys drove almost 140 miles a day for nineteen days.

We have been taking advantage of the Abernathy trip to call your attention to the utility side of the BRUSH. This trip demonstrated, however, in just as big a way, the pleasure side of this wonderful car. No car offers more as a pleasure vehicle than the BRUSH, except size and carrying capacity. No car in the world offers as much, considered both from the standpoint of utility and pleasure, as the BRUSH.

Ask yourself the same question which you did at the beginning of this advertisement, and remember that there is a BRUSH dealer near you who will be glad to show you how to prove what the BRUSH will do for you. If you are busy, he will be glad to come to you if you will write or telephone him.

Brush Runabout Company, Detroit, Michigan

Kemp Brothers Automobile Company
1514 Hennepin Avenue, Distributors for Minneapolis and Vicinity

---

[251] The *Minneapolis Journal* (Minneapolis, Minnesota) August 21, 1910 Pg. 16.
[252] *Star Tribune* (Minneapolis, Minnesota) August 21, 1910, Pg. 8.

Ask Yourself This Question

"Would an Automobile that I Could Buy for $485.00 and Operate for Less than One Cent a Mile, be a Good Investment for Me?"

The way to arrive at a sensible conclusion as to whether or not you should buy an automobile, is to talk it over with yourself. You know all about your own business. You know how you make your money. If you have much getting around to do, you know how much time it takes and what it costs you to do it. So you are the best judge of whether or not you could increase your efficiency or that of some of your employees by the use of an automobile.

If time is worth anything to you, the chances are you would save a great deal of it by the use of any automobile. But its first cost would have to be so low and the up-keep of it so small that the result would show a net profit.

The BRUSH RUNABOUT, because of its first low cost, because of the very small amount of money necessary to operate and maintain it, is the logical car for you to use as a basis for making your investigation. If the BRUSH will not do the things that you want an automobile to do and show a profit, then no motor car built will. If you have much getting about to do, a BRUSH will do it for you cheaper than carfare. If you are now using a horse or horses, a BRUSH will enable you to cover twice the ground, and your gasoline and oil bills will be much less than you are now paying for feed and blacksmith's bills. This may sound to you like a strong statement. The proof is found in the testimony of thousands of BRUSH owners who are proving it to their satisfaction every day. It is a simple matter for you to prove it for yourself.

Think for a moment about the 2,500-mile trip of the Abernathy kids! After riding from Oklahoma City to New York on horseback to pay their respects to Colonel Roosevelt, these youngsters decided to make the return journey by automobile. Louie, the elder of the two (and he is only nine years old), chose a Brush Runabout to make the long drive, because it is the only car which is so simple mechanically and so easy to handle that a boy of his age could run it as well as a professional driver operates a large machine. Louie Abernathy drove the BRUSH all the way himself. They "honked" up the main street of Oklahoma City just twenty-three days after they left New York. They stopped a day each in four of the larger cities to see the sights. So they were on the road nineteen days, averaging about 140 miles a day.

Louie Abernathy demonstrated in a way that admits of no argument, that the BRUSH features which we have been telling you about in our advertising are REAL features. He demonstrated that the BRUSH is simple to operate and easy to handle. He demonstrated its easy-riding qualities, both the boys arriving home feeling better than when they left New York. He demonstrated that a nine-year-old boy could crank it and that the motor starts without fuss and trouble. He demonstrated that the BRUSH driver is practically free from mechanical worries. He demonstrated that the BRUSH can travel any road, can climb any hill, has the strength to stand any strain.

These are the things which should go a long way toward helping you solve the automobile question for yourself. The Abernathy boys attracted the attention of the whole country. Thousands greeted them and cheered them along the roads. The sight of seeing this youngster actually starting, driving and stopping his car was such proof of BRUSH simplicity that even the most skeptical could doubt no longer.

For every effect there must be a cause. We can make claims for the BRUSH that no other automobile manufacturer can make for his product—because no other automobile is like the BRUSH either in its mechanical or important construction features. The motor in the BRUSH is simplicity itself. You can learn all about it in five minutes. The BRUSH has a spiral-spring suspension, the like of which is found on no other motor car built. You can drive a BRUSH over rough, rutty roads at a speed impossible for any other automobile. It is so light you can lift one wheel and prop it up to make a tire repair without the aid of a jack. Weight, more than anything else, is responsible for tire trouble. The easiest car on tires is the lightest car. The lightest car, by wide margin, is the BRUSH.

We could go on enumerating BRUSH features which make the car loom up so big purely as an investment. The best we can do, however, in any piece of advertising, is to arouse your curiosity to the point of making a personal investigation of the BRUSH. The way to find out all about the BRUSH RUNABOUT, the way to prove to yourself that the things we say about it are true, the way to know just what it will do for you—is to examine it, ride in it, drive it. It will not take you long to go to the dealer nearest you who handles the BRUSH. He is more than willing to give you an actual BRUSH demonstration. And remember, the car that you can buy for $485, is an exact duplicate of the BRUSH car which the Abernathy boys drove almost 140 miles a day for nineteen days.

We have been taking advantage of the Abernathy trip to call your attention to the utility side of the BRUSH. This trip demonstrated, however, in just as big a way, the pleasure side of this wonderful car. No car offers more as a pleasure vehicle than the BRUSH, except size and carrying capacity. No car in the world offers as much, considered both from the standpoint of utility and pleasure, as the BRUSH.

Ask yourself the same question which you did at the beginning of this advertisement, and remember that there is a BRUSH dealer near you who will be glad to show you how to prove what the BRUSH will do for you. If you are busy, he will be glad to come to you if you will write or telephone him.

Brush Runabout Company, Detroit, Michigan

The Belmont Garage Co.

1711 Fourteenth Street

Distributors for Washington, D. C.

Ask Yourself this Question

"Would An Automobile that I Could Buy for $485.00 and Operate for Less than One Cent a Mile, be a Good Investment for Me?"

The way to arrive at a sensible conclusion as to whether or not you should buy an automobile, is to talk it over with yourself. You know all about your own business. You know how you make your money. If you have much getting around to do, you know how much time it takes and what it costs you to do it. So you are the best judge of whether or not you could increase your efficiency or that of some of your employees by the use of an automobile.

If time is worth anything to you, the chances are you would save a great deal of it by the use of any automobile. But its first cost would have to be so low and the up-keep of it so small that the result would show a net profit.

The BRUSH RUNABOUT, because of its first low cost, because of the very small amount of money necessary to operate and maintain it, is the logical car for you to use as a basis for making your investigation. If the BRUSH will not do the things that you want an automobile to do and show a profit, then no motor car built will. If you have much getting about to do, a BRUSH will do it for you cheaper than carfare. If you are now using a horse or horses, a BRUSH will enable you to cover twice the ground, and your gasoline and oil bills will be much less than you are now paying for feed and blacksmith's bills. This may sound to you like a strong statement. The proof is found in the testimony of thousands of BRUSH owners who are proving it to their satisfaction every day. It is a simple matter for you to prove it for yourself.

Think for a moment about the 2,500 mile trip of the Abernathy kids! After riding from Oklahoma City to New York on horseback to pay their respects to Colonel Roosevelt, these youngsters decided to make the return journey by automobile. Louie, the older of the two (and he is only nine years old), chose a Brush Runabout to make the long drive, because it is the only car which is so simple mechanically and so easy to handle that a boy of his age could run it as well as a professional driver operates a large machine. Louie Abernathy drove the BRUSH all the way himself. They "honked" up the main street of Oklahoma City just twenty-three days after they left New York. They stopped a day each in four of the larger cities to see the sights. So they were on the road nineteen days, averaging almost 140 miles a day.

Louie Abernathy demonstrated in a way that admits of no argument, that the BRUSH features which we have been telling you about in our advertising are REAL features. He demonstrated that the BRUSH is simple to operate and easy to handle. He demonstrated its easy-riding qualities, both the boys arriving home feeling better than when they left New York. He demonstrated that a 9-year-old boy could crank it and that the motor starts without fuss and trouble. He demonstrated that the BRUSH

driver is practically free from mechanical worries. He demonstrated that the BRUSH can travel any road, can climb any hill, has the strength to stand any strain.

These are the things which should go a long way toward helping you solve the automobile question for yourself. The Abernathy boys attracted the attention of the whole country. Thousands greeted them and cheered them along the roads. The sight of seeing this youngster actually starting, driving and stopping his car was such proof of BRUSH simplicity that even the most skeptical could doubt no longer.

For every effect there must be a cause. We can make claims for the BRUSH that no other automobile manufacturer can make for his product—because no other automobile is like the BRUSH either in its mechanical or important construction features. The motor in the BRUSH is simplicity itself. You can learn all about it in five minutes. The BRUSH has a spiral-spring suspension, the like of which is found on no other motor car built. You can drive a BRUSH over rough, rutty roads at a speed impossible for any other automobile. It is so light you can lift one wheel and prop it up to make a tire repair without the aid of a jack. Weight, more than anything else, is responsible for tire trouble. The easiest car on tires is the lightest car. The lightest car by a wide margin, is the BRUSH.

We could go on enumerating BRUSH features which make the car loom up so big purely as an investment. The best we can do, however, in a piece of advertising is to arouse your curiosity to the point of making a personal investigation of the BRUSH. The way to find out all about the BRUSH RUNABOUT, the way to prove to yourself that the things we say about it are true, the way to know just what it will do for you—is to examine it, ride in it, drive it. It will not take you long to get to the dealer nearest you who handles the BRUSH. He is more than willing to give you a free BRUSH demonstration. And remember, the car that you can buy for $485, is an exact duplicate of the BRUSH car which the Abernathy boys drove almost 140 miles a day for nineteen days.

We have been taking advantage of the Abernathy trip to call your attention to the utility side of the BRUSH. This trip demonstrated, however, in just as big a way, the pleasure side of this wonderful car. No car offers more as a pleasure vehicle than the BRUSH, except size and carrying capacity. No car in the world offers as much, considered both from the standpoint of utility and pleasure, as the BRUSH.

Ask yourself the same question which you did at the beginning of this advertisement, and remember that there is a BRUSH dealer near you who will be glad to show you how to prove what the BRUSH will do for you. If you are busy, he will be glad to come to you if you will write or telephone him.

Brush Runabout Company, Detroit, Michigan

LICENSED UNDER SELDEN PATENT

---

254 *Detroit Free Press* (Detroit, Michigan) August 21, 1910, Pg. 20.

The Brush Runabout Ride

The Abernathy boys' decision to return home by car added a new dimension to their growing fame. They had demonstrated their versatility and willingness to embrace the future, embodying the spirit of an America on the cusp of modernization. Their journey showcased the promise of the automobile, inspiring others to see the possibilities of this new technology.

255 256

The boys have mastered bronchos, now automobiles, proving their adaptability and adventurous spirit in this ever-changing world.[257]

---

[255] The *Boston Globe* (Boston, Massachusetts) August 28, 1910, Pg. 53.
[256] The *Daily Oklahoman* (Oklahoma City, Oklahoma) August 28, 1910, Pg. 11.
[257] *Boston Evening Transcript* (Boston Massachusetts) January 10, 1911, Pg. 8.

The trip home in the Brush Runabout became one of the most celebrated chapters in the Abernathy boys' story, cementing their status as national icons and trailblazers of their time.

And so, with New York's lights twinkling behind them and their little Brush cars pointed west, the Abernathy family closed the year on the move once more. They had crossed a nation, swapped their bridle reins for steering wheels, saddles for seat cushions, and met both the lion-hearted Colonel and the elusive President. They had seen the lights of Broadway and flown with Wilbur Wright. They had ridden into the hearts of Americans, not just as riders or showmen, but as symbols of youthful daring and frontier spirit.

Journey of the Abernathy Boys — Who rode their horses from Oklahoma City to New York City to greet the former President Roosevelt and their modern trip home in a Brush Runabout.

Louie, the 9-year-old son of Marshal "Jack" Abernathy, drives the car on the long tour, and his brother, Temple, aged 6, keeps him company.

It is the greatest journey ever made by two boys, and even smashes the record of the outgoing journey on horseback.

The Abernathy boys are accompanied by their father, Marshal "Jack" Abernathy, also known as "Eat 'Em Alive Jack" and a warm friend of former President Roosevelt.

More than 100 miles will be made each day by the Abernathy boys in the Brush runabout. A record of the running time will be kept, with explanations for all stops and delays.

Young Abernathy learned to operate the Brush machine in three short lessons, and immediately afterward mastered the intricate details of the traffic of New York City, where an extraordinary farewell was given to them by the press and municipal officials.

Each night a stop will be made at a hotel, and when this is not convenient the Abernathy party will not scorn to sleep in their blankets on the road.

The route is as follows:

New York City, Albany, Schenectady, Utica, Syracuse, Auburn, Geneva, Canandaigua, Rochester, Batavia, Buffalo, Erie, Conneaut, Ashtabula, Cleveland, Lorain, Vermillion, Sandusky, Toledo, Ypsilanti, Detroit, Ann Arbor, Jackson, Albion, Battle Creek, Kalamazoo, Paw Paw, Decatur, Niles, South Bend, La Porte, Valparaiso, Hammond, South Chicago, Chicago, Joliet, Bloomington, Springfield, Staunton, Litchfield, Mt. Olive, Edwardsville, East St. Louis, St. Louis, Wellston, Warrenton, Montgomery, Willsville, Armstrong, Marshall, Odessa, Independence, Kansas City, Shawnee, Williamsburg, Emporia, Cottonwood Falls, Elmdale, Newton, Wichita, Riverdale, Caldwell, Enid, Hennessey, Kingfisher, El Reno and Oklahoma City. Stops will be made at many intermediate points, where the boys will also visit the places of interest. They will also call upon mayors of cities and governors of states.

It is, in all, a distance of 2434 miles, or more than two-thirds of the distance across the United States. This remarkable journey has never before been attempted by boys of any age. The cost of running the car will be almost nothing compared with the expense of the great horseback ride of 2100 miles.

The Brush runabout was chosen by Marshal Abernathy for the boys after experts made a thorough examination of the car. Abernathy found that it was the simplest for the boys to handle, the most comfortable and the sturdiest little car that could be found.

The car was shipped from the factory in Detroit like any other car and nothing special has been added to it. It was tested on the streets of New York, and the fact that this 9-year-old boy mastered it in less than three days is proof that his father made a wise choice.

The Abernathy boys are sons of Marshal "Jack" Abernathy and come of good stock, as is manifest in their sturdiness and their absolute lack of fear. After seeing their father for months, he permitted them to ride to Santa Fe.

Then they accomplished the tour which made the world talk, by riding their ponies from Oklahoma City, Oklahoma, to New York City: They wanted to see the former President Roosevelt arrive from his African hunting trip, and when he stepped foot on the Battery, New York City, these two boys were among the first to come forward and shake the hand of the man who thundered through Africa and Europe. They heard the twenty-one guns of welcome that sounded from the battleship South Carolina, and again heard the guns speak when

Roosevelt stepped foot onshore. Wearing khaki suits and puttee leggings, they were in the famous parade that welcomed the former president. Afterward, they were entertained by scores of high officials in New York City and won favor by their wonderful appreciation of things and their peculiarly winsome ways.

There was one question of which they tired in New York City: that was, "Well, how far did you ride, boys?" Sometimes they answered it, and at other times they treated the questioner with disdain, thinking that there was an implication that their ride was so wonderful that they had not accomplished it. Neither Temple, the 6-year-old, nor Louie, the 9-year-old, speaks of the horseback ride unless asked about it.

The boys visited Mayor Gaynor, the big man of New York. Without trepidation these youngsters entered his office. Louie walked boldly forward, hat in hand, and said, "How do you do?" to Mayor Gaynor.

"What!" said the mayor, when he learned who they were, "these boys rode that long, long journey on horseback?"

"Yes," answered Louie.

"Do you wish to become a mayor?" asked Gaynor.

"No," replied the boy, "I want to be a hotel clerk." And at this the mayor laughed.

Meanwhile Temple, who had entered the mayor's office, turning his little straw hat above his head on the top of a diminutive cane, amused himself and many others by making grimaces in a mirror under the mayor's big table. The boys said they enjoyed their visit when, on taking leave, their small hands grasped that of the mayor.

When the mere statement is made that these boys made a 2100-mile journey on horseback unaccompanied except by two ponies and a dog, and that they had to look after themselves en route, pay their own hotel bills through checks furnished by Marshal Abernathy, find their way to New York City, and brave the dangers of traveling.

"How did you find your way on such a tremendous journey?" inquired a stranger.

"Inquired," answered Louie, and he turned on his heel to look at a boy of 18 who was running an automobile. "That's the way I'd like to go back home," he mused aloud.

The stranger heard the boy. "Why don't you ask your father to buy an auto?"

Louie pondered an instant, and then his face lighted up. "I will, and I believe pop'll do it, too. Say, then we'll return the modern way."

That was the beginning of the auto trip. Marshal "Jack" had no peace from either of the boys until he bought the runabout for them and the Maxwell car for himself. The very moment Louie was seated in the auto, he was a traitor to the horse. "It will be ever so much better going back this way," he remarked naively. "You must come, too, pop," said Temple. And right there was where the marshal decided to drive the touring car through instead of having it shipped.

On their horseback journey the boys often had to sleep out in their blankets, and for more than eight days they covered seventy-five miles each day. They tell of this in a simple manner, with the same unconcern the older city boy would talk of a ten-mile trip on horseback. Fortunately, they are strangers to fear on the plains and mountains. They always had something to keep their little eyes and their little tongues busy. They appreciate scenery as much as they do a plate of ice cream. When hospitality was offered as a favor they refused it all along the line. But when friends of their father—and he has many—offered them a room they accepted it gladly, and told the story of their travels, which always was listened to with more than usual interest.

In Baltimore, they were met by a party of New York newspaper men, several of whom accompanied them on the journey to New York City. The journey of less than 200 miles was felt more by the grown-ups than the whole two thousand had been by the Abernathy kids.

In Baltimore, a dry goods merchant with a big store sent around to the hotel where the boys were staying, telling them to come to his store the next morning and they would receive as many toys as they wished. In the morning papers, there appeared an advertisement that the Abernathy boys would be in the department store at 11 o'clock. Five thousand persons were outside the place long before the time for the boys to come, and when the young Abernathys understood why the merchant wanted them there, these boys turned their horses' heads around and returned to the hotel. They are brimful of pride, these boys.

Every evening in New York City, they were "on the go." They went to visit friends, to the theater, to a prize fight, to Coney Island, and kept themselves busy generally. At last came the news that they were going to return to their native heath[258] in an auto. Marshal Abernathy was by this time anxious to return to his home state as soon as possible, and he resolved that he would leave the boys in charge of a friend if he had to hurry on to Oklahoma City.

The boys are not afraid to be in the machine alone. The big Maxwell car that leads the way on the route was an incentive to the kids to make the little Brush runabout go as fast as possible. However, the boys are obedient and they promised their father that if he bought them the Brush runabout they would be careful and drive the car at a moderate pace.

Temple Abernathy, the smaller boy, is able to ride horseback, but his legs are not yet long enough to permit him to manipulate the brake on the car, and his little arms are too short to reach the control lever. This is not pleasing to young Temple, and he rages within himself that his brother can do something which he can not—as yet.

Temple, Louie's passenger, so to speak, is a child who can not bear fondlings from any one except his father. One day in New York City the boy was going up in the elevator of a big hotel with his brother and father.

---

[258] Original text.

"And you rode such a long, long way," said a pretty woman. "How many miles was it?" She placed her jeweled fingers on the boy's head. Temple shook his head free and turned to his father. "Tell her, pop," he said, and then watched the boy stop the elevator. When Marshal Abernathy told her how far the boys had ridden unaccompanied, the pretty woman marveled.

While his brother was taking lessons to become a competent driver, Temple amused himself in the big hotel in New York City by playing at being a call boy. When the "bell hops" marched in to report at 7 o'clock one night, Marshal Abernathy was astounded, yet amused, to see the line broken by the form of his sturdy younger son, marching with the other boys, even if he did have to run to keep up with them.

And still more astonished was the marshal when, later in the evening, he heard a shrill voice piping out, "Mistah Abernathy, Mistah Abernathy." It was his son greeting him in his new amusement as page boy in the Broadway hotel.

The first time that Temple was placed beside his brother in the Brush runabout he turned to the 9-year-old boy and said, "Let her out, Louie."

"You can't spur this like you can a horse," said the older boy, "and I promised pop not to go too fast. So, Temp, you must content yourself with this speed while you are in the city."

The automobile trip of the boys will be followed by an account of what they think of riding the distance in an auto and how it compares with their journey on horseback. "Helen's Babies," that *amusing book of two children, is nothing compared with the humor of the questions asked by the Abernathy boys.*[259]

Return to Gotham

As the final days of 1910 ticked away, the Abernathy brothers again found themselves far from the quiet plains of Oklahoma on a return trip to New York City.

ABERNATHY BOYS TO GOTHAM.

Two Famous Youngsters Will Join Father in New York.

The "Abernathy kids" are off again on one of their cross-continent trips. This time the destination is New York City. The trip is not to be made on ponies, but on the conventional method of Pullman cars. The boys left Tuesday afternoon on the Frisco for New York, where they will be guests of the American Automobile association in the annual show at Madison Square Garden.[260]

---

[259] The *Waco Times-Herald* (Waco, Texas) October 9, 1910, Pg. 15.
[260] The *Wichita Eagle* (Wichita, Kansas) December 15, 1910, Pg. 2.

From the roar of crowds in New York to the awe of onlookers at the Brush Runabout booth in Madison Square Garden, their fame had swelled to near-mythic proportions. But amidst the holiday galas and mechanical marvels, the boys were still boys—Temple marveling at Santa's sleigh-shaped tree at Durland Riding Academy, Louie dreaming of getting back in the saddle with Wiley Haynes and Sam Bass. [261]

> The two Abernathy boys, Louis and Temple, who came to town to see Colonel Rosevelt las june when he arrived in New York, riding horseback, have returned to Gotham and will be a feature of the Brush machine exhibit at the Licensed Automobile Manufacturers' show which opens at Madison Square Garden January 6. The famous kids will probably remain in the east for some time, as it is said they have developed a healthy liking for metropolitan life.

Answer Many Questions and Demonstrate Car Running to Engineers at Show. —

Louis and Temple Abernathy passed through the crucial test at the Madison Square Garden last

ABERNATHY BOYS BUSY.

Answer Many Questions and Demonstrate Car Running to Engineers at Show.

NEW YORK'S HUMAN SIDE

Two Abernathy Boys From Oklahoma Features Of The Big Automobile Show.

[*From the Brooklyn Eagle.*]

---

[261] *East Oregonian* (Pendleton, Oregon) January 5, 1911 Pg. 6.

evening. The boys faced batteries of lorgnettes and fusillades of questions during most of the time they were in attendance, but held the fort in a manly fashion. The management raised the price of admission and the "class" of the attendance last night and dubbed it "society" night. Salesmen and distinguished guests, including the Abernathy boys, added tone to the occasion with boiled shirts and tuxedos.

"Did you little boys really cross the country in a small machine like that?" asked one matron, whose own stylishly clad children were held tightly in leash at some distance by an assiduous man servant. "Yes'm, Bud drove the car all the way, but I steered part of the time," answered Temple, the six-year-old. Then followed a demonstration by the youngest salesman at the show. Temp crawled into a Brush roadster, advanced the spark and throttle, and gave a complete and noiseless pantomime of the way to run the car.

NO FREAK CARS SEEN AT THE LICENSED SHOW

Makers Display Special Features in Cars.

DUCK BOAT WAS ONE

Martha Washington Coupe and George Washington Coach Are Attractive Designs. Abernathy Boys Very Much in Evidence.

Bystanders declare that the lady is surely "sold" and that all Temple needs to do is to have the contract signed.[262] [263] [264]

Those Abernathy Kids.

No motorcar company had a better advertising medium than the Abernathy boys, those Western ponies riders who rode the "bronchos from Oklahoma to New York to greet former-President Roosevelt when he returned from his hunting trip and who turned up at the show in a Brush runabout. One of these boys is about 10 and the other 6 years of age, and having become perfect masters of riding the "bronchos," they waited until they had mastered the art of running an automobile.

Dressed in their khaki uniforms during the day and their little tuxedo suits at night, these two boys were on duty all the week, answering all manner of questions and doing more to boom the Brush business than any other kind of an advertisement could possibly do.

---

[262] The *Brooklyn Daily Eagle* (Brooklyn, NY) January11, 1911, Pg. 25.
[263] The *Evening Sun* (Baltimore, Maryland) January 13, 1911, Pg. 6.
[264] The *Morning Union* (Springfield, Massachusetts) January 15, 1911 Pg. 19.

The Brush Complete $450.

No Race, No Tour, No Endurance Run ever answered so many questions about an automobile as the trip of the Abernathy Boys from New York to Oklahoma in a Brush Runabout—when they returned from meeting Roosevelt.

The feat of their driving a BRUSH car 2546 miles has made them famous the world over. Thousands saw 9 year old Louie at the wheel, in their triumphant drive across many States.

This alone proved conclusively the utter reliability, durability and power of the BRUSH—the car for Every Man.

The Brush is the simplest car built, the least liable to trouble, the easiest to understand and learn to operate, the safest to run, the most economical to maintain, and, last, but not least, the easiest-riding car in the world.

In the Brush is contained as high a grade of material and workmanship as you will find in any other car sold within three or four times its price.

Ask for a demonstration.

Address correspondence to 1171 West Eldorado Street.
Agent for the Sampson "35"

Clyde L. Emery, Agent
AT SHELLABARGER'S FIRE-PROOF GARAGE.

---

[265] *Herald and Review* (Decatur, Illinois) May 7, 1911, Pg. 10.

Louie and Temple Abernathy, the Oklahoma youngsters who drove their Brush runabout from New York to Oklahoma, following their horseback trip to New York to greet Colonel Roosevelt upon his return from the jungle, received a spontaneous welcome from 150 members of the American Boy Scouts on Saturday afternoon when they started from their New York hotel to go to the Automobile Show.

The appearance of the American Boy Scouts at a time when the youngsters were headed for the Brush exhibit to tell visitors about their long overland trip was in the nature of a tribute from an organization of amateur scouts to two sturdy American boys, who have earned the reputation of being real scouts.

As the boys jumped into their Brush and Louie was about to start the car the sound of a bugle drew his attention and he discovered the khaki-clad scouts approaching him, formed in platoons and each commanded by a signal service officer. Louie stopped to acknowledge the greeting, and after a cordial handshaking all around, the uniformed scouts fell in line behind the automobile and *escorted the boys downtown. After passing the building of the United States Motor Co., in Sixty-first street, near Broadway, they swung into East Fifty-ninth Street and then turned south on Fifth avenue.*

Through all the congestion of motor and other vehicular traffic in this thoroughfare Louie piloted the car with remarkable ease of control and at a pace of two miles an hour, to enable the scouts to follow. On arrival at Madison Square Garden the Abernathys showed their appreciation of the welcome by purchasing and presenting to the scouts a large silk American flag.[266]

Their father, was now navigating a different kind of frontier. No longer a U.S. Marshal, he turned from public service to private ventures, ready to chase wolves for New York millionaires and perhaps chase new dreams far from Washington's political games. "It is an expensive job," he told reporters of his role as U.S. Marshal, noting the toll the marshal's post had taken.[267] The headlines, once filled with his legendary exploits, now focused more on his sons—two boys who had become folk heroes while their father faded from officialdom.

---

[266] The *Pittsburgh Press* (Pittsburgh, Pennsylvania) January 22, 1911, Pg. 14.
[267] The *Dothan Eagle* (Dothan, Alabama) December 13, 1910, Pg. 2.

Guthrie, Okla., Dec. 16. — The resignation of John R. Abernathy, as United States marshal of Oklahoma, takes effect Jan. 1, and on that day he will pull off a cross-country wolf and fox hunt for a New York millionaire, who desires such an entertainment for a party of holiday house guests in New Jersey. Abernathy gets a $5,000 guarantee for the day.

His three wolf-hunting ponies, "Sam", "Wiley Haines" and "Geronimo", have been shipped to New York from the Abernathy farm near Frederick, for the event. Abernathy's two boys, who recently rode overland to New York, will assist their father in the New Year's Day hunt.[268]

The nature of their ride was not obvious to the boys as described by the following account the ride by Louis as recorded in the Fall River Massachusetts Globe,

The following is Louis Abernathy's account of the ride, clipped from the Delineator:

I don't know as I can tell you all about the ride, but I'll try. We started out from Frederick and we went through Oklahoma, Kansas, Missouri, Illinois, Indiana, Ohio, Pennsylvania, Virginia, and New

---

[268] The *Perry Republican* (Perry, Oklahoma) December 22, 1910, Pg. 1

Jersey. When it rained, we put on slickers—that's a kind of a rain coat and just kept on. Of course, if a man had got sick we'd have to lay up for a couple of days and get a doctor. But we didn't get sick or tired. We weren't scared of anything. Sometimes the roads were pretty bad but not as bad as they were on the one, we took before this to Mexico. The West ain't like the East. When we got to Cincinnati, though there were some too about St. Louis. We picked my horse because he's my favorite, in fact he is the favorite of the whole family, and we just felt that he could do the trip. He did too. We ate at hotels or railroad stations. When we stopped, we left our horses at the livery stables and if it was just one meal told them how to feed, but if we stayed over a day we only went to see them once a day, not every meal. I understand how to take care of horses. We didn't have any plans as to how far we would go every day, we just went on until it seemed a good place to stop. We only had one accident. You see we was kind of running in a race and the road was bad, and my horse, he slipped and fell. Didn't hurt the horse any, but it hurt my leg some, but not bad.

    I don't remember when I began to ride. I must have been a baby. Any boy could take that trip. — Louis Abernathy[269]

---

[269] *Fall River Globe* (Fall River, Massachusetts) August 23, 1910, Pg. 2.

Oklahoma City, Okla., Aug. 31. — This is the home of two of the most remarkable youngsters in the country—the Abernathy boys, who have just completed a round trip to New York City, where they greeted Colonel Theodore Roosevelt on his return from the jungles. While this in itself is sufficient to make the lads the envy of all youngsters in the universe, still more honor was achieved by them. After a tedious, tiresome drive astride bronchos from their home to Gotham, the boys discarded their ponies for a Brush runabout in which to make the return journey.

> **ABERNATHY'S BOYS HOME.**
> Given a Cordial Reception on Their Arrival at Oklahoma City.

Louis and Temple, who are nine and six years old respectively, were given ovation on their arrival at the Oklahoma metropolis, the like of which was never before equaled—not even when Colonel Roosevelt himself as President made an official visit to the city.

The boys made a record run from Omaha to Oklahoma City, leaving the former city Monday morning and arriving home Thursday afternoon. Night stops were made at Kansas City, Emporia, and Wichita, Kans. The speedometer indicated 2,315.2 miles when the trip ended.[270]

---

[270] The *News Journal* (Wilmington, Delaware) August 31, 1910, Pg 3.

As 1910 faded into history, the road ahead promised more adventure—maybe the West Indies, maybe Alaska, maybe something wilder still. But one thing was certain: the Abernathy boys were just getting started.

Newspapers often run looking back in history columns and by 1911 newspapers were already looking back at the adventures of the Abernathy boys.

> **June 11 In American History.**
> 1776—The Continental congress named the committee of five to draft the Declaration of Independence.
> 1844—William R. Brooks, American astronomer, born.
> 1870—William Gilmore Simms, novelist of southern life, died; born 1806.
> 1898—Spaniards attacked United States marines at Guantanamo; first fight of Americans in Cuba.
> 1910—Abernathy boys, aged ten and six years, reached New York city, completing horseback ride from Oklahoma.

[271]

272 273 274 275 276 277 278 279

---

[271] *Stockton Evening 7 Sunday Record* (Stockton, CQ) June 10, 1911, Pg. 2.
[272] The Zanesville Signal (Zanesville, Ohio) June 10, 1911, Pg. 4.
[273] *Muscatine News-Tribune* (Muscatine, IA) June 11, 1911, Pg. 2.
[274] The *Alexandria Times-Tribune* (Alexandria, Indiana) June 12, 1911, Pg. 2.
[275] *Mount Carmel Item* (Mount Carmel, PA) June 12, 1911, Pg. 2.
[276] *Leader-Tribune* (Marion, Indiana) June 12, 1911, Pg. 4.
[277] The *Neenah Daily Times* (Neenah, Wisconsin) June 12, 1911, Pg. 2.
[278] The *Prolocutor* (Garden City, Kansas) June 15, 1911, Pg. 4.
[279] The *Boonville Standard* (Boonville, Indiana) June 16, 1911, Pg. 6.

Chapter 8:
1911 — The Elephant and Donkey Race

Just now a very novel race is being run from New York to Washington. The chief figures are a big elephant and a lop-eared donkey. It all grew out of a conversation held not long ago between "Uncle Joe" Cannon and a New York showman[280].

These boys have mastered riding bronchos and now lead exotic animals through America's cities.[281]

In the summer of 1911, Louis and Temple Abernathy again found themselves at the center of an American spectacle—this time not on horseback, but guiding two rather unusual companions: a Republican elephant named Judy and a Democratic donkey named Jennie. The peculiar duo was at the heart of a politically charged stunt—a wager made between Luna Park amusement mogul Frederic Thompson and former Speaker of the House "Uncle Joe" Cannon. The Abernathy brothers had earned a name for themselves as fearless travelers, representing, the rugged can-do attitude that many saw as the heart of the American spirit.

The bet? That the outcome of the 1912 presidential election could be predicted by a symbolic race from Coney Island, New York, to the steps of the White House in Washington, D.C. If Jennie, the Democratic donkey, arrived first, it was said, the Democrats would win the

---

[280] The *Evening News* (Ada, Oklahoma) July 12, 1911, Pg. 2.
[281] *Boston Evening Transcript* (Boston, Massachusetts) January 10, 1911, Pg. 8.

presidency. If Judy, the Republican elephant, prevailed, the GOP could take heart.

On the evening of July 7, 1911, Judy and Jennie departed Luna Park amid much fanfare. Temple, age 7, rode the donkey while 11-year-old Louis perched on the elephant's back. The boys, already famous for their cross-country rides, lent legitimacy—and charm—to what might otherwise have been dismissed as a mere publicity gimmick.[282]

Well, the way the press agent tells it, and he ought to know, Frederic Thompson, who built Luna Park, in New York, and has organized a large bank account out of it, bet Uncle Joseph Cannon, of Washington, D.C., that the next President would be a Democrat and Uncle Joe, biting a cigar between his teeth, took him up. To decide the bet it was settled that they wouldn't wait until 1912 but would race a donkey and an elephant, representing the parties of which they are emblems, from Luna

> **PARTY EMBLEMS RACING HERE**
>
> Judy, The Elephant, And Jennie, The Donkey, On The Way.
>
> **IT'S BET WITH "UNCLE JOE"**
>
> Frederic Thompson, In Washington, Saw Mr. Cannon And Fixed Up Fine Advertising Trick.
>
> Incidentally, Watch For Those Abernathy Lads.
>
> The donkey and the elephant started out from Luna Park at 9.30 o'clock last night, with a brass band tooting them to the mark, and Col. Jack Abernathy and the everlasting Abernathy boys—the same boys who rode from the West to meet Roosevelt—are leading the procession over the long route. Incidentally, these boys don't seem to be able to get away from New York since butting into the Roosevelt parade made them as famous as some soaps. They are advertising values.

---

[282] *The Evening Sun* (Baltimore, Maryland), July 8, 1911, Pg. 2.

Park to Washington. If the donkey finished first the next President would be a Democrat, so far as the bet was concerned, and vice versa.[283]

The sight of two boys managing these party mascots delighted the press. As the *Evening Sun* of Baltimore observed, "These boys don't seem to be able to get away from New York since butting into the Roosevelt parade made them as famous as some soaps".[284]

With guidance from animal handlers and a plan to stick to major travel routes, they began their journey in the heart of New York City. Crowds gathered to witness their departure, captivated by the sight of two young boys calmly managing such strikingly different animals.

Their journey began with much fanfare in New York City. Judy the elephant, enormous and lumbering, contrasted sharply with the boys' smaller frames and youthful energy. Jennie the donkey, stubborn and slower, added an element of comedy to the procession. Newspapers were quick to highlight the absurdity and charm of the event.

---

[283] The *Evening Sun* (Baltimore, Maryland) July 8, 1911, Pg. 2.
[284] *The Evening Sun* (Baltimore, Maryland) July 8, 1911, Pg. 2.

PRINCIPALS IN THE NOVEL RACE FROM NEW YORK TO WASHINGton, D. C. The photograph shows the huge elephant which will represent the traditional G. O. P.; and Jennie II., a slate-colored, lop-eared donkey, representing the O. B. B. (Order of Bill Bryan), both of Luna Park, Coney Island. Accompanying them are the famous Abernathy boys of Oklahoma, who will act as pathfinders. The donkey, the elephant and the Oklahoma "bear cats" have left Luna Park on a Presidential race to the national capital. On the elephant is a big white flag upon which is inscribed "White House or Bust in 1912." The donkey has nothing but a ribbon on its saddle. The race started as the result of a conversation between Fred Thompson of Luna Park and "Uncle Joe" Cannon two weeks ago in Washington. "You're going to get licked good and plenty next year," said Thompson to Cannon. "The Democrats will win sure." "Nonsense," returned "Uncle Joe," never was a donkey could lick an elephant." "All right," said Thompson, "I'll show you one that can." The race is the result.

285 286 287 288 289 290 291 292 293 294 295

---

[285] The *Gazette* (York, Pennsylvania) July 10, 1911, Pg. 1.
[286] The *Central New Jersey Home News* (New Brunswick, New Jersey) July 11, 1911, Pg. 3
[287] The *Tennessean* (Nashville, Tennessee) July 11, 1911, Pg. 1.
[288] The *Daily Oklahoman* (Oklahoma City, OK) July 11, 1911, Pg. 1.
[289] The *Hutchinson Gazette* (Hutchinson, KS) July 15, 1911, Pg. 6.
[290] The *Miami Herald (*Miami, Florida) July 14, 1911, Pg. 3.
[291] The *Billings Gazette* (Billings, Montana) July 18, 1911, Pg. 8.
[292] *Midland Empire News* (Billings, Montana) July 18, 1911, Pg 8.
[293] The *Ottawa Daily Republic* (Ottawa, Kansas) July 25, 1911, Pg.1.
[294] The *Evansville Journal* (Evansville, Indiana) July 11, 1911, Pg. 1.
[295] *Marion News-Tribune* (Marion, Indiana) July 11, 1911, Pg 5.

> **Incidentally, Watch For Those Abernathy Lads.**
>
> The donkey and the elephant started out from Luna Park at 9.30 o'clock last night, with a brass band tooting them to the mark, and Col. Jack Abernathy and the everlasting Abernathy boys—the same boys who rode from the West to meet Roosevelt—are leading the procession over the long route. Incidentally, these boys don't seem to be able to get away from New York since butting into the Roosevelt parade made them as famous as some soaps. They are advertising values. [296]

At every stop, the sight of two young boys leading an elephant and a donkey down Main Street left townsfolk awestruck. In one small town, a group of children followed Judy, giggling as her trunk playfully snatched at their hats. Local shopkeepers offered the boys food and supplies, eager to be part of the journey. 'It's not every day you see an elephant outside your storefront,' one shopkeeper remarked to a reporter.

Despite the unconventional nature of the journey, the Abernathy brothers treated it with their usual professionalism and focus. Along the way, the boys continued to captivate crowds, who marveled at their ability to manage such large and temperamental creatures.

---

[296] The *Evening Sun* (Baltimore, Maryland) July 8, 1911, Pg. 2.

"Crowds gathered to cheer the boys and their companions, with Judy the elephant often stealing the show. Temple, ever the showman, waved his hat while Jennie the donkey plodded along behind."[297]

A Race Unlike Any Other

The caravan passed through New Jersey towns like Perth Amboy, New Brunswick, and Princeton. In each town, they drew large crowds. Children tugged at Judy's tail, while Jennie plodded ahead, cheered by Democrats who saw her as a symbol of coming victory.

Judy suffered foot pain along the hard roads, requiring her handlers to bathe her feet and fit her with custom Oxford-style shoes. Jennie, meanwhile, showed surprising agility and stamina. In Trenton, it was reported that she had a four-hour lead over Judy.[298] Still, the elephant's team claimed she would make up time by traveling longer hours each night.[299]

In Camden, a local policeman presented the Abernathy boys with the key to the city. They were housed at the Camden Hotel and given a hero's breakfast before continuing into Philadelphia. There, the Inquirer noted, *"Old Judy, a 7600-pound elephant…was the cynosure of thousands of eyes,"* while Jennie followed behind, drawing applause from onlookers.[300]

---

[297] *Boston Evening Transcript* (Boston, Massachusetts) January 10, 1911, Pg. 8.
[298] *The Central New Jersey Home News* (New Brunswick, NJ) July 12, 1911, p. 6.
[299] *Springfield Evening Union* (Springfield, Massachusetts), July 10, 1911, p. 4.
[300] *Courier-Post* (Camden, New Jersey), July 14, 1911, p. 1.

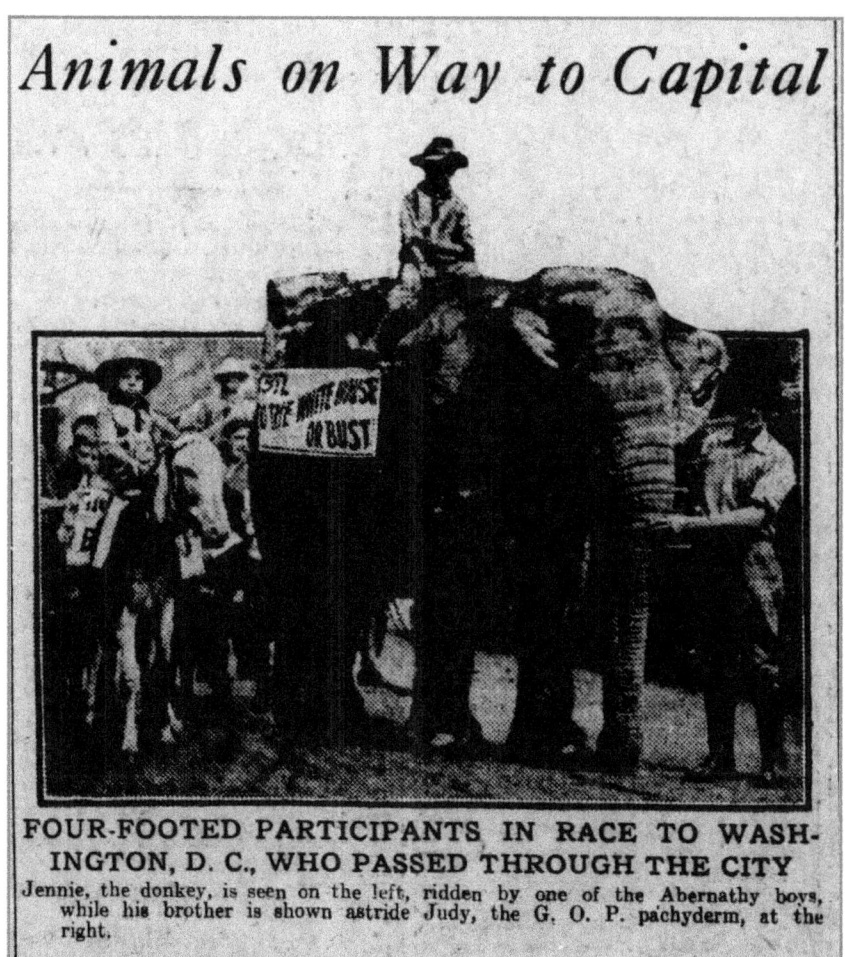

FOUR-FOOTED PARTICIPANTS IN RACE TO WASHINGTON, D. C., WHO PASSED THROUGH THE CITY

Jennie, the donkey, is seen on the left, ridden by one of the Abernathy boys, while his brother is shown astride Judy, the G. O. P. pachyderm, at the right.

Trouble on the Trail

But the excitement was not without chaos. Outside Perth Amboy, Judy's appearance spooked a milk wagon team, causing them to bolt,

---

[301] The *Philadelphia Inquirer* (Philadelphia, Pennsylvania) July 15, 1911, Pg. 2.

spill their cargo, and crash. The incident, while humorous in hindsight, led to outrage among local parents whose children missed out on their Sunday milk.[302]

As temperatures climbed, both animals began to show signs of fatigue. Judy became increasingly restless, reportedly refusing to lie down due to unsafe stable conditions. Jennie, unused to her iron shoes, developed sore feet.[303]

ADMIRING EYES GAZE AT JUDY AND JENNIE

Ridden by Abernathys, Elephant and Donkey Pass Through City on Race

Lumbering through the streets of Philadelphia yesterday with a small boy mounted on its swaying back, Old Judy, a 7600-pound elephant, emblematic of the Republican Party, was the cynosure of thousands of eyes. Behind it ambled a little donkey, Jennie, astride which was another boy, who smilingly acknowledged the plaudits of the throngs that gazed upon him and his miniature steed with undisguised approval.

The boys were Temple Abernathy and his brother, Louis Abernathy, who gained national fame by riding ponies from their native Oklahoma to greet former President Roosevelt when the latter returned from his hunting expedition to Africa and his subsequent tour of Europe.

The elephant and the donkey are participants in a novel race from Luna Park, Coney Island, to Washington, the result of a wager as to the fleetness and staying qualities of the two animals, which was made by Frederic Thompson, the amusement man, and "Uncle Joe" Cannon, former Speaker of the House. "Uncle Joe" bet several of his favorite cigars that the elephant, like the Republican Party, could not be beaten by the Democratic donkey.

Judging by the record the elephant had already made when it entered the city, with the donkey at its heels, "Uncle Joe" will probably win the bet. The elephant had outdistanced the donkey in their walk through New Jersey, and it was in the lead when it passed the City Hall. The competing animals are expected to cover the distance between Luna Park and Washington in eleven days. The route pursued by them and their boy riders in this city was out Market street from the Delaware River ferries to the City Hall, south on Broad street to Locust, to Twenty-first, to Walnut, to Forty-first, to Woodland avenue, to Darby and thence along the Chester pike.

The S. P. C. A. yesterday sent Agent Hoot to meet Jennie and Judy at Market street ferries the instant they set foot on Pennsylvania soil. The agent reported that the beasts showed every mark of good care.

[304]

---

[302] *The Philadelphia Inquirer* (Philadelphia, PA) July 15, 1911, Pg. 2.
[303] *Springfield Evening Union* (Springfield, MA) July 10, 1911, Pg. 4.
[304] The *Philadelphia Inquirer* (Philadelphia, Pennsylvania) Jul 15, 1911, Pg. 2.

ABOVE: Photograph shows the Republican elephant, Judy, and the Democratic donkey, Jennie, in Coney Island preparing to go to Washington; on the right, on horseback, are the two famous Abernathy boys, Louis and Temple waiting to accompany the elephant and the donkey; animals wear banners "1912 to the White House or bust!"[305]

Donkey-Elephant Race Called Off

The much-anticipated race between Judy, the Republican elephant, and Jennie, the Democratic donkey, did not reach a triumphant

---

[305] Republican elephant Judy, etc. New York Coney Island, ca. 1911. Photograph. https://www.loc.gov/item/2012649403/.

conclusion. Announced with great fanfare and driven by the adventurous Abernathy brothers, Louis and Temple, the race ended in disappointment when both animals became unable to continue.

Announcing that the national race from New York to Washington between Judy, the Republican elephant, and Jenny, the Democratic donkey, had been abandoned, owing to the disability of the two contestants, Jack Evans, the official manager of the speed trial, shipped both animals back to Coney Island yesterday afternoon, over the Pennsylvania Railroad, from Seventy-second street and Woodland avenue. This action was taken by order of the owner, Fred Thompson, after Manager Evans had telephoned him that both elephant and donkey had become ill and footsore.[306]

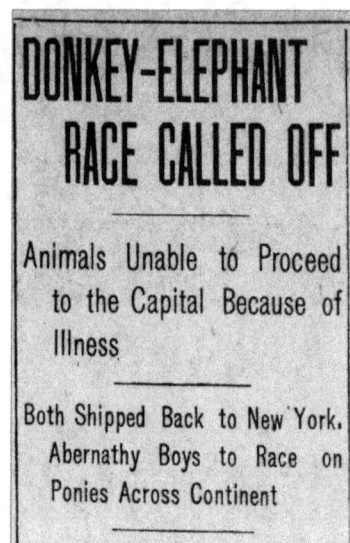

The journey, which began with enthusiasm and political humor, quickly became a struggle. Judy, the elephant, struggled to rest properly and developed a fever, likely exacerbated by her discomfort

---

[306] The *Philadelphia Inquirer* (Philadelphia, Pennsylvania) July 16, 1911, Pg. 4.

in unfamiliar environments. Jennie, the donkey, suffered from foot injuries, as she was unaccustomed to wearing horseshoes. Despite their handlers' best efforts, the combination of hot weather and rough roads proved overwhelming for the animals.

On July 15, the *Philadelphia Inquirer* reported that both animals had been quietly shipped back to Coney Island, their condition too poor to continue. The race was over. Though it had captured headlines across the country, the conclusion came not with a finish line celebration, but with a practical admission of defeat.[307]

Both contestants were officially withdrawn near Philadelphia and shipped back to Coney Island via train.

While the race itself ended prematurely, the spectacle was far from a failure. The Abernathy boys once again captivated public attention with their resilience and charm, becoming a key part of the story as they cared for the animals and managed the challenging circumstances. The event solidified their reputation as intrepid young adventurers, and they were already preparing for their next daring feat: a 3,600-mile ride to San Francisco, further proving their unyielding spirit.

The abandoned race serves as a reminder of the challenges inherent in mixing spectacle with endurance, even when humor and lighthearted competition are the driving forces. Though the elephant and donkey couldn't finish the course, their journey added another memorable chapter to the Abernathy boys' story.

---

[307] *The Philadelphia Inquirer* (Philadelphia, PA) July 16, 1911, p. 14.

The Abernathy boys, always calm and collected, managed the journey with grace, earning the admiration of everyone who met them and their unusual companions.[308]

They returned to New York with their reputations only enhanced. Their professionalism, poise, and good humor once again earned admiration across the political spectrum. And though neither the elephant nor the donkey made it to Washington, the symbolism of the race wasn't lost on the public, and as for the presidency, the following year, Democrat Woodrow Wilson won.

If a donkey could outrun an elephant—even briefly—perhaps the tide really was turning.

Elephant-Donkey Race Ended

Judy, the elephant, and Jenny, the donkey, ended their race from Coney Island to the White House in Washington, at Darby, just outside of Philadelphia, on Saturday. Jenny had never been rode previous to entering the race, and her feet became so sore that she finally balked. Judy ran a nail in her hoof at New Brunswick and was all out at Darby. Fred Thompson, owner of both and backer of Jenny, called the race off, and both animals were shipped back to Coney Island in a box car. The Abernathy boys, Louis riding Judy, and Temple, Jenny, were each confident of the outcome of the contest, and gave it up reluctantly.

[309]

---

[308] *The Evening Sun* (Baltimore, Maryland) July 8, 1911, Pg. 2.
[309] The *Cecil Whig* (Elkton, Maryland) Jul 22, 1911, Pg. 1.

Chapter 9: 1911 — Coast to Coast

When the boys arrived in San Francisco they galloped their horses out through Golden Gate Park, and when the animals stood knee-deep in the water of the Pacific Ocean the boys stood up in their stirrups and waved their hats exultantly. "Gee, but it's great to get here," said Temple on his arrival. "I liked the trip all right, but sometimes it got cold, and then I didn't like it so well. I want the deepest feather bed I can get in this town."[310]

"The Abernathy boys, Temple and Louis, start on a trip across the continent next Monday from Luna Park, to settle a bet of $5,000 made between their father and Frederic Thompson.[311]

By 1911, the Abernathy brothers were no strangers to epic adventures. Their latest challenge—to ride horseback from New York City to San Francisco in under 60 days—promised to be the most demanding yet. The journey would cover more than 3,600 miles and test every ounce of their endurance, adaptability, and resilience. In order to secure the prize money they would have to average 60 miles a day and spend at least 12 hours a day in the saddle for 60 days! They would not be allowed to eat or sleep indoors. Although only 11 and 7 years old, Louis and Temple Abernathy, according to multiple news reports, approached the task with their trademark confidence and grit.[312] Early in the trip, they were accompanied by their father. While

---

[310] The *Boston Globe* (Boston, Massachusetts) November 7, 1911, Pg. 3.
[311] The *Day* (New London, Connecticut) June 12, 1911, Pg. 5.
[312] The *Boston Globe* (Boston, Massachusetts) August 1, 1911 Pg. 7.

the exact point where he left the journey is uncertain, evidence suggests he continued with them at least as far as Nebraska. From there, the boys pressed on alone, determined to prove that age was no obstacle to greatness.

A Wager with Weight

The origin of this ride came from a bet between their father and showman Frederic Thompson of Luna Park. The *New York Times* reported, "They will try to ride from the Atlantic to the Pacific in sixty riding days, during which time they agree not to sleep or eat under cover" [313] The prize was initially $5,000—a princely sum for the time—and the rules were strict.

At some point during the journey, it inexplicably doubled to $10,000. While the reason for this increase remains unclear, the higher stakes only added to the pressure and spectacle of the Abernathy boys' daring cross-country ride.

In the days leading up to their departure, the Abernathy boys became the toast of New York City. Crowds gathered outside their hotel to catch a glimpse of the intrepid brothers, while newspapers buzzed with speculation about their chances of completing the journey. Winning the $5,000 prize would defy expectations. For Louis and Temple, this was another chance to prove that adventure knew no age.

---

[313] *The New York Times* (New York, New York) July 30, 1911, Pg. 68.

> **FOR PRIZE OF $5,000.**
>
> Abernathy Boys Will Ride From New York to Frisco.

[314]

The $5,000 prize offered for completing the journey within the allotted time added extra motivation, but the rules were strict.[315] The boys could not eat or sleep indoors, forcing them to rely on their ingenuity and the kindness of strangers for sustenance and rest. As they set out from New York City, the nation watched in awe, captivated by the spectacle of two young boys embarking on such a trip.

> **ABERNATHY AND BOYS RIDING TO OAKLAND ON $5,000 WAGER**
>
> NEW YORK, Aug. 1.—From Atlantic to Pacific on horseback on a wager of $5000, is the feat which Jack Abernathy and his two sons, Louis and Temple, have undertaken. The start was made at midnight from Coney Island Beach, and to win the bet the trio must reach Oakland by October 15, without riding Sundays.

[316]

---

[314] The Topeka State Journal (Topeka, Kansas) August 1, 1911, Pg. 5.
[315] *The Buffalo Commercial* (Buffalo, New York) August 1, 1911, Pg. 1
[316] *Oakland Enquirer* (Oakland, California) August 1, 1911, Pg. 1.

New York, July 31. — From Coney Island to the Pacific coast on horseback is the trip which is being undertaken by the Abernathy boys, the two little veterans of the saddle, who last year rode into New York from Oklahoma. It was one minute after midnight tonight when Louis Abernathy, 11 years old, and his brother, Temple, 4 years his junior, started on the trip which will take them 3,600 miles. [317] [318]

> **ABERNATHY BOYS LEAVE N. Y.**
>
> **Oklahoma Youngsters Off on Ride Across the Country.**
>
> NEW YORK, July 31. From Coney Island to the Pacific coast on horseback is the trip which is being undertaken by the Abernathy boys, the two little veterans of the saddle who last year rode into New York from Oklahoma. It was one minute after midnight tonight when Louis Abernathy, 11 years old, and his brother, Temple, four years his junior, started on the trip which will take them 3,600 miles.

The Launch Westward

Their route was set to begin at Luna Park in Brooklyn, where thousands gathered to witness the departure. However, the celebrated start was delayed as Temple was taken ill. Despite all the planning, Temple's sweet tooth nearly postponed history. Too many Coney Island confections left him with stomach pains, and the family physician ordered a short delay in the start. Newspaper reports indicated the following, *A few minutes before starting time Temple was in tears. He said he had a pain about the belt, and he was taken to the home of Dr. John W. Pierce, in Coney Island, and put to bed. The*

---

[317] *Kansas City Journal* (Kansas City, Missouri) August 1, 1911, Pg. 3.
[318] *Saline County Democrat* (Friend, Nebraska) August 8, 1911, Pg. 2.

physician advised that the long ride be postponed for at least three days.[319] [320] [321]

> **PAIN ABOUT THE BELT HALTS ABERNATHY BOYS' TRIP.**
>
> Because one of them had eaten too many sweets, the Abernathy boys, who planned to start on horseback for the Pacific Coast from Coney Island to-day, had to postpone the trip. Last night Temple, who is 7 years old, complained of a pain about the belt. Then Col. Jack Abernathy, their father, decided that Louis, 11 years old, and Temple should wait three days. The boys plan to reach Oakland, Cal., in sixty days.

[322]

After finally starting they first rode to City Hall and up Broadway, the boys crossed into the Bronx and continued toward Yonkers, planning to rest briefly before pushing on toward Albany. Their trusty mounts were the same companions who had carried them through previous adventures: Louis rode "Sam," the white horse once favored by Theodore Roosevelt, and Temple rode "Wiley," the bay who had carried him into New York the year before.

---

[319] The *Kansas City Star* (Kansas City, Missouri) August 1, 1911, Pg. 12.
[320] The *Wichita Eagle* (Wichita, Kansas) August 2, 1911, Pg. 1.
[321] *Battle Creek Enquirer* (Battle Creek, Michigan) August 2, 1911, Pg. 1.
[322] The *Standard Union* (Brooklyn, New York) August 1, 1911, Pg. 2.

LUNA PARK—"Luna Park is ready to receive one of the greatest crowds of its busy season on Monday night, when the Abernathy boys and their father, Col. Jack Abernathy, start on their record-breaking horseback ride of 3,600 miles to the Pacific Coast. They will leave Luna Park at one minute after midnight. Horses and riders are in fine fettle for the trip, and the latter are confident they will make it in sixty days, exclusive of Sundays, as Col. Abernathy has wagered that they will. Much interest has been manifested in the undertaking, several army officers, for one thing, having visited the park to look the horses over. Their sentiments are that neither man nor beast will be able to stand such a strain. Louie Abernathy will ride 'Sam,' the famous white horse that Col. Roosevelt made so much of when Col. Abernathy took him wolf hunting on the Comanche Indian reservation. Temple, the 7-year-old youngster, will ride 'Wiley,' the bay horse that made the trip from Oklahoma here last summer, and Col. Abernathy has a rangy sorrel for his mount.[323]

[323] *Times Union* (Brooklyn, New York) July 29, 1911, Pg. 5.

The boys departed New York City with a fanfare of cheering crowds and media coverage. Mounted on their trusted horses, Louis and Temple waved goodbye to onlookers as they began their long trek westward. Despite the urban start, they were soon to be challenged by the open road.

Military officers inspecting the boys' gear before departure questioned whether the horses—or the boys—could endure such a journey. But the Abernathys, already known for defying expectations, weren't fazed.[324]

As the boys rode through Manhattan, the clatter of hooves against cobblestones mixed with the din of bustling streets. Temple, perched confidently on his pony, tipped his hat to onlookers, while Louis focused on the route ahead. The transition from city streets to the rolling hills of Pennsylvania brought its own challenges—muddy trails, sudden downpours, and the ever-present whinny of their horses.

---

[324] *The Kansas City Times* (Kansas City, Missouri) August 1, 1911, Pg. 11.

Their itinerary early today took them through Brooklyn, across the bridge, across Newspaper Row, and City Hall Square to Broadway, and up that metropolitan backbone to the Bronx. Before starting Abernathy declared that they would not stop until they got to Yonkers, soon after daylight, when they would rest a bit before starting for Albany.[325] [326]

The story of their journey made front pages across the country. From the *New York Times* to the *Minneapolis Journal*,[327] [328] [329] readers followed their progress with amazement. The sheer novelty of two boys braving the vastness of America on horseback captured the public imagination like few tales ever had.

> **Boys to Ride from Coney Island to Pacific Coast**
>
> **Abernathy Youngsters Start on Another Journey Across the Continent.**
>
> By Associated Press.
>
> NEW YORK, Aug. 1.—From Coney Island to the Pacific Coast on horseback, is the trip that is being undertaken by the Abernathy boys, who last year rode into New York from Oklahoma. It was one minute after midnight this morning when Louis Abernathy, 11 years old, and his brother Temple, four years his junior, started on the trip which will take them 3600 miles, according to the route which they have picked. If they make the ride in 60 riding days and abide by certain conditions they will win $5000.
>
> The boys have agreed that they will not eat or sleep under a roof during the ride. Their beds will be on the grass and they will eat their meals by the roadside.
>
> Before leaving Coney Island they drove their horses into the Atlantic Ocean, knee deep, and then started toward the Pacific.

---

[325] *Wilkes-Barre Times Leader, The Evening News* (Wilkes-Barre, Pennsylvania) August 1, 1911, Pg. 2.
[326] *Springfield Evening Union* (Springfield, Massachusetts) August 1, 1911, Pg. 5.
[327] *The New York Times* (New York, New York) July 30, 1911, Pg. 4.
[328] *The Minneapolis Journal*, (Minneapolis, Minnesota) August 1, 1911, Pg. 3.
[329] *The Buffalo News* (Buffalo, New York) August 1, 1911, Pg. 5.

Other papers ran front-page headlines celebrating their grit and gumption.[330] Public interest was intense—not only because of their age but because of the sheer audacity of the plan.

In those first days, the journey unfolded with all the spectacle of a Wild West show. Clad in frontier gear, the boys became media darlings once more. Their departure and every subsequent mile made headlines. In Cleveland by mid-August, they were already 90 miles behind schedule—but they maintained their usual cheer and determination. Temple told reporters, "We're having a great time with Dad. He weighs almost 200 and it's hard on him and the horse too".[331]

In Toledo, Ohio, the trio faced a brief crisis. They tied their ponies while grabbing breakfast. When they returned, the horses were gone. Jack Abernathy eventually tracked them down two miles away—mischief or miscommunication, no one knew.[332]

KENDALLVILLE, Ind., Aug. 12.—A. R. Otis, of this city, has received word from Doubleday, Page & Co., of New York, that the Abernathy boys, who are going across the continent on horseback, will be here on

---

[330] *The Topeka Daily Capital* (Topeka, Kansas) August 1, 1911, Pg 1.
[331] *The Plain Dealer* (Cleveland, Ohio), August 16, 1911, *Pg. 12.*
[332] *The Tipton Daily Tribune (*Tipton, Indiana), August 19, 1911, Pg. 2.

Aug. 17. The boys are seven and 11 years old and riding from New York to San Francisco. [333]

Crowds greeted the boys in small towns across the Midwest, offering food and encouragement. The boys became minor celebrities along their route, with townsfolk often organizing parades or gatherings in their honor. Temple, the more outgoing of the two, entertained audiences with stories of their adventures, while Louis focused on planning their next steps.

Though not documented in surviving press reports, one might picture a moment like this: on a scorcher of an afternoon on the open plains, Temple slumps in his saddle and groans, "Louie, I'd trade all the $5,000 for a cold lemonade." Louis, brushing dust from his hat, pragmatically replies, "We'd have to stop riding to drink it, so let's keep going." Whether such a moment occurred or not, it would have fit perfectly within the rhythm of their epic journey—equal parts grit and brotherly wit.

Such imagined exchanges, while fictionalized, are inspired by the many recorded newspaper anecdotes of generosity and perseverance that surrounded the boys' ride. In countless small towns, strangers opened barns, shared meals, and listened wide-eyed as Temple spun tales of their ride under the stars. These glimpses of everyday American hospitality became as essential to the boys' success as their own indomitable resolve.

---

[333] The *South Bend Tribune* (South Bend, Indiana) August 12, 1911, Pg. 6

The Ride in Real Time

To ground these stories in their historical reality, the following section presents an additional curated collection of original newspaper clippings that documented the Abernathy boys' 1911 coast-to-coast ride as it unfolded. These articles, drawn from publications across the country, capture the wonder, skepticism, and admiration their journey inspired in real time. From the bustling cities of the East to the quiet towns of the Midwest and beyond, these voices from the past help illuminate not only where the boys went—but how the nation watched, reacted, and remembered.

Abernathy Kids, on 3600-Mile Ride On Horseback, Will Travel West — *NEW YORK, Aug. 14. — (Spl.) — Scarcely tall enough to reach their horses' heads, Louie and Temple Abernathy, 11 and 7 years old respectively, have started on the longest and hardest ride of their strenuous career — a little jaunt on horseback of about 3600 miles across the continent. As an example of boy scouting, their ride will probably stand unexcelled for a long time.*[334]

---

[334] The *Kentucky Post* (Covington, Kentucky) August 14, 1911, Pg. 2.

Abernathy Kids, on 3600-Mile Ride On Horseback, Will Travel West

LOUIS AND TEMPE RESTING THEIR BRONCHOS

NEW YORK, Aug. 14.—(Spl.)— Scarcely tall enough to reach their horses' heads, Louie and Temple Abernathy, 11 and 7 years old respectively, have started on the longest and hardest ride of their strenuous career—a little jaunt on horseback of about 3600 miles across the continent. As an example of boy scouting their ride will probably stand unexcelled for a long time.

"Yes," admitted their father, Col. Jack, "it's a long, hard trip, and we may not make it in 60 days, but we are going to do our best. The boys wanted to go so bad I couldn't refuse 'em. Oh, they could take care of themselves all right. I just want the exercise."

The Abernathys will ride up the east side of the Hudson to Albany, thence through Schenectady, Utica, Syracuse, Rochester, Buffalo, Cleveland, Chicago, Des Moines and Omaha. They will then ride northwest over the great plains, more barren than any they ever rode in Oklahoma, through Cheyenne, and the mountains to Salt Lake City, from where they will shape their course to San Francisco.

Program for Start

The program for the start was very different from the start of the journey that had its ending in the riotous welcome to Col. Roosevelt. In "The Ride of the Abernathy Boys," published by Doubleday, Page & Co., it is described how on April 5, 1910, Louie and Temple arose before daylight, and cheered only by their relatives and the cowpunchers, rode away from their father's ranch at Frederick, Okla., near the Texas line, on their long ride to New York. That was a ride of about 2500 miles.

Last Wednesday the boys had such a send-off as only gay Coney Island can give.

The boys had rested and were fresh for their ride when they cantered down Surf-av. shortly before 12 midnight and prepared to ride their horses into the water. Their father rode beside Temple, the youngest of the boys, and the contrast only served to accentuate the smallness of the plucky youngsters.

Try to Break Girl's Record

Since spring the boys have been in and around New York and both of them, as well as their father, Col. Jack, have heard the call of the trail—the same call that is heard by the boy scouts, except that with these boys it is inbred. So they're off to try to lower the only existing transcontinental horseback record, which was made by Miss Nan Aspinwall, of Montana, who rode from San Francisco to New York in 180 riding days. Miss Aspinwall started last Sept. 1 and reached New York July 8. She rode a California mare, Lady Ellen. Miss Aspinwall's feat was a notable one, and the boys realize it will take the hardest riding of their career to lower her record. If they succeed they win a large money prize.

It's More Fun Ridin'

In preparing for the ride the greatest precaution as to the choice of mounts was used. It is part of the compact that the riders shall not eat nor sleep under a roof during their ride, so they will have to carry their blankets, tarpaulins, slickers, grub and a few cooking utensils with them, making very heavy loads for the horses.

"Are you glad to go?" Louie and Temple were asked. The elder of the two little boys replied with his Southwestern accent, "Sure we are. It's more fun ridin' than just stayin' around here."

"But don't you like New York and Coney Island?" he was urged.

"Of course we do, don't we Temp? But you can't beat the fun o' gettin' out yonder an' ridin' over those plains all day."

The 7-year-old child who is to make the ride that nearly baffled a strong young woman whose whole life had been spent in the saddle, nodded assent and explained that, as their book told, the strawberry soda pop was just as good in small towns along the road as at Coney Island. When Temple wants to mount his horse, and his brother is not around to help him, he just shins up the animal's foreleg. It matters not to Temple if the animal be a "sunfisher" and on the point of starting a session of bucking and pitching.

Louis is the responsible one. From having the care of his little brother on their other two rides he has developed a great sense of his duties, which include seeing to his little brother's health, mind and soul. He strictly enforces their rule of never working nor riding on Sunday, and whenever in a town on Sunday takes Temple to Sunday school.

RIDE AGAINST TIME ACROSS CONTINENT - *To ride 3,600 miles horseback, from Coney Island, N.Y., to the Golden Gate, San Francisco.*

To cover the route in sixty days, averaging 60 miles daily, in order to win $10,000 awarded by Coney Island Amusement Co.

To sleep entirely in the open and to avoid hotels absolutely except to get meals and attend church if possible.

To rest all day Sundays and to attend church if possible.

To reach San Francisco Oct. 10, having left New York Aug. 1.

"Catch-'em-alive" Jack Abernathy, formerly United States marshal at Lawton, Okla., and his two sons, Louie, 11, and Temple, 7, reached Cleveland yesterday afternoon on their overland horseback jaunt from Coney Island, New York, to San Francisco. They will receive an award of $10,000, offered by the Coney Island Amusement Co., [336]*if they cover the 3,600 miles between the two coasts within sixty days.*

"We're having a great time with dad," said Temple Abernathy, the smaller of the boys. "He weighs almost 200 and it's hard on him and on the horse, too. The last time we went through Cleveland was after Col. Roosevelt got back from Africa. We met him in New York after loping all the way from Oklahoma City to New York. That was a great ride, but this is going to be a better one because it's longer."

---

[335] The *Kentucky Post* (Covington, Kentucky) August 14, 1911, Pg. 2.
[336] NOTE: It is unclear why or where the prize changed.

The boys are riding the same cow ponies which they rode triumphantly into New York more than a year ago to meet the former president. They hope their mounts will stand the wear and grind on the ocean-to-ocean jaunt. The father, because of his bulk, wore out his first mount at Syracuse, N.Y., and purchased a more powerful horse there.

The trio reached The Hollenden at 3 o'clock yesterday afternoon, having ridden from Madison, O., since daybreak. Yesterday they were ninety miles behind in their schedule but hoped to make up lost time when they reach the plains and higher altitude where the heat is less oppressive to the horses.

Abernathy said this is the first vacation he ever has enjoyed. He went east several weeks ago to visit his daughter, Kittie, a student in Ursuline college, New York. The boys, he said were standing the trip much better than he was.

> **RIDE AGAINST TIME ACROSS CONTINENT**
>
> Abernathy Boys and Their Father Pass City in Coast-to-Coast Jaunt.
>
> Are Behind Schedule but Hope to Strike Better Gait in West.
>
> ATTEMPTED BY ABERNATHYS

The trio drove away from The Hollenden late in the afternoon to hit the trail again for the west. The riders have no set stopping places, rolling up in blankets for the night wherever they happen to be.[337]

ABERNATHY BOYS Are 90 Miles Behind Schedule in Their Horseback Trip To Coast. — SPECIAL DISPATCH TO THE ENQUIRER. — *Toledo, Ohio, August 18—Brown as the proverbial berry Jack Abernathy, erstwhile United States Marshal of Oklahoma, and his two sons, Louis and Temple, 11 and 7 years old respectively, passed several hours in this city today on their way from Coney Island, New York, to San Francisco to win a reported wager of $10,000.*

Abernathy and his two sons reached the outskirts of the city early this morning and tied their bronchos to a tree trunk while they sought "chow." When they returned their horses were missing. Parent Abernathy took up a trail and about two miles further from the camp they found the horses.

Abernathy and the boys have had good luck all through the trip, according to the father. They left New York August 1 and are to complete their trip to the Golden Gate in 60 days. They left here this afternoon. They are 90 miles behind their schedule.[338] [339]

---

[337] The *Plain Dealer* (Cleveland, Ohio) August 16, 191, Pg. 12.
[338] The *Tipton Daily Tribune* (Tipton, Indiana) August 19, 1911, Pg. 2.
[339] The *Cincinnati Enquirer* (Cincinnati, Ohio) August 19, 1911, Pg. 2.

"Temp" and "Bud" Abernathy, 7 and 11, respectively, who rode from New Mexico to New York on horseback to meet Roosevelt when he returned from Africa, passed through Cleveland Tuesday on their third long ride. They are going from Coney Island to San Francisco on a $10,000 wager.

They ignored Cleveland hospitality and hotels and plugged on to a few miles from Lorain, where they spread their blankets in the open for the night.

"Jack" Abernathy, the boys' father, is with them.

"Temp" began his first big ride when he was five. Tuesday he looked conspicuously tiny on his chestnut bronco.

His broad-brimmed Stetson shades his whole body when he is in saddle. But as far as the horse is concerned "Temp" is master of the situation, even in crowded downtown crossings.

"We must ride about 15 miles yet to make our 60 miles for to-day," said "Temp," while a crowd of about 500 crowded around him. "We're 90 miles behind schedule."

The boys left Coney Island Aug. 1 and must reach San Francisco Oct. 1 to win the money.[340]

ABERNATHY BOYS ARE CROSSING INDIANA ON OCEAN-TO-OCEAN RIDE WATERLOO, Ind., Aug. 21.—The Journal-Gazette correspondent met the Abernathy boys at 6:30 Monday morning on the south road en route on their great horseback ride from New York City to San Francisco. They left Coney Island, August 1, and are due at the other end of the trip October 10. The party consists of John R. Abernathy, former Rough Rider and United States marshal of Oklahoma, and known to fame as the "man who with bare hands caught wolves," and his two sons, Louie, age 11, and Temple, age 7.

The boys are the central figures. They are making the endurance trip, and their father rides with them for protection. Under the terms of the contract they cannot sleep or eat under a roof, must not ride on Sundays, and must at least stay miles ahead. The boys are well mounted and are "born horsemen." The animals carry, besides their

---

[340] The *Kentucky Post* (Covington, Kentucky) August 21, 1911, Pg. 2.

living burdens, blankets, cooking utensils, food, and other necessary articles for camping out of doors.

On the trip, Temple, the little fellow, tried to stop and eat at Waterloo, but his father commanded that they move on. They had spent Sunday at Edgerton, and horses and boys looked fresh from the rest. The two boys made friends as they passed through the area.

The Abernathy family started the trip from their family ranch in Oklahoma to New York. There they met with Colonel Roosevelt in New York City. A book has been published giving a description of the remarkable ride of these two boys. [341] [342]

KENDALLVILLE, Ind., Aug. 21.—The Abernathy boys, Louis and Temple, arrived in this city shortly after 11 o'clock today accompanied by their father, Col. John R. Abernathy. They stopped in this city three-quarters of an hour. Temple, the seven-year-old lad, rides "Jim," which was one of the horses used in the trip from Oklahoma to New York when the boys went to see Roosevelt. Temple is very short and his spurred feet do not come more than halfway down the horse's side. Both boys are in good health. Somewhere east of Syracuse, N.Y., a stranger wanted to trade a horse and follow them "some distance." The father did not go to sleep until after 12 o'clock that night as he had told the boys he believed this fellow would give them trouble, but

---

[341] The *Fort Wayne Journal Gazette* (Fort Wayne, Indiana) August 22, 1911, Pg. 1.
[342] NOTE: The coast to coast trip did not start immediately after their ride to see Roosevelt, which this newspaper entry seems to imply?

as they were very tired, sleep came anyway and in the morning they found their horses had been run off. Securing a fresh horse from a farmer, he started after them and came up with them about eight miles from where they had camped for the night. They were delayed about four hours by this trouble. The horse "Jim," which was purchased by the boys from Louisiana while on this trip to Mexico and before starting on this New York trip. They are scheduled to reach San Francisco October 10th and hope to be there ahead of time.[343]

---

[343] The *Fort Wayne Journal Gazette* (Fort Wayne, Indiana) August 22, 1911, Pg. 1.

ABERNATHY BOYS ARE CROSSING INDIANA ON OCEAN-TO-OCEAN RIDE

WATERLOO, Ind., Aug. 21.—The Journal-Gazette correspondent met the Abernathy boys at 6:30 Monday morning on the south road en route on their great horseback ride from New York city to San Francisco. They left Coney Island, August 1 and are due at the other end of the trip October 10. The party consists of John R. Abernathy, former Rough Rider and United States marshal of Oklahoma, and known to fame as the man who with bare hands caught wolves, and his two sons, Louie, age 11, and Temple, age 7.

The boys are the central figures. They are making the endurance trip and their father rides with them for protection. Under the terms of the contract they cannot sleep or eat under a roof, must not ride on Sundays and go at least sixty miles a day. The boys are well mounted and are born horsemen. The animals carry, besides their living burdens, blankets, cooking utensils, food and other necessary articles for camping out doors.

On the trip Temple, the little fellow, wanted to stop and eat at Waterloo, but his father commanded that they move on. They had spent Sunday at Edgerton, and horses and boys looked fresh from their rest. The two boys last year made the ride of 2,500 miles from the family ranch in Oklahoma to New York, and were the attraction at the home-coming of Colonel Roosevelt in New York city. A book has been published giving a description of the remarkable ride of these two boys.

KENDALLVILLE, Ind., Aug. 21.—The Abernathy boys, Louis and Temple, arrived in this city shortly after 11 o'clock to-day accompanied by their father, Col. John R. Abernathy. They stopped in this city three-quarters of an hour. Temple, the seven-year-old lad, rides "Jim," which was one of the horses used in the trip from Oklahoma to New York when the boys went to see Roosevelt. Temple is very short and his spurred feet do not come more than half way down the horse's side. Both boys are in good health. Somewhere east of Syracuse, N. Y., a stranger wanted to trade horses and followed them some distance. The father did not go to sleep until after 12 o'clock that night as he had told the boys he believed this fellow would give them trouble, but as they were very tired, sleep came easy and in the morning they found their horses had been run off. Securing a horse from a farmer he started after them and came up with them about eight miles from where they had camped for the night. They were delayed about four hours by this trouble. The horse ridden by Louis was purchased by the boy from the Indians while on his trip to Mexico and before starting on the New York trip. They are scheduled to reach San Francisco October 10th and hope to be there ahead of time.

[344] The *Fort Wayne Journal Gazette* (Fort Wayne, Indiana) August 22, 1911, Pg. 1.

"Yes," admitted their father, Col. Jack, "it's a long, hard trip, and we may not make it in 60 days, but we are going to do our best. The boys wanted to go so bad I couldn't refuse 'em. Oh, they could take care of themselves all right. I just want the exercise."

The Abernathys will ride up the east side of the Hudson to Albany, thence through Schenectady, Utica, Syracuse, Rochester, Buffalo, Cleveland, Chicago, Des Moines, and Omaha. They will then ride northwest over the great plains to Cheyenne, through Denver, Salt Lake City, from where they will shape their course to San Francisco.

Program for Start

The program for the start was very different from the start of the journey that had its ending in the riotous welcome to Col. Roosevelt. In "The Ride of the Abernathy Boys," published by Doubleday, Page & Co., it is described how on April 5, 1910, Louie and Temple arose before daylight, and cheered only by their relatives and the cowpunchers, rode away from their father's ranch at Frederick, Okla., near the Texas line, on their long ride to New York. That was a ride of about 2500 miles.

Last Wednesday the boys had such a send-off as only gay Coney Island can give.

The boys had rested and were fresh for their ride when they cantered down Surf-av., shortly before 12 midnight and prepared to ride their horses into the water. Their father rode beside Temple, the youngest of the boys, and the contrast only served to accentuate the smallness of the plucky youngsters.

Try to Break Girl's Record

Since spring the boys have been in and around New York, and both of them, as well as their father, Col. Jack, have heard the call of the trail — the same call that is heard by the boy scouts, except that with these boys it is inbred. So they're off to try to lower the only existing transcontinental horseback record, which was made by Miss Nan Aspinwall of Montana, who rode from San Francisco to New York in 180 riding days. Miss Aspinwall started last September and arrived in New York, July 8. She rode a California mare, Lady Ellen. Miss Aspinwall's feat was a notable one and the boys realize it will take the hardest riding of their career to lower her record. If they succeed, they win a large money prize.

It's More Fun Ridin'

In preparing for the ride the greatest precaution as to the choice of mounts was used. It is part of the compact that the riders shall not eat nor sleep under a roof during their ride, so they will have to carry their blankets, tarpaulins, slickers, grub and a few cooking utensils with them, making very heavy loads for the horses.

"Are you glad to go?" Louie and Temple were asked. The elder of the two little boys replied with his Southwestern accent, "Sure we are. It's more fun ridin' than just stayin' around here."

"But don't you like New York and Coney Island?" he was urged.

"Of course we do, don't we, Temp? But you can't beat the fun of gettin' out yonder an' ridin' over the plains all day."

The 7-year-old child who is to make the ride that nearly baffled a strong young woman whose bride life had been spent in the saddle, nodded assent and explained that, in their book told, the strawberry soda pop was just as good as in many towns along the road as at Coney Island. When Temple wants to mount his horse, and his brother is not around to help him, he just shins up the animal's foreleg. It matters not to Temple if the animal be "sunfisher" and on the point of starting a session of bucking and pitching.

Louis is the responsible one. Of the care of his little brother on their other two rides he has developed a great sense of duty in the absolute seeing to his little brother's health, mind and grit. He strictly enforces their rule of never working or riding on Sunday, and whenever they come to Sunday takes Temple to Sunday school. [345]

Saturday morning Louie and Temple Abernathy with their father, John R. Abernathy of Oklahoma, stopped at the Ten-cent Barn in Wauseon to feed and rest their horses. They were on their 19th day since their start from Coney Island on August 1st, for their long ride across the continent to San Francisco and the waters of the Pacific. The boys propose to break the record for endurance riding by making the trip from ocean to ocean in sixty days; they are not to eat or sleep under a roof until the journey is completed. Sixty miles a day is their aim and they are not to ride Sundays. The boys, Louie aged 11 and Temple aged 7, have already made enviable records as riders of endurance. In 1909 they rode from Guthrie, Oklahoma, to Santa Fe and

---

[345] The *Kentucky Post* (Covington, Kentucky) August 14, 1911, Pg. 2.

returned, a distance of 2340 miles. In 1910 they rode from Frederick, Okla., to New York City, a distance of 2200 miles to meet their friend Ex-President Roosevelt on his return from his lion hunt in the Eastern jungles. The boys were alone on both of these rides. Mr. Abernathy is with them on this trip; he told the Tribune reporter that he had nothing else to do just now and was with the boys just because he wanted to take the trip with them.[346]

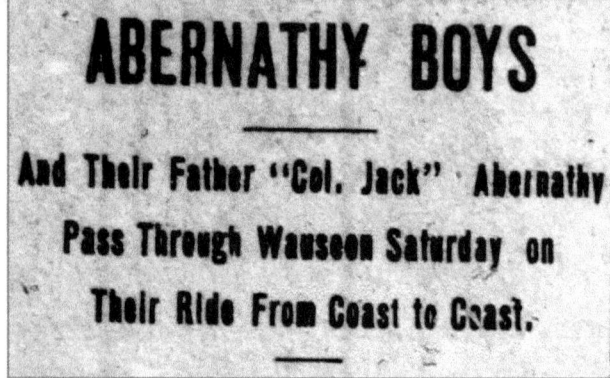

Mr. Abernathy, who was formerly a U.S. Marshal in Oklahoma and owns a ranch in Oklahoma near the Texas line, is one of the men it is a pleasure to meet and has a record as a wolf hunter. The boys and their father have been in and about New York City for some months and have been helping to write the history of the boys' horseback trip, which has just come off the press of Doubleday, Page & Co.

---

[346] *Fulton County Tribune* (Wauseon, Ohio) August 25, 1911, Pg. 1.

There is a large money prize coming to the boys if they meet all the conditions of the test of their endurance and hand to San Francisco officials before October 10th, letters which they are carrying with them from New York officials. The accompanying picture was taken just as the party started out of the barn in Wauseon to continue the long trail to the West."[347]

---

[347] *Fulton County Tribune* (Wauseon, Ohio) August 25, 1911, Pg. 1.

> **ABERNATHY BOYS REACH CHICAGO.**
> Chicago, Aug. 24.—Louis and Temple Abernathy, sons of John Abernathy, of Oklahoma, passed through Chicago late today on horseback. The boys, who are making a horseback trip from New York to San Francisco, were two days behind schedule time when they left Chicago. [348]

[349 350 351 352 353 354 355 356 357 358 359 360 361]

The famous Abernathy 'kids' the two Oklahoma youngsters whose long distance riding stunts brought them all kinds of fame the past few years, passed through Dixon Saturday evening enroute from New York to San Francisco.

The two boys, Louis, aged 11 and Temple, aged 7, were accompanied by their father, an old scout who is a personal friend of Col. Roosevelt. In fact, it was his friendship for Mr. Roosevelt that first won the boys national fame. When the Colonel reached America

---

[348] The *Topeka Daily Capital* (Topeka, Kansas) August 25, 1911, Pg. 1.
[349] The *Boston Globe* (Boston, Massachusetts), August 25, 1911, Pg. 10
[350] *Boston Evening Transcript* (Boston, Massachusetts) August 25, 1911, Pg. 2.
[351] *Fort Worth Star-Telegram* (Fort Worth, Texas) August 25, 1911, Pg. 3
[352] *Arkansas Democrat* (Little Rock, Arkansas) August 25, 1911, Pg. 2
[353] *Albuquerque Journal* (Albuquerque, New Mexico) August 25, 1911, Pg. 1
[354] *Springfield Evening Union* (Springfield, MA) August 25, 1911, Pg. 18.
[355] The *Waco Times-Herald* (Waco, Texas) August 25, 1911, Pg. 5.
[356] *Palladium-Item* (Richmond, Indiana) August 25, 1911, Pg. 2.
[357] The *Morning Union* (Springfield, Massachusetts) August 26, 1911, Pg. 3.
[358] The *Santa Fe New Mexican* (Santa Fe, New Mexico) August 26, 1911, Pg. 2
[359] The *Barre Daily Times* (Barre, Vermont) August 26, 1911, Pg. 3.
[360] Arizona Daily Star (Tucson, Arizona) August 27, 1911, Pg. 7.
[361] The State Journal (Frankfort, Kentucky) August 27, 1911, Pg7.

from South Africa the Abernathy boys made their second long distance ride on their ponies going from Oklahoma City to New York, 2209 miles, alone. This won for them the plaudits of the entire nation.

Their first long ride on their bronchos was in 1909 when they rode to Mexico from their home and around through the greasers' country a distance of 2340 miles. Their ride to meet Roosevelt was in 1910 and on their return to Oklahoma they drove a runabout which was purchased for them in New York.  *They lately got their names into the papers by driving an elephant and a donkey from Coney Island to Washington.*

Their present jaunt was started Aug. 1st and their schedule calls for the finish of the trip Oct. 10th. They are guided on their trip by their father and are at present six days behind their schedule. The trip is to be made all the way on horseback and the party is not to sleep indoors at all.[362]

---

[362] *Dixon Evening Telegraph* (Dixon, Illinois) August 28, 1911, Pg. 4.

The famous Abernathy boys, Louie and Temple, whose long rides across country have been featured in the newspapers, will pay a visit to Cedar Rapids tomorrow. They will arrive in the forenoon. They are making another trip, and are headed west this time, coming to this city from Clinton.

The Abernathy boys are the sons of the well-known Marshal Abernathy of Oklahoma, a personal friend of Roosevelt. Cedar Rapids boys, who have read Miles Abernathy's account of 'The Ride of the Abernathy Boys' will be interested in seeing the youngsters. It is expected they will make their headquarters tomorrow at the Geo. A. Mullin Co. store.

The boys will be received here by the boys' division of the Y.M.C.A., and all the boys in the city are invited to be on hand to greet the young travelers.[363]

The Abernathy boys, Temple and Louis, spent half an hour in Cedar Rapids yesterday, calling on the George H. Mullin company, which is selling their book; stopped to greet The Gazette force, left their regrets for the Boy Scouts of the Y.M.C.A. with whom they had expected to have a little visit, and then pushed ahead to camp a few miles west of town.

---

[363] *The Gazette* (Cedar Rapids, Iowa) August 29, 1911, Pg. 3.

'We'd like to stop,' said Temple, the eleven-year-old manager of the trip, 'but dad isn't used to the road and he has been holding us back a little. If we get to San Francisco on time we've got to keep a-going.'

The boys rode in alone about five o'clock in the afternoon. Their father, Marshal John L. Abernathy, of Oklahoma ("Eat 'em alive Jack") old time scout, and companion of Roosevelt's hunting trips in the southwest, followed the boys and confirmed their story that the ride 'is pretty tough on an old man.'

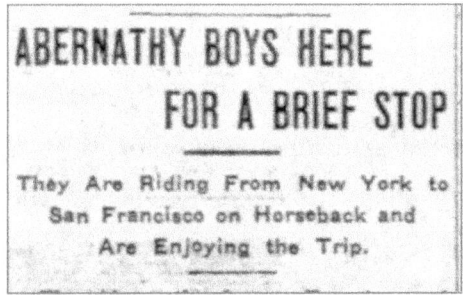

Temple Abernathy is eleven years old this summer while Louie is seven.[364] The latter says that he commenced riding when he was eighteen months old. Two years ago the two boys without any companion made a long trip on their ponies down to Old Mexico[365]; a year later they rode from Oklahoma to New York to welcome Roosevelt on his return from Africa. While in New York their father bought them an automobile which they drove on the return trip. The story of these trips is told in their book recently published.

---

[364] Their ages are occasionally mixed up, but with thousands of articles that might be expected.

[365] NOTE: This refers to their New Mexico Trip. Occasionally you see it referred to as "Old Mexico."

The present ride commenced in New York on the first day of August and it is the purpose of the boys to push right on to San Francisco. Marshal Abernathy will leave them in a few days, however, as he says he has had 'enough of the drill.'

All the boys' baggage is carried on their ponies and consists of a blanket apiece, a tarpaulin for a cover at night and a few cooking utensils. The boys are happy, freckle-faced little chaps and seem to be enjoying every minute of their trip. Their chief care seemed to be for their ponies. Light as their load is the horses seem to be feeling the effects of the long trip and the boys are trying to spare them in every possible way.

The boys do not ride on Sunday and spent last Sunday at Dixon. Their next objective point is Marshalltown where they will call tomorrow morning.[366]

> **Abernathy Boys at Cedar Rapids.**
> Cedar Rapids, Ia., Aug. 31.—The Abernathy boys, en route from New York to San Francisco, reached here last night. They are making the trip on horseback.

[367]

Not every encounter was positive, however. The boys occasionally faced skepticism from those who doubted the wisdom of allowing children to undertake such a dangerous journey. Chapter 12

---

[366] The *Gazette* (Cedar Rapids, Iowa) August 31, 1911, Pg. 3.
[367] *Quad-City Times* (Davenport, Iowa) August 31, 1911, Pg. 1.

investigates this further, but by 1911 you began seeing increasing news commentary such as the following:

The Abernathy boys have started on another horseback ride. This time it is from New York to San Francisco. What a pity those boys are not put to work at something that will be a benefit to somebody. —Broken Arrow Ledger.[368]

Yet their maturity and composure often silenced critics. Louis, in particular, impressed adults with his calm demeanor and ability to manage the logistics of their journey.

> The Abernathy boys, who are making a trip against time on horseback from New York to the Paiific coast, were two days behind time when they left Chicago.[369]

[370] [371] [372] [373] [374] [375] [376] [377] [378] [379] [380] [381] [382] [383] [384] [385]

---

[368] The *Guymon Herald* (Guymon, Oklahoma) August 24, 1911, Pg. 2.
[369] The *Munden Press* (Munden, Kansas) August 31, 1911, Pg. 2.
[370] *News Letter Journal* (Newcastle, Wyoming) September 1, 1911, Pg.3
[371] *The Lincoln Herald* (Lincoln, Nebraska) September 1, 1911, Pg 2.
[372] *The Free Press* (Grand Island, Nebraska) September 1, 1911, Pg. 2.
[373] *The Juniata Herald* (Juniata, Nebraska) September 6, 1911, Pg. 2.
[374] *The Brock Bulletin (*Brock, Nebraska) September 7, 1911, Pg. 2.
[375] *The Citizen-Patriot* (Atwood, Kansas) September 7, 1911, Pg. 2.
[376] *The Beaver Crossing Times* (Beaver Crossing, NE) September 7, 1911, Pg.2.
[377] *Woodruff Budget* (Woodruff, Kansas) September 7, 1911, Pg. 2.
[378] *Wahoo Newspapers* (Wahoo, Nebraska) September 7, 1911, Pg. 6.
[379] *Red Willow County Reporter* (Indianola, Nebraska) September 7, 1911, Pg. 2.
[380] *The Deshler Rustler (*Deshler, Nebraska) September 7, 1911, Pg. 2.
[381] *Harlan County Journal* (Alma, Nebraska) September 8, 1911, Pg. 6.
[382] The *Hubbell Standard* (Hubbell, Nebraska) September 8, 1911, Pg. 2
[383] The *Shubert Citizen* (Shubert, Nebraska) September 8, 1911, Pg. 2
[384] The *Mahaska Leader* (Mahaska, Kansas) September 15, 1911, Pg. 6.
[385] The *Byron Blade* (Byron, Nebraska) Fri, September 8, 1911, Pg. 2.

THE ABERNATHY BOYS.

En route from New York to San Francisco on a wager, the Abernathy boys, sons of "Eat-em-Alive" Jack Abernathy, were in Cedar Rapids Wednesday evening. They stopped to register at the Geo. A. Mullin book store, which is introducing their book, recently published, which tells of their other trips. They left New York August 1.

Louis and Temple Abernathy, aged 11 and 7, and their father, John R. Abernathy, former United States marshal of Oklahoma, and the friend and hunting companion of Theodore Roosevelt, reached Marshalltown on their trans-continental journey on horseback a few minutes before 5 o'clock Friday evening.

---

[386] The *Gazette* (Cedar Rapids, Iowa) September 1, 1911, Pg. 9.

Looked for since morning there was more or less disappointment shown when the day wore along and there was no sight of the youngsters. They showed up from the east toward evening, however, and remained here two hours before leaving.

Three Days Behind Schedule.

In order to win the $10,000 purse the lads must reach San Francisco within sixty days after leaving New York, and already they have spent a month on the journey. An average of sixty miles must be maintained, and with their arrival here the lads were about three days behind their schedule. They are confident of reaching 'Frisco in time, however, but realize that if they do so they can not encounter many more obstacles of delay.

ABERNATHY BOYS BEHIND SCHEDULE

MISHAPS RESULT IN LOSS OF THREE DAYS ON TRANSCONTINENTAL TRIP.

LADS IN FINE HEALTH, AND ENJOYING JOURNEY

Feel Confident That They Will Make the Trip on Time, But Realize That Not Many More Things Can Arise to Interfere—Horses Must Last Thru Nebraska.

Has Chase For Postcards.

When Master Temple lost from the pommel of his saddle Friday a bag containing postcards there was a chase of sixteen miles before he found them. The boys had traveled four miles before the cards were missed, and upon going back over the route Louis found that they had been picked up by a passerby and taken on four miles farther east. This caused a delay, and the day being so warm for both riders and horses, it was necessary to "lay up" a part of the day. Mr. Abernathy's horse, too, was giving out, and at Montour a trade was effected whereby the elder Abernathy secured a new mount

Two Horses Must Last.

According to the terms of the trip the two original mounts on which the boys left New York must be ridden until the state of Nebraska before they are discarded for fresh horses. The boys are allowed to "switch" horses, however, in their riding, as a change in mount is refreshing to a rider. When the party reached here neither of the boys was on his own mount. Louis riding Temple's horse, Temple riding his father's, and Mr. Abernathy Louis' mount. The gray horse, Sam, is Louis' regular mount, and the bald face, Wiley, is Temple's horse. The Wiley horse has already carried his owner from Guthrie, Okla., to New York, and the Sam horse has carried Louis from Guthrie to the Mexican border line, and from New Mexico to Guthrie. Sam was also used by Colonel Roosevelt while hunting with Mr. Abernathy and Mr. Abernathy says the animal is the best wolf hunting horse he ever saw.

Rest on Sundays.

The Abernathy boys do not travel on Sundays. They expect to make more than sixty miles today, and to reach Omaha on Wednesday. The Transcontinental route is being followed across Iowa, but from Cedar Rapids to this city another road was taken, which took the travelers thru Toledo instead of Tama.

The boys were entertained during a part of their stay at the George A. Mullin store, and it was planned by McCord and McCord to entertain them at lunch. This, however, could not be done, as one of the rules of the trip is that no meal shall be eaten under a roof, and no night shall be passed indoors.[387]

Louie and Temple Abernathy, bound for San Francisco in a cross-country ride, are expected here today and great preparations are being made for their reception and entertainment. Louie is now 11 and Temple 7 years of age. They are sons of "Catch 'em Alive Jack" Abernathy, former marshal of Oklahoma and crony of Colonel Roosevelt. Omaha is on the way from New York to San Francisco, and so they stop here in their cross-country ride on a wager.

These two midgets created a sensation in their ride from Oklahoma to New York City and have been in Omaha before on that occasion. They are now riding from Coney Island to the Presidio, which is a distance of 3,600 miles, in sixty riding days. In other

---

[387] *Evening Times-Republican* (Marshalltown, Iowa) September 2, 1911, Pg. 6.

words, they must average sixty miles a day, including[388] Sundays, on which days they are forbidden to ride. They cannot sleep or eat under a roof during their journey, which began on August 1. Incidentally, the paternal "Catch 'em Alive" accompanies them on the trip.

> **ABERNATHY BOYS TO REACH OMAHA TODAY**
>
> On Their Way From Coney Island to 'Frisco on Horseback—Father Along.
>
> Henry Kieser Will Meet and Entertain Them, Accompanied by Boy Scouts.

The reception in Omaha will be in charge of Henry Kieser, manager of the Bennett store book department and the Omaha boy scouts. They will be given a dinner and all the good times they can stop to enjoy. A large supply of red pop and red lemonade, which is "Temp's" favorite beverage, will be provided. Mr. Kieser will give the dinner to the guests and Omaha scouts.

A telegram was received by Mr. Kieser yesterday stating their progress from Des Moines toward Omaha, and he will meet them as soon as he hears again from the tourists. A great deal of noise and pow wow were made over the boys when they started from Coney Island. A book has been issued by Doubleday & Page, written by their

---

[388] NOTE: The context would seem to indicate this should be excluding, but this is the original text.

uncle on "The Ride of the Abernathy Boys," describing the trip from Oklahoma to New York.[389] [390]

Louis and Temple Abernathy of Oklahoma, 11 and 7 years old, respectively, will arrive in Omaha Wednesday on the transcontinental horseback ride they are making alone from New York City to San Francisco.

A monster reception, to be headed by the boy scouts of Omaha and participated in by all boydom[391] *of the city, has been arranged by Henry Kieser, manager of the Bennett book department. The reception and a "grub" will be held at the north entrance of the Bennett store, immediately on the arrival of the "Abernathy kids.*

---

[389] *Omaha World-Herald* (Omaha, Nebraska) September 6, 1911, Pg. 12
[390] *Evening World-Herald* (Omaha, Nebraska) September 5, 1911, Pg. 1.
[391] Original text.

The "grub" will consist of the things boy scouts have to eat when out on a hike, and will be supplemented with a bottle of red pop for every boy. Red pop is a favorite drink with Temple Abernathy, and one he insists on having whenever they reach a town.

The exact hour of the arrival here of the famous youthful scouts will not be known until this evening, when they telephone Mr. Kieser. If they reach here at noon the "grub" will be held as a luncheon, and if later it will be a supper.

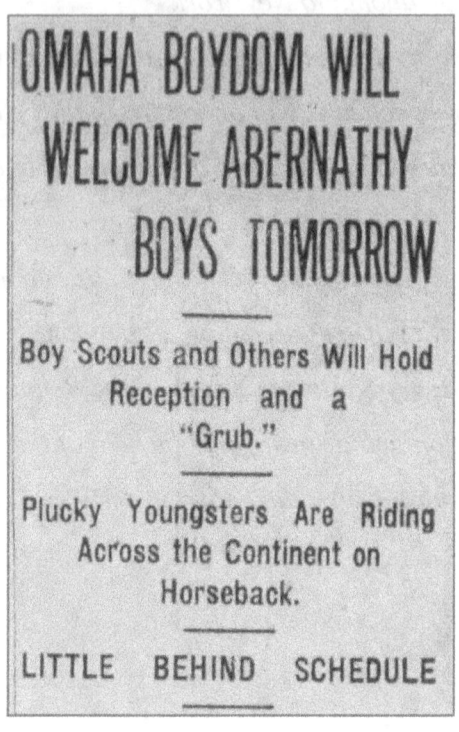

All Boys Are Invited.

All boys of Omaha, South Omaha and Council Bluffs are invited by Mr. Kieser and the local troops of boy scouts to participate in the reception and meet the Abernathys.

The two boys left New York on August 1, to win a money prize if they rode from Coney Island, New York to Presidio, San Francisco, 3,600 miles, in sixty days. At the present time they are a couple of days behind their schedule.

Under the conditions of the ride the boys must not sleep under a roof, must not eat under a roof, must average sixty miles a day for the whole distance, and must deliver a letter at San Francisco not later than Tuesday, October 10.

The boys left Coney Island one minute after midnight on Tuesday, August 1. Thousands of people were on hand to see them off. Since leaving New York they have ridden through Albany, Syracuse, Rochester, Cleveland, Chicago, and Des Moines. From Omaha, they will go through Cheyenne, over the mountains to Salt Lake City, and then on to San Francisco.

Have Had But Two Accidents.

The boys have met with a couple of accidents. Between Albany and Buffalo, Temple's horse fell off the bridge into the river. His elder brother plunged in after him and the father had to go in for his two sons. In Indiana, Louis' horse fell on him, inflicting injuries that held them up for five hours.

This is the second long ride the boys have taken. They became famous in 1910 when they rode from Frederic, Okla., to New York, 2,200 miles. They were then 10 and 6 years old. In 1909 they rode from Guthrie, Okla., to Santa Fe, N.M., and return, 2,340 miles. They were then 9 and 5 years

Raised in Saddle.

The two boys have been almost raised in the saddle. When Temple, the elder, was 18 months old, he was carried in front of his father on the horn of the United States marshal's saddle when the incident occurred that gave Abernathy the reputation of catching wolves with his bare hands. This occurred when he took President Roosevelt hunting and gave him the title of "Catch 'Em Alive Jack." The incident is described in the book, "The Ride of the Abernathy Boys," written by an uncle, as follows:

"Making a lightning grab the hunter threw his bare hand into the mouth of the angry wolf and soon subdued him. Meantime, Temple had succeeded in pulling out of the mud and slush and instead of crying or being excited he said triumphantly to his parent, 'Well, daddy, you shore dot him.'"[392]

Abernathy Youths Delayed by Storm

Young Plainsmen Enroute from New York to 'Frisco Arrive Here Thursday Morning.

The Abernathy boys, Louis and Temple, who are in the saddle from New York to 'Frisco, sent word Wednesday to Henry Kieser of Bennett's book department that they had been delayed at Logan by a rainstorm and would reach Omaha at 8:15 Thursday morning, in time to meet the school children before the bell rings. The young plainsman were scheduled to arrive here Wednesday.

[393]

---

[392] *The Omaha Daily News* (Omaha, Nebraska) September 5, 1911, Pg. 1.
[393] *Omaha Daily Bee* (Omaha, Nebraska) September 7, 1911, Pg. 5.

Storm be-draggled and weary, but nevertheless exhibiting every sign of the robustness of their young natures, the Abernathy boys, Louie and Temple, 11 and 7-year-old sons of "Catch 'Em-alive Jack" Abernathy, rode into Omaha this morning on their cross-continent horseback jaunt from Coney Island.

> **ABERNATHY BOYS EAT BREAKFAST ON SIDEWALK**
>
> Reach Omaha on Long Ride Across Continent Rather Weary and Bedraggled.
>
> Start for Lincoln Before Noon —Boy Scouts Fail to Turn Out.

The boys were expected in Omaha yesterday, but delays in travel forced a postponement of their entry into the Gate city. As a result, extensive plans for their reception and entertainment had to be abandoned.

The boys, accompanied by their father, crossed the Douglas street bridge a few minutes before 8 o'clock. They were met on the Nebraska side by a committee composed of Henry Kiser, manager of Bennett's book department, the Rev. M. O. McLaughlin, and others. It was the original intention to have had the Omaha boy scouts in the reception line and to serve as escort to the midget horsemen on their triumphal entry, but the weather and school days combined to thwart this part of the program.

(Continued On Page Eleven.)[394]

ABERNATHY BOYS EAT BREAKFAST ON SIDEWALK

(Continued from First Page.)

(Continued from First Page.)[395]

From the bridge the boys were taken to the Bennett store, where a breakfast was served to the travelers. The meal was tendered to the boys and their father by Mr. Kiser and was staged on the sidewalk near the Sixteenth street store entrance.

At the conclusion of the breakfast newspaper photographers had their innings and then the trio were whisked away for an automobile tour of the city.

According to the schedule as mapped out by the Abernathys their journey will be resumed at 10:30 o'clock, when they start for Lincoln.

Their trip from Coney Island to the Presidio of California represents a distance of 3,600 miles and must be completed in sixty riding

---

[394] NOTE: This is how the article was broken up and continued in the original text.
[395] NOTE: I inserted this as I thought the title on the continuation page was interesting.

days. They are forbidden to sleep or eat under a roof during the entire ride.[396]

[397]
398 399 400

---

[396] *Evening World-Herald (*Omaha, Nebraska) September 7, 1911, Pg. 1.
[397] *Evening World-Herald* (Omaha, Nebraska) September 7, 1911, Pg 1.
[398] The *Omaha Evening Bee* (Omaha, Nebraska) September 7, 1911, Pg. 1
[399] *Omaha Daily Bee* (Omaha, Nebraska) September 8, 1911, Pg. 3.
[400] *Omaha World-Herald* (Omaha, Nebraska) September 8, 1911, Pg. 1.

> **Abernathy Youths Delayed by Storm**
>
> **Young Plainsmen Enroute from New York to 'Frisco Arrive Here Thursday Morning.**
>
> The Abernathy boys, Louis and Temple, who are in the saddle from New York to 'Frisco, sent word Wednesday to Henry Kiser of Bennett's book department that they had been delayed at Logan by a rainstorm and would reach Omaha at 8:15 Thursday morning, in time to meet the school children before the bell rings. The young plainsmen were scheduled to arrive here Wednesday. [401]

Riding from New York to San Francisco on horseback with the big outdoors as their dining room and sleeping apartment, Louis and Temple Abernathy, 11 and 7 years old, respectively, stopped in Fremont a few hours last evening. They are accompanied on the long ride by their father "Catch-'em-Alive Jack" Abernathy, former marshal of Oklahoma and crony of Col. Roosevelt.

The midgets and their father had supper at a table prepared for them on the sidewalk in front of Hauser's bookstore where a crowd of curious people gathered to watch the little fellows satisfy their big, healthy appetites.

---

[401] *Omaha Daily Bee* (Omaha, Nebraska) September 8, 1911, Pg. 3.

By the terms of a $10,000 wager, they must ride from Coney Island to San Francisco in sixty days, actual riding time, an average of sixty miles a day. They are about two days behind their schedule, since, Oh, before I can remember.

When they rode into Fremont "Temp" was on the back of one of the horses on which they made their famous ride from Oklahoma to Washington to see Col. Roosevelt. The old white horse has carried one or the other of the boys 4,500 miles and is now making the trip across the country as far as Wyoming, where the riders will get a change of mount.

Company Manners.

Louie and Temple held an informal reception at Hauser's store while their supper was being prepared. They politely doffed their Stetsons when anyone stepped up to shake hands with them. They answered questions about their trip quite freely, showing not the least embarrassment.

"New York is on the bum," announced Temple in answer to a question. "When I went there first I thought I'd like it, but I changed my mind."

When asked if it tired them to ride, Temp spoke up quickly, "Oh no sir; we have been riding ever since."

Toys Interested Him.

Tho he is doing a stunt that few men would undertake, Temp is, after all, a real boy with a boy's love of play. The toys on the counter held heaps of interest for him. He found a musical top that just suited him and a little train of cars that looked just like the big ones. His joy knew no limit when Harry Hauser made him a present of the toys that so struck his fancy.

"Let's see if I've got a string to spin the top." With that he plunged a chubby little hand into his pocket and pulled forth a roll of twine large enough to stake his horse out with. Louie was fitted out with a top and twine which he says he will learn to play "Yankee Doodle."

The two are then romped off with a picture show man and spent an hour at the show. So interested had they become that "Catch-'em-Alive" Abernathy had to round them up when it was time to mount their horses again. At 10 o'clock they rode out westward expecting to catch a few winks of sleep on the road somewhere this side of North Bend.[402] [403]

---

[402] *Fremont Tribune* (Fremont, Nebraska) September 8, 1911, Pg. 8.
[403] *Fremont Tri-Weekly Tribune* (Fremont, Nebraska) September 9, 1911, Pg. 2.

> **Abernathys at Grand Island.**
>
> GRAND ISLAND, Neb., Sept. 11.— The Abernathy boys and father, making a trip across the continent on horseback, arrived from Central City today, and left a few hours later hoping to reach Kearney tonight.[404]

Fresh from a sleep on the prairie near Gibbon, the Abernathy party riding from New York to San Francisco, arrived in Kearney at eight o'clock on Tuesday morning. They spent less than an hour in the city and after posing for a photograph and pleasantly answering the questions of interrogators who were desirous of hearing how they turned their weary ponies toward the west and at a brisk canter rode away on the last half of the 3,619 mile journey.

The party consists of "Jack" Abernathy, Louis Abernathy, and Temple Abernathy. The owner is the father, forty years old; Louis is eleven and Temple is seven. They are riding from New York City to San Francisco and at the end of the journey, if completed by October 10, they will receive ten thousand dollars. They left New York August 1. They rode their horses out of the Atlantic ocean and by the terms of the contract must ride them into the Pacific before midnight of October 10.

---

[404] *Lincoln Nebraska State Journal* (Lincoln, Nebraska) September 12, 1911, Pg. 7.

By agreement, the party will change horses in Wyoming. Mr. Abernathy says they are plentifully provided with money and that it is no "charity trip." The party rode from Grand Island to a mile west of Gibbon Monday. Although they were now behind their schedule, they expect to make it up before reaching the Rockies.

Jack Abernathy is a personal friend of Theodore Roosevelt, having served with him on the plains years ago and rode with him up San Juan Hill. He is large, good-natured, and brown from the sun and wind and rain until his face shines with the reflection of the out of doors.

Mr. Abernathy was riding a bay pony while the boys rode gray, the same horse they have ridden from New York. Although Mr. Abernathy has been compelled to change as the horse he left New York on became disabled. By their agreement, the party may change horses in Wyoming.

> **ABERNATHY PARTY REACHES KEARNEY**
>
> FIRST HALF OF LONG JOURNEY IS NOW COMPLETED.
>
> **SPEND BUT A SHORT TIME HERE**
>
> Off on Weary Horses For the West—Left New York City August 1—Must Be in San Francisco October 10—Will Win $10,000 If Trip is Finished O. T.

The party is well-equipped for the trip, carrying their blanket rolls, extra clothing, and such other paraphernalia as they may need strapped to their regular cowboy saddles. They expect to encounter some snow before reaching San Francisco.

While the father was making some purchases, a crowd of admiring boys gathered about the youngsters and plied them with questions. "They were ready," answered little Temple, the younger, didn't approve of the way in which Louis fastened himself into a rower all looped and called him a snare.

The boys then turned to Temple and asked him if he liked this place as well as Oklahoma City, the home of the Abernathys.

"This place," he said, "would hold just about three of them. Louis doubled up his little horn and threw it in a lasso at Temple. The younger flashed a grin and bent to "snag" his older brother. Louis had asked what kind of an academy they would find.

"A boys' academy?"

"For boys?" he asked.

"No for girls," said seven-year-old Temple. "Don't you see who stopped there? He's a ladies boy," he said to the crowd while further describing the stoppage.

The Abernathy boys are called "Roosevelt boys" because they rode horseback from Oklahoma City to Washington, D.C., where they were received by President Roosevelt. They also made a trip to Mexico on horseback, and this is their third long journey.

They are to ride from Cheyenne on fresh horses before they completed the journey.

"But we don't know yet where," said Temple, "nobody knows. Daddy doesn't himself!"[405]

SMALL BOYS' LONG RIDE — Abernathy Boys, Crossing Continent Horseback, Pass Through Junction City.

(Special to The Herald-Republican.)

Ogden, Oct. 6. — The famous "Abernathy kids," aged seven and nine, who first sprang into fame as "pals of President Roosevelt" during his bear hunts in the south, stopped in Ogden for a few hours today on their long ride from New York to San Francisco.

Their first journey of moment was from their home in Oklahoma to New York City to "meet Mr. Roosevelt" on his return from the old world. The ex-president extended the kids an enthusiastic welcome, and they have since

---

[405] *Kearney Semi-Weekly Hub* (Kearney, Nebraska) September 14, 1911, Pg. 5.

undertaken the coast-to-coast trip, their father preceding them by rail and maintaining a general supervision of their trip.[406]

The youngsters had their ponies shod at P. R. Shupe's blacksmith shop on Washington avenue and resumed their way immediately in the direction of Brigham City. They expressed their happiness and told of the fun they are having on the trip.

They left Coney Island August 1 and will try to reach San Francisco October 15. Their average rate is forty miles a day.[407]

> **Abernathy Boys' Trip.**
>
> Cheyenne.—J. R. Abernathy of New York, who is accompanying his young sons, Louie and Temple, across the continent on horseback, arrived ahead of the boys, who are en route from Sidney. The horses ridden by the boys are the same they started with at Coney Island. The ride is being made on a wager of $10,000.

[408]

---

[406] NOTE: Their father is never far from them, joining for rides as far as Kearney, NE.
[407] *Salt Lake Herald* (Salt Lake City, Utah) October 7, 1911, Pg. 6.
[408] *Natrona County Tribune* (Casper, Wyoming) October 11, 1911, Pg. 2.

The Silent Stretch: Crossing the Great Divide

As the Abernathy boys rode out of Nebraska in the late summer of 1911, the clatter of headlines and the hum of public excitement began to fade behind them. Their journey westward from the heartland marked a curious shift—not in momentum, but in visibility. After weeks of intense media coverage that followed their every trot and trotline from New York through Ohio, Indiana, and into the Midwest, a strange quiet settled in.

News from the trail went sparse as they entered the vast, open expanses between Nebraska and California. This wasn't due to a lack of determination or progress—the boys were still riding strong, their eyes set firmly on the Pacific. But they had entered a part of the country where small towns dotted a much more rugged landscape, and newspapers were fewer, slower, or maybe just uninterested in the daily happenings of two dusty young adventurers passing through.

Yet this stretch—often overlooked in newsprint—was in many ways the most grueling and formative part of their transcontinental ride. It is also the stretch that cost them the most time on their journey. Here, in the high plains and mountain passes, far from the curious stares and crowded street corners of the East, the boys faced what might have been their most challenging days. Heat shimmered off the plains. Water became scarce. Their horses grew leaner, and rest was earned only under the stars, never beneath a roof, in keeping with the strict terms of their $10,000 wager.

Jack Abernathy, riding alongside his sons for portions of the trip, had found himself sometimes struggling more than the boys. At one point, as reported before they went radio silent, he had to replace his horse due to overexertion—a telling sign of the toll this journey was taking on even seasoned riders. But Louis and Temple, though small in stature, continued on with an endurance that confounded skeptics and amazed supporters.

For hundreds of miles, the boys rode in near anonymity, stopping in unmarked fields and unknown valleys, moving ever westward through the hush of history. This "silent stretch" was not without drama—Temple's pony reportedly went lame and required makeshift re-shoeing; Louis's saddle wore thin, patched with bits of burlap and ingenuity. They navigated by instinct and inquiries, sometimes guided only by the sun and the kindness of a passing rancher.

Then, just as suddenly as they had vanished from the public eye, they reemerged in California. Newspapers began to buzz again. The boys were spotted near the Sierra foothills, the Pacific now within reach. They were weathered, yes—but unbroken.

This quiet portion of their ride, lacking in headlines but rich in perseverance, underscored what made the Abernathy boys so compelling. They didn't ride for the cameras or the clamor. Did they ride for the challenge, for the thrill, and, perhaps most of all, maybe they just rode for each other? And it was in this unsung part of the journey that their legend quietly deepened.

Losing Their Horses in Utah

As the boys crossed into Utah, disaster struck. One of their horses fell ill, likely from the combined strain of long days, rugged terrain, and limited forage. Despite their efforts to nurse the animal back to health, it became clear that continuing on horseback was no longer viable. The loss was a devastating blow to the Abernathy brothers, whose bond with their horses had carried them through countless adventures.

Though historical reports don't detail the moment, one can imagine how the loss might have felt to the boys—two riders whose bond with their horses had carried them through so many miles. The animal was not just transportation, but a trusted companion.

The Rockies: A New Challenge

The approach to the Rockies continued to bring fresh challenges. Altitude, unpredictable weather, and steep trails made every step forward a test. Snowfall, though early, turned sections of their route treacherous. Paths vanished under the early snow. Breaths came shorter. Progress slowed.

While there is no exact record of their conversations, Temple may have gazed at the towering peaks ahead and whispered something like, "It's like the edge of the world." Though imagined, such a remark captures the awe and tension of that ascent.

Later, Temple would describe the experience of crossing the mountains as "riding through the clouds"—a poetic reflection from a boy whose youthful wonder seemed to survive even the harshest conditions.

ABERNATHY BOYS HAVE REACHED SACRAMENTO.

Sacramento, Cal., Oct. 30.—Temple and Louis Abernathy, seven and eleven years old respectively, arrived in Sacramento on horseback Saturday, after a ride that has taken them almost across the continent. The boys started from Coney Island on August 1st, and were to make the trip in sixty days to win a purse of $10,000. They were delayed in Utah and Wyoming when their horses got away and again lost five days in Wyoming because of high water.

---

[409] The *Sioux City Journal* (Sioux City, Iowa) October 29, 1911, Pg. 1.
[410] The *Star Press* (Muncie, Indiana) October 29, 1911, Pg. 1.
[411] *Nevada State Journal* (Reno, Nevada) October 29, 1911, Pg. 1.
[412] The *Buffalo Commercial* (Buffalo, New York) October 30, 1911, Pg. 5

ABERNATHY BOYS FAIL ON TRIP.

A Cross-Continent Ride Was to Have Been Made in Sixty Days.

SACRAMENTO, CAL., Oct 28.—Temple Abernathy and his brother Louis, 7 and 11 years old, arrived in Sacramento on horseback today after a ride that has taken them almost across the continent. The boys started from Coney Island, August 1, and were to make the trip to San Francisco in sixty days. They were delayed in Utah and Wyoming when their horses got away and again lost five days in Wyoming because of high water.

The boys were accompanied by their father, J. R. Abernathy from the Rocky Mountains.

ABERNATHY BOYS HERE

Louis and Temple Abernathy, the two boys from Oklahoma who are on their way fom New York to San Francisco on horseback, passed through this city yesterday.

The boys will win a substantial wager if they make the trip to the metropolis on scheduled time and every indication points to their success.

---

[413] The *Courier-Journal* (Louisville, Kentucky) October 29, 1911, Pg. 11.
[414] The *Kansas City Star* (Kansas City, Missouri) October 29, 1911, Pg. 1.
[415] *Detroit Free Press* (Detroit, Michigan) October 30, 1911, Pg. 4.
[416] *Vallejo Times-Herald* (Vallejo, California) October 31, 1911, Pg. 5.

ABERNATHY BOYS ON LONG RIDE FROM CONEY

Two days behind their schedule and losers of a $10,000 purse as a result, Louise and Temple Abernathy, sons of Jack Abernathy, the wolf hunting friend of Roosevelt's, rode their horses into the Pacific ocean here yesterday, completing a horseback ride from Coney Island.

The two Oklahoma lads started from Coney Island in August, on a wager. They were to receive $10,000 did they make the trip in 60 days.

Part of the time the boys were accompanied by their father, who rode on the the last miles of the journey to San Francisco with them.

The escape of their mounts and subsequent loss for six days in Utah, coupled with inclement weather and sickness kept the boys from the rich prize.

---

[417] *San Francisco Bulletin* (San Francisco, California) October 31, 1911, Pg. 20.

Temple Abernathy, aged 7, is shown at the left, with Louis Abernathy, aged 11, at the right. Their father, John R. Abernathy, is between them. The boys yesterday completed their coast to coast saddle trip.

[418] *The San Francisco Call & Post* (San Francisco, California) October 31, 1911, Pg. 4.

Long Journey Is Ended By the Abernathy Boys — *Breaking the record for crossing the continent on horseback, Louis and Temple Abernathy, aged seven and eleven respectively, rode their mounts into the waters of the Pacific last evening at sundown, and ended their 4,500-mile ride begun at Coney Island, New York, August 1.*

They made the trip in sixty-two riding days, and the only known record is 182 days, made by an army officer years ago.[419]

LOUIS ABERNATHY, mounted on "Wiley," and portraits of brother and father.

Louis Abernathy, mounted on "Wiley."

Temple Abernathy
John R. Abernathy

---

[419] NOTE: An earlier reference indicated Miss Nan Aspinwall of Montana rode from San Francisco to New York in 180 riding days.

If they had reached this city by October 10th, they would have won $10,000 offered by a syndicate of sporting men of New York, who made up the purse with the understanding that they should cross the continent between August 1st and October 10th.

The young horsemen did not show any signs of fatigue or weariness from their long stay in the saddle, although they have had many hard experiences since leaving New York, from losing their horses in Kelton, Utah, to being poisoned by eating canned tomatoes.

"Wiley," the pony of Louis, the younger, went into the flooded river with him, and horse and rider barely escaped from the torrents.

The boys were accompanied 2,200 miles of the way by their father, John R. Abernathy, a rancher of Oklahoma City, Oklahoma, who has been on many hunting trips with former president Roosevelt. Since leaving New York they have ridden 4,500 miles.

They lost six days at Kelton, Utah, when their horses escaped. The pony of Louis was recaptured, but the horse of Temple was never found. A new horse was purchased there for Temple. They lost four days in Wyoming owing to rains and high water.

"I'm pretty glad to get here," said Louis last evening at the ferry building as he rode off the boat from Vallejo. "I'm going to get a feather bed two feet deep and sleep as long as I want to. Ain't I dad?"

"You sure are," said Abernathy. "You can sleep your head off, son."

The only equipment carried by the lads is a double blanket, tarpaulin, mess kit and pistols. When possible, they purchased their meals on the road, but when on the plains cooked their own food.[420]

> ABERNATHY BOYS RIDE TO COAST.
> SAN FRANCISCO, Nov. 1—"Jack" Abernathy, United States marshal, of Oklahoma, yesterday welcomed his two sons Temple and Louis, seven and eleven years old respectively, who had just completed a horseback ride from New York to San Francisco in sixty-two days. He bade them alight and rest their saddles, but the boys insisted on first riding into the Pacific ocean. Through losing their horses at Kelton Utah, the boys missed an opportunity to win $10,000, offered by New York men, if they crossed the continent in sixty days.

[421]

San Francisco, Calif., Nov. 6. —Louis and Temple Abernathy of Frederick, Okla., accompanied by their father, John R. Abernathy, rode into San Francisco last week, thus completing a horseback jaunt from Coney Island, N. Y. In making the trip, the boys, who are only 11 and 7 years old respectively, have covered a direct distance of close

---

[420] The *San Francisco Examiner* (San Francisco, California) Oct 31, 1911, Pg. 4.
[421] *Transcript-Telegram* (Holyoke, Massachusetts) November 1, 1911, Pg. 9.

to 4,000 miles, the side trips, such as one when they were obliged to change their horses for 114 miles, adding greatly to this figure.

The ride was made as a result of a bet between Fred Thompson of Luna Park, Coney Island, and Gilda Davis. Davis bet $10,000 that the children could not make the trip to the coast in sixty days of actual riding. The wager was subscribed by a number of wealthy New Yorkers, and the boys, accompanied by their father, left New York on August 1. The time actually occupied in riding has been sixty-two days, so the boys have lost the prize of $10,000 which they were to receive by the narrow margin of two days. Abernathy says that the boys lost because of delays in Wyoming and Iowa due to floods. Part of the rules which governed the contest prohibited the boys from

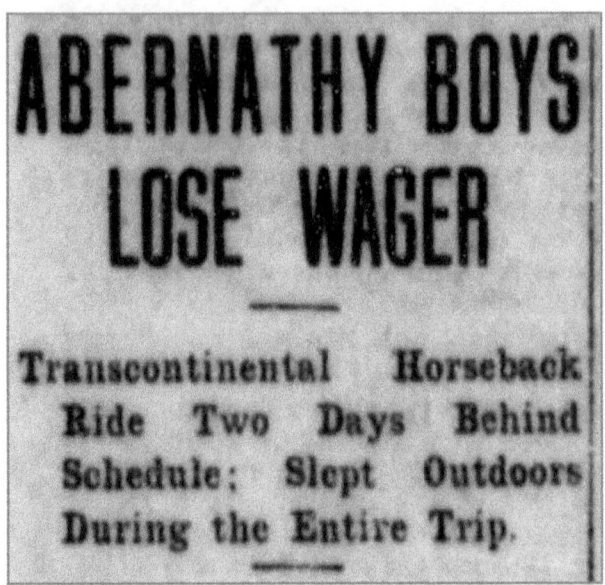

sleeping under a roof or eating within a house during the trip, and last night they ate their first meal indoors since leaving New York.

The boys gained fame last year when they rode from Oklahoma to New York for the purpose of meeting former President Roosevelt on the latter's return from Europe.

Previously they had ridden from their home to Santa Fe and return, a distance of 2,340 miles. The boys will now remain here, it being their father's intention to place them in some school in this vicinity before returning to Oklahoma.[422]

The Final Push: California Dreaming

As the boys descended into California in late October 1911, the end of their journey seemed tantalizingly close. Yet, the final stretch was no less challenging. The heat of the Central Valley pushed both horses and riders—where possible—to their limits, and the boys were forced to take longer breaks to ensure their own health and safety.

Word of their impending arrival spread, and excitement built in San Francisco. Crowds gathered to await their arrival, eager to witness the culmination of this journey. Despite their best efforts, Louis and Temple arrived two days past the 60-day deadline. While they missed out on the $10,000 prize, their achievement was celebrated as a monumental success.

---

[422] The *Albuquerque Tribune* (Albuquerque, New Mexico) November 6, 1911, Pg. 5.

They arrived two days behind schedule, but their spirits remained high, and their journey was celebrated.

San Francisco greeted the boys with parades and accolades. Reporters clamored for interviews, and the boys' story dominated headlines across the country. Temple, ever the showman, quipped that they might have made it on time if only they had "less rain and fewer mountains to climb."

ABERNATHY BOYS END LONG JOURNEY

They Ride Nearly Across the Continent on Horseback With Their Father.

SACRAMENTO, Cal., Oct. 28.—Temple Abernathy and his brother, Louis, 7 and 11 years old, respectively, arrived in Sacramento on horseback today, after a ride that has taken them almost across the continent.

The boys started from Coney Island Aug. 1 and were to make the trip to San Francisco in 60 days to win a purse of $10,000 said to have been offered by several millionaires of New York. They were delayed in Utah and Wyoming when their horses got away and again lost five days in Wyoming because of high water.

The boys were accompanied by their father, J. R. Abernathy, from the Rocky Mountains.

---

[423] *St. Louis Post-Dispatch* (St. Louis, Missouri) October 29, 1911, Pg. 30.

Abernathy Boys Wrte Taft.

Abernathy Boys Write Taft. *— Louie and Temple Abernathy, the two small sons of "Jack" Abernathy, noted throughout Oklahoma and the West as the man who "kills 'em alive," meaning wolves, have written President Taft a letter of their arrival in San Francisco at the end of their long ride across the continent by horseback. These boys are the only human beings who ever attempted this feat. They began their feats of horsemanship when they were only a few years old, and several years ago, when Roosevelt was in the White House, they rode from Oklahoma to New York by horse, stopping at the White House. This year they tried riding from New York to San Francisco. This is the day the boys address the President:*

"To Our Friend: We left the Atlantic August 1, 1911. We hadn't ridden a step Sunday or hadn't been under a roof to eat or sleep. We lost fifteen riding days..."

(Continued on Seventh Page)[424]

... leaving sixty-two days' actual travel. We have covered a distance of 3,619 miles; only one of our horses held out all the way. The trip cost us over $2,800. We accepted no favors, paid our own expenses, found our own way and lost the prize by two days, and we have suffered all kinds of hardships.[425]

---

[424] NOTE: This is how the article was broken up and continued in the original text.
[425] The *News and Advance* (Lynchburg, Virginia) November 14, 1911, Pg. 1.

"Respectfully,
TEMPLE ABERNATHY,
LOUIE ABERNATHY."

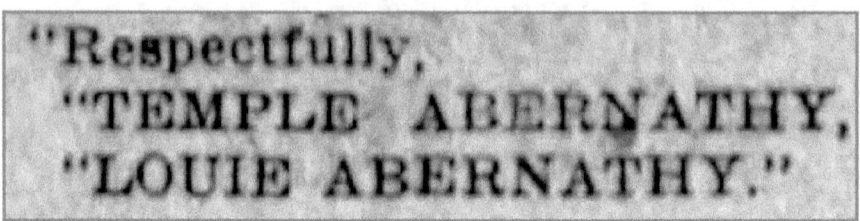

ABERNATHY BOYS LOST THE $10,000[426]
BUT HAD LOTS OF FUN ON THEIR OCEAN TO OCEAN TRIP FROM EAST TO WEST — 3,600 MILES WERE TRAVELED

A San Francisco, California, paper of October 31, published a picture of Temple and Louie Abernathy, the two Tillman county[427] *boys, and their father, John R. Abernathy, made at the completion of the boys' 3,600-mile coast-to-coast ride. Accompanying their picture was this story:*

---

[426] NOTE: I have not found any formal notice that the prize changed from $5,000 to $10,000 but this is the first mention of it in the archives I have reviewed.

[427] County was not capitalized in the original text.

ABERNATHY BOYS LOST THE $10,000

BUT HAD LOTS OF FUN ON THEIR OCEAN TO OCEAN TRIP FROM EAST TO WEST—3,600 MILES WERE TRAVELED

"Sleepy and saddle-weary, but happy because the long coast-to-coast ride was ended, Temple and Louie Abernathy, who started from Coney Island, New York, on August 1, and reached San Francisco from Vallejo, at 5:30 o'clock last evening.

"The young riders turned their horses up Market street, galloped out 6:30 o'clock through Golden Gate park and at 6:30 o'clock eight steel shod hoofs were planted in the sands of the Pacific ocean while two exultant boys rose in their stirrups and waved their hats.

"Accompanying the boys on several stages of their journey was 'Jack' Abernathy, their father, for 11 years a United States marshal at Oklahoma City, and a personal friend of Theodore Roosevelt.

"Temple Abernathy is 7 years old, Louie is 11. The boys' actual time was 91 days. The distance, as taken, covered 3,619 miles. Neither would consent to riding on Sunday, and in addition to this, they were delayed by sickness, accident and weather long enough to lose a prize offered by New Yorkers if they made the trip in 60 days.

"Since they left the starting point neither of the boys has eaten or slept under a roof. This was one of the terms of their contract. They ate and slept out in all kinds of weather. The trip cost the father $2,600.

"Neither appeared disheartened at having lost the prize.

"'Gee, but it's great to get here,' said Temple. 'I liked the trip all right, but sometimes it got cold and then I didn't like it so well. I want the deepest feather I can get in this town.'

"'It was too hard,' said Louie. 'We averaged nearly 60 miles a day, when we rode, and it was too far.'

"The boys two years ago gained fame by riding to New York City from Oklahoma and greeted Col. Roosevelt upon his return from his African hunting trip. Another long trip was the 2,340-mile journey on horseback from Guthrie, Okla., to Old Mexico and return by way of Santa Fe.

"The boys will enter the San Francisco public schools next week. For the present, the Abernathy boys are at the Golden West hotel."[428] [429]

---

[428] The *Frederick Leader* (Frederick, Oklahoma) November 10, 1911 Pg. 3
[429] *Mangum Weekly Star* (Mangum, Oklahoma) November 16, 1911, Pg. 5

Chapter 10:
1912 — A Lull in the Action?

> *The Abernathy boys from Oklahoma, who created quite a stir some years ago by riding their ponies to Washington to see President Roosevelt were in Lawrence last evening. They are traveling on motorcycles this time and had come from Burlingame since yesterday morning.*[430]
>
> *Louis and Temple, who are 9 and 13 years old*[431]*, are known throughout the country for numerous cross-country trips which they have made on horseback. The two youngsters have crossed the continent several times and immediately after reaching New York this summer they will go to Europe with their father.*[432]

After their triumphant coast-to-coast horseback journey in 1911, Louis "Bud" Abernathy, age 12, and Temple, age 8, found themselves back in Oklahoma, temporarily trading fame for a brief period of quiet. But the year 1912 was far from a footnote. It marked a transitional phase—where the Abernathy story began shifting from saddle to spark plug, from hooves to horsepower.

From Horseback to the Stage

Even as they stepped back from new long-distance rides horseback, the Abernathy brothers stayed in the public eye. Newspaper ads and clippings from the spring and summer of 1912 document a new

---

[430] The *Daily Gazette* (Lawrence, Kansas) May 30, 1913, Pg 1.
[431] These ages should be flipped around to match the order of the names, but more importantly they show the many variations of the boys' ages which were presented in the media.
[432] *Columbia Daily Tribune* (Columbia, Missouri) June 5, 1913, Pg. 2.

venture: public lecture appearances and vaudeville-style shows featuring lantern slides and moving pictures recounting their 1911 San Francisco ride.

The *Morning Press* (Santa Barbara, California) advertised the "famous Abernathy kids" appearing at the La Petite Theater, promising audiences a presentation that included "two reels of moving pictures, together with stereopticon views of their long horseback ride across the continent." They were described as "the most talked about in the country today.".[433]

In 1912, the Abernathy brothers did however find themselves caught up in the raucous energy of American politics—not as candidates, but as youthful symbols of the Progressive movement. Their father, a staunch supporter of Theodore Roosevelt and former U.S. Marshal, was actively involved in organizing Roosevelt clubs across Oklahoma. Temple, dressed in a Rough Rider outfit, reportedly walked through a Republican convention hall shouting, "I want Teddy," while another boy rode a pony through the same hall amid cheering Roosevelt supporters. The convention itself was a political spectacle, filled with balloon ascensions, shouted slogans, and

> Among the other methods used by Perry to stimulate Roosevelt sentiment was the presence of Temple Abernathy, the youngest of the famous Abernathy boys, who, dressed in Rough Rider costume, walked about the hall, crying, "I want Teddy!"

---

[433] *The Morning Press* (Santa Barbara, CA), May 24, 1912, Pg. 2.

even physical altercations between Taft and Roosevelt supporters. Though Jack Abernathy ultimately returned to Oklahoma to continue organizing support for Roosevelt, the image of his sons participating in such theatrical political displays once again captured the public's attention. The boys' presence helped underscore Roosevelt's branding of the Progressive Party as youthful, vigorous, and deeply rooted in frontier values. [434] [435] [436] [437]

> Dynamite explosions, a fight between a Choctaw governor and a Rough Rider, a balloon ascension and a wild ride on a broncho through the convention hall by one of the Abernathy boys, son of "Catch-'Em-Alive" Jack, featured the efforts of Perry to get delegates instructed for Roosevelt for president.

[438]

Getting Into Gear

The spotlight wasn't their only new stage. As early as 1912, hints began surfacing about the boys' fascination with motorized travel. Although their most famous motorcycle journey wouldn't come until

---

[434] The *Pittsburgh Press* (Pittsburgh, Pennsylvania) January 24, 1912, Pg. 2.
[435] *Daily Local News* (West Chester, Pennsylvania) January 24, 1912, Pg. 1.
[436] The *Republican (*Springfield, Massachusetts) January 24, 1912, Pg. 2.
[437] *Marion News-Tribune* (Marion, Indiana) January 24, 1912, Pg. 8.
[438] The F*ranklin County Observer* (Washington, Missouri) January 5, 1912, Pg. 2.

1913, *Indian Motorcycle Media* and later retrospectives describe this period as when their interest in the machine was sparked.[439]

Meanwhile, reports from 1912 indicated that Jack Abernathy had given the boys a 40-horsepower Buick touring car—a significant upgrade from horseback. According to one article, this vehicle was "as much their playground as the prairie had once been."[440] It's likely the boys began honing their mechanical skills during this time, practicing driving and handling tools with the same dedication they had shown on horseback.

A Moment You Can Picture

No reporter was present the first time they tried riding a motorcycle, but the moment practically writes itself:

When Louis first kicked the starter on the Indian, a sputtering cough turned into a full-throated roar. Temple, perched on the seat next to his brother, clutched his brother's coat.

"Faster than any bronco we ever rode!" he might've shouted, his voice trailing behind them as the machine lurched forward.

Townsfolk, already used to seeing the boys on horseback, now stood at the edges of Oklahoma City's dusty streets to watch them go by—part wonder, part worry etched into their faces.

---

[439] *Indian Motorcycle Media*. "Be Legendary: The Abernathy Brothers Rode from Oklahoma to New York on an Indian Motorcycle Aged 14 and 10 Years Old." Published January 26, 2017. https://www.indianmotorcycle.media/be-legendary-the-abernathy-brothers-rode-from-oklahoma-to-new-york-on-an-indian-motorcycle-aged-14-and-10-years-old-112392

[440] The *Oregon Daily Journal* (Portland, Oregon) January 21, 1912, Pg. 36.

While imagined, scenes like this reflect the tone of admiration—and sometimes controversy—that surrounded their every move.

> **ABERNATHY BOYS IN SCHOOL.**
>
> Juvenile Long Distance Horseback Riders to Study in Frisco.
>
> Guthrie, Jan. 29.—Louis and Temple Abernathy, sons of John R. Abernathy, former United States marshal, have entered school in San Francisco. The boys recently completed an overland trip with their father from New York city to Los Angeles and prior to that time they took two other long distance horseback trips.
>
> The father of the lads will return to Oklahoma soon to assist Ed Perry of Coalgate, and others, in the organization of Roosevelt clubs. [441]

The Road Ahead

The rest of 1912 seems to have passed without another epic ride, but not without purpose. Between school, stage appearances, and mechanical tinkering, the Abernathy brothers were preparing. Their next great chapter would begin in 1913—with roaring engines and an Indian motorcycle carrying them from Oklahoma to New York.

---

[441] *Morning Examiner* (Bartlesville, Oklahoma) January 30, 1912, Pg. 6.

Chapter 11:
1913 — The Indian Motorcycle Ride

The Abernathy boys from Oklahoma, who created quite a stir some years ago by riding their ponies to Washington to see President Roosevelt were in Lawrence last evening. They are traveling on motorcycles this time and had come from Burlingame since yesterday morning.[442]

Louis and Temple, who are 9 and 13 years old, are known throughout the country for numerous cross-country trips which they have made on horseback. The two youngsters have crossed the continent several times and immediately after reaching New York this summer they will go to Europe with their father.[443]

MOTORCYCLES THIS TIME
Abernathy Boys Will Go to New York in Quicker Time Than Year Ago.

[444]

---

[442] The *Daily Gazette* (Lawrence, Kansas) May 30, 1913 Pg 1.
[443] *Columbia Daily Tribune* (Columbia, Missouri) June 5, 1913 Pg. 2.
[444] The *Wichita Beacon* (Wichita, Kansas) May 9, 1913, Pg. 2.

A Different Kind of Ride

The Abernathy boys had already made headlines across the country for their adventures on horseback and in automobiles. But their latest endeavor brought an entirely new element of modernity to their repertoire: the Indian motorcycle. The boys, now 13 and 9 years old, decided to ride the cutting-edge machine from Oklahoma to the American Midwest, marking their first foray into the rapidly evolving world of motorized travel.

By 1912, horses were no longer the only steeds in the Abernathy stables. The boys had turned their sights toward something louder, faster, and far more modern: the Indian motorcycle.

Motorcycles in the early 20th century were still in their infancy—temperamental machines that required skill, strength, and a good dose of luck to operate.

The Abernathy boys—Louie, 13 years old, and Temple aged 9 years—spent a few hours in Topeka yesterday on their way to New York from Frederick, Okla. This time the boys are making their cross-continent trip on a motorcycle. It will be remembered that they journeyed all the way from Oklahoma to New York on horseback in 1910 to see Theodore Roosevelt.

At their various stops the boys are showing moving picture films of their rides and of scenes in Oklahoma. The two kids looked like seasoned travelers yesterday when they stopped at the Central Cycle

ABERNATHY BOYS ON A POP-POP TRIP

company. Temple's face was a little dirty with dust and Louie had a hard time to get his brother to wash as the little fellow wanted to hear all about the roads from here to Kansas City.

The boys wore similar costumes—a red sweater, brown trousers, leggins, leather cuffs—and had their eyes shaded with huge goggles. They both ride the same motorcycle and are making the trip for the fun of it. They left Frederick on May 21.[445]

Motorcycles in 1912 also represented the cutting edge of modern transportation, symbolizing speed, freedom, and technological progress. For many Americans, these roaring machines were an exciting yet intimidating glimpse into the future. The Abernathy boys' decision to tackle the open road on an Indian motorcycle again captured the nation's imagination, showcasing their willingness to embrace the modern age while retaining their frontier spirit.

For most adults, let alone children, such a journey would seem impossible. But for Louis and Temple Abernathy, it was just another challenge to conquer.

The Indian Motorcycle Company, eager to promote the durability and reliability of its machines, sponsored the boys' journey. Their father, Jack Abernathy, supported the venture wholeheartedly, recognizing it as both a personal challenge for his sons and an opportunity to embrace the future.

---

[445] The *Topeka Daily Capital* (Topeka, Kansas) May 30, 1913, Pg. 5.

Before setting off, Louis and Temple spent several days learning to ride and maintain their motorcycle. Louis, the elder of the two, quickly mastered the controls, while Temple rode pillion, acting as co-pilot and navigator. Their training sessions drew curious onlookers, who marveled at the sight of two young boys confidently handling such a machine.

Learning to maneuver the heavy machine wasn't easy. These early motorcycles required real muscle and skill—there were no automatic transmissions, and every gear shift demanded full-body coordination. But the Abernathy boys, already seasoned from horseback adventures across the continent, approached this new challenge with the same enthusiasm that had already captivated the nation.

The boys packed lightly, bringing only the essentials: a small tool kit, spare parts, and their bedrolls. Unlike their earlier adventures, this journey required a mechanical mindset. They would need to understand the inner workings of the motorcycle to address inevitable breakdowns.

446

Hitting the Open Road

The journey began with the roar of the Indian's engine as the boys set out from Oklahoma City. The novelty of the motorcycle and the fame of the Abernathy brothers ensured that crowds gathered at every town they passed through. Spectators cheered as the boys rode by, many running to keep pace with the motorcycle until it disappeared into the distance.

The roads, however, were far from smooth. Early highways were often little more than dirt paths, riddled with potholes and prone to

---

[446] Bain News Service, Publisher. *Abernathy Kids*. ca. 1910. [Between and Ca. 1915] Photograph. https://www.loc.gov/item/2014693521/.

turning into muddy quagmires after a rainstorm. The Indian motorcycle, though state-of-the-art for its time, struggled on such terrain.

Despite the challenges those early roads presented, the boys pressed on. Townspeople often offered help, whether it was a meal, a place to camp, or assistance with repairs. The boys graciously accepted, their charm and humility winning over even the most skeptical observers.

ABERNATHYS HERE AGAIN
Sons of Wolf Catcher Are Making 2,000-Mile Trip on Motorcycles.

Those Abernathy boys are at it again. They're making a 2,000-mile trip from Frederick, Ok., to New York on motorcycles this time. They made the trip on horseback in 1910, their object at that time being to visit Colonel Roosevelt at Oyster Bay. Louis, aged 13, and Temple, aged 9, arrived in Kansas City early yesterday morning and joined their father. "Jack Abernathy," formerly United States marshal, who won fame by his feats of catching wolves alive. Together the trio celebrated Memorial Day in Kansas City and this morning the boys will proceed on their journey.

"We're really having more fun with the motorcycles. They're less trouble and they go faster," said Louis. "Sometimes that other trip of ours got a little slow. But we're going to make great time on this trip

as soon as we get used to our machines. You see we only got them a month ago and haven't got saddlebroke to them yet. But we are learning."

"No, we aren't afraid of losing our way. We are taking the same route that we did three years ago and we remember the road pretty well. It's lots of fun to shift for yourself without any older person to interfere. Everybody treats us nicely on the road."

"We usually stop at a hotel or a farm house at night, but if it's too much trouble to find either one, we sleep out of doors. Nothing like sleeping out of doors, anyhow."

The boys have been on the road since May 21. They have put in five days of actual travel, having been delayed by rains. They have no schedule and do not use road maps.

"We'll get there in plenty of time," said Louis. "We have all the time there is."[447]

Mechanical Troubles and Ingenuity

The motorcycle's engine was put to the test during the long journey. Flat tires, overheating, and mechanical failures were frequent occurrences. Louis, now a seasoned problem-solver from their previous adventures, proved adept at fixing the bike on the roadside, but the mechanical difficulties caused delays.[448]

---

[447] *Kansas City Journal* (Kansas City, Missouri) May 31, 1913, Pg. 5.
[448] *Manchester Evening News* (Manchester, Greater Manchester, England) July 12, 1913 Pg. 6.

Their ability to overcome these obstacles further cemented their reputation as resourceful and fearless adventurers.

Welcomed by the Crowds

As they progressed, the boys' fame continued to grow. Reporters eagerly covered their journey, and newspapers printed glowing accounts of their progress. At towns along the way the boys gave illustrated lectures on their travels.[449] Crowds gathered to greet the boys, fascinated by their story and eager to see the remarkable machine they were riding.

The boys made a habit of demonstrating the motorcycle's capabilities, revving the engine and explaining its mechanics to curious onlookers. Temple, ever the entertainer, delighted children by inviting them to sit on the bike while he explained how it worked.

---

[449] *Columbia Daily Tribune* (Columbia, Missouri) June 5, 1913, Pg. 2.

ABERNATHY BOYS VISIT DAYTON

The Abernathy boys, sons of the famous "Jack" Abernathy, formerly U. S. marshal for Oklahoma and member of Roosevelt's rough rider regiment, who passed through Dayton Wednesday morning on motorcycles. They are on their way to Oyster Bay, N. Y., where they will visit their father's old friend, Col. Roosevelt.

They achieved considerable space in the news columns recently because of their trip on horseback from Oklahoma to New York to visit "the colonel." The boys remained in Dayton several hours Wednesday morning before resuming their journey. They came via Richmond.

[450] The *Dayton Herald* (Dayton, Ohio) June 26, 1913, Pg. 6.

A New Era for the Abernathy Kids

The motorcycle adventure marked a turning point for the Abernathy brothers as they moved from horses to automobiles and then to motorcycles with ease. The journey also highlighted the promise of modern transportation, inspiring many young readers to dream of taking on the open road. The boys obviously embraced the technological innovations of their time.

When the boys finally returned to Oklahoma City, on the batted Indian motorcycle they were greeted by another admiring crowd. The boys, smiling broadly, declared the journey a success and expressed their excitement for future challenges. Their story had even aquired a following outside the U.S. The World News in Australia reported the following:

The two Abernathy boys, Louis, aged 13, and Temple, aged 9, who distinguished themselves by riding on ponies from Oklahoma to New York, a distance of 3,000 miles, to greet Mr. Roosevelt on his arrival from his African expedition, have again made a record. Wishing to attend their sister's school graduation in New York, the two boys have this time come the 3,000 miles on a tandem motor-cycle.

They left home at the end of May, and were 35 days on the way, as far as actual riding was concerned, a few days being lost through tyre and mechanical difficulties. This works out at 86 miles a day, which is extremely good going when the rough Western roads are taken into consideration.

The boys are the sons of "Catch-'em-alive" Jack Abernathy, a ranchman, who gained his sobriquet from his habit of catching wolves with his hands. He was one of Colonel Roosevelt's Roughriders in the Cuban war.[451].

This journey solidified their place in history and as ambassadors of a modernizing America. By taking on the challenge of the Indian motorcycle, Louis and Temple Abernathy bridged the gap between the rugged frontier and the new mechanical age, showing that the pursuit of adventure knows no boundaries.

9 Year Boy Crosses Continent on an INDIAN!

With his brother. The two Abernathy boys, over mountains, deep canyons, swamps and all kinds of difficulties, rode our Indian. The cradle spring frame, combined with all the other advantages an Indian possesses, made this possible. Big Twin $250, Big Single $200. Easy payments. Immediate deliveries.

USED MOTORCYCLES, $35 UP. **NEAL, CLARK & NEAL CO.,** 643-645 MAIN STREET. Open Evenings.

[452]

---

[451] The *World's News* (Sydney, New South Wales, Australia) August 23, 1913, Pg. 18.
[452] The *Buffalo Enquirer* (Buffalo, New York) August 8, 1913, Pg 6.

Chapter 12: The Imitators

The boy's daring horseback journeys, mastery of automobiles, and groundbreaking motorcycle rides inspired a few imitators. Across the country, other young people—some as young as the Abernathys themselves—set out to replicate their feats, hoping to achieve fame and admiration. Newspapers picked up any reference to adventurous young riders copying the Abernathy boys as stories of these would-be adventurers began to surface.

While some may have reached their goals, most found that the strength, smarts, and staying power those trips demanded weren't easy to come by. The Abernathy brothers made their challenges look easy, but as the imitators discovered that is wasn't easy as Louis and Temple made it appear

> The Abernathy boys had barely time to get settled in their home, when Oklahoma starts two young women to make a "hobo" trip around the world. Depend on Oklahoma to be in the limelight. [453]

Even when they weren't being copied, their adventures were referenced,

---

[453] *Butler Citizen* (Butler, Pennsylvania) August 22, 1910, Page 4.

> Monday, George Tredway and Chas. Martin donned their Sunday go-to-meetin' clothes and left on the noon train for the wilds of Wyoming. They go from here to Greely, Col., in the "kivered kyars" and from there they expect to charter an authmobile for the rest of the journey. They say they are going up to Wyoming to look for a piece of land suitable to raise a few dollars on. The boys are pretty young to go so far away by themselves, but when we remember that the Abernathy boys returned safe and sound from their late expedition, we have hopes of seeing George and Charlie again.

454 455

In contrast to the Abernathy boys, aged nine and six years, respectively, who traveled from New York to Oklahoma City in a Brush runabout, C. W. Poole, seventy years old, is making a trip from Detroit to Springdale, Ark., in a car of the same type. Mr. Poole, a

---

[454] The *Hominy Herald* (Hominy, OK) October 20, 1910, Pg. 1.
[455] The P*awhuska Capital (*Pawhuska, Oklahoma) October 1910, Pg. 8.

veteran of the Civil War, is secretary of the Commercial Club of Springdale, and, although he has completed threescore years and ten, is hale and hearty and says that driving the car does not fatigue him in the least. He is using a ten horsepower runabout, and will pass through St. Joseph.[456] [457]

The First Wave of Imitators

The first wave of imitators emerged in 1910, shortly after the Abernathy boys completed their legendary horseback ride from Oklahoma to New York. Inspired by their fame, children from towns across the Midwest and West began undertaking their own ambitious

---

[456] The *Guthrie Daily Leader* (Guthrie, OK) June 21, 1911 Pg. 5.
[457] The *Springfield News-Leader* (Springfield, Missouri) July 2, 1911 Pg. 11.

journeys on horseback. Local communities often celebrated these efforts, hopeful that their own young riders might capture national attention.

One such figure was seven-year-old Glen Pendergrast of Homestead, Oklahoma, who was recognized in the press and compared to the Abernathy's for his exceptional grit. At age five, he rode six miles daily to Homestead alone, managed cattle across snake-infested land, and once survived a rattlesnake bite—administering first aid to himself before help arrived. Though he never sought approval or public adoration, Glen's feats as recorded in the Bartlesville *Morning Examiners* stated he exemplified the same rugged independence that made the Abernathy brothers famous.[458]

Others left even fainter historical footprints. Brian Baldwin, who the author grew up with in Southeast Colorado, relates an old family story that his great-granddad Earl Baldwin and his older brother Pearl Baldwin rode from their homestead in Hooker, Oklahoma to Chicago around 1910, tasked with handling some family estate business. After talking to his father, Brian believes Earl would have been about 10 and Pearl around 12 years old at the time, and that the journey took place during the summertime. Brian's father also recalls that they attended a fair while they were in Chicago. If the story holds true, it's

---

[458] *Morning Examiner* (Bartlesville, Oklahoma) Jun 26, 1910, Pg. 6.

one of those bits of family lore that echoes the boldness of the Abernathy rides—quiet adventures that lived on not in headlines, but in family memory.[459]

A lone 14-year-old rider from Washington was featured in newspapers during his trip to Connecticut, celebrated for his youthful ambition, though his journey ultimately didn't match the scale of the Abernathy's achievements.[460]

Stirred by the stories of the long horseback ride of the Abernathy boys, of Oklahoma, Bradley Lee Dawley, 1309 N street northwest, [Washington, DC] set out yesterday afternoon on a horseback trip to the northern part of Connecticut. Bradley, who is 14 years old, will

Lad on Horseback Starts 450-Mile Journey Alone

Fourteen-Year-Old Bradley Dawley, of Washington, Off on Saddle Trip to Connecticut to Visit Cousin—Youngster Was Stirred by Glowing Stories of Abernathy Brothers' Ride From Oklahoma. Thinks It Will Take Ten Days.

---

[459] Brian Baldwin, personal communication with the author, 2025. Baldwin recounted a longstanding family story that his great-grandfather and great-uncle rode on horseback from their homestead in Hooker, Oklahoma, to Chicago around 1910 to attend to family estate matters. According to Baldwin, the boys were approximately 10 and 12 years old at the time.

[460] The *Washington Post* (Washington, DC) July 5, 1911 Pg. 12.

make the entire trip unaccompanied. By his schedule, he expects to make the 450-mile trip in about ten days. He is going to visit a cousin.

Bradley, an ardent equestrian, has had his horse, "Rubberneck," for two years, and has made several short trips. He started from in front of The Post building at 5 o'clock yesterday, and stopped last night at Laurel, Md. This morning he will go to Baltimore.

No Fear of Failure

Bradley, who has no knowledge of the roads, will be guided by persons along the way and by a road map. His saddle bags are stuffed with food and clothing.

"I had a hard time getting my father to consent to my going," he said yesterday, "but he finally thought it would be all right. I know I will get through, but I hope I will have no trouble finding places at which to eat and sleep. I have money to pay for everything.

"I will go through Baltimore, Wilmington, Philadelphia, Trenton, Jersey City, N.J., and New York City. I know I will stop at all those places, but my route from New York has not yet been decided upon.

Will Write Regularly

"I will write to father every morning and every night, so he will know I am all right."

Bradley is the youngest child of Thomas R. Dawley, Jr. He is in the seventh grade at Thomson School.[461] [462] [463]

IOWA RIVALS OF ABERNATHY BOYS — *Fort Madison, IA., Aug. 22.* — *The Misses Helen Willard and Bessie Gordon, high school graduates, left here Monday on horseback for Carrollton, Mo. The young women announced that they would go every step of the distance of 160 miles by horseback, stopping overnight at hotels in the various towns along the route.*[464]

One of the individuals inspired by the spirit of cross-country adventure popularized by the Abernathy boys was **Miss Alberta Claire**, known as the "Girl from Wyoming." Born and raised on the frontier, Claire set out alone from Sheridan, Wyoming, aiming to ride on horseback all the way to Buffalo, New York — a journey of thousands of miles. Traveling with only a dog and a .44 Colt revolver for protection, she endured brutal weather, harsh trails, and long stretches

---
[461] *News-Democrat* (Paducah, Kentucky) July 12, 1911, Pg. 8.
[462] The *Topeka State Journal* (Topeka, Kansas) July 15, 1911 Pg. 9.
[463] The *Pittsburgh Press* (Pittsburgh, Pennsylvania) July 18, 1911 ·Pg. 4.
[464] *Quad-City Times* (Davenport, Iowa) August 22, 1911, Pg. 2.

without reliable shelter. Standing just four feet, eleven inches tall and weighing only 97 pounds, Claire embodied the rugged, independent image of the American West.

Claire financed her trip by giving concerts and selling her own photographs in the towns she passed through. Along her route, she navigated the same kind of hardships that Louis and Temple Abernathy had faced years earlier: starvation, loneliness, exposure to the elements, and the vastness of the open country. Like the Abernathys, her daring enthralled the public. Newspapers marveled at her determination, noting that she often rode 40 to 80 miles a day. Her plan was to complete her journey by April 7 and eventually write a book about her travels, further cementing her place among the early pioneers of long-distance endurance rides.

While Claire may have been driven partly by a desire to promote her home state of Wyoming, her bold solo journey resonated with a national audience already captivated by young riders proving themselves against a vast and untamed landscape. [465]

The imitators' stories—both successes and failures—underscore the nature of the Abernathy brothers' achievements. While others tried to follow in their footsteps, few could match their resilience, adaptability, and sheer courage.

Louis and Temple's fame had sparked a nationwide movement of youthful adventurers, proving that their story was more than just a collection of journeys—it was an inspiration for an entire generation.

---

[465] *Daily Republican-Register* (Mount Carmel, Illinois) February 26, 1912, Pg. 1.

Chapter 13: School of the Open Road

A few days ago they finished another horseback ride, one that made their previous attempts look as mild as a game of tiddlywinks or pingpong. They rode alone—this boy of 11, with his brother of 7—from the Atlantic to the Pacific, from New York to San Francisco—and now that they have finished their jaunt of 3619 miles they are sitting at their desks and studying their books just like any other youngsters.[466]

Both boys are clad in well-worn and much-soiled clothes and blue flannel shirts. They are guiltless of cravats and wear big sombreros perched on the backs of their heads. The pleasant boyish faces are burned brick red by the sun and fairly radiate good-humored independence from every freckle. The boys are utterly without shyness and do not know what fear is.[467]

They started from Frederick the first of May. Marshall Jack gave them both check books so that each boy could spend his money as he saw fit. No one but the girls knew where they were going. Louis rode Sam, the horse upon which Colonel Roosevelt had hunted when he visited them, and Temp rode Geronimo, his favorite.[468]

A Controversial Approach to Parenting

Jack "Catch-'Em-Alive" Abernathy was no ordinary father, and his parenting style was as unconventional as his life as a wolf hunter and U.S. Marshal. Raising Louis and Temple, he adopted a philosophy rooted in self-reliance, resilience, and hands-on experience.

---

[466] The *Boston Globe* (Boston, Massachusetts) November 7, 1911, Pg. 3.
[467] The *Evening Journal* (Wilmington, Delaware) June 9, 1910, Pg. 2.
[468] *Fall River Globe* (Fall River, Massachusetts) August 23, 1910, Pg. 2.

Critics often questioned his decisions, particularly in allowing his young sons to embark on arduous, often dangerous journeys across the country. Yet, to Abernathy, these adventures were not reckless—they were formative.

The Abernathy boys' mother had passed away prior to the events described in *Guthrie to Gotham*. While the newspapers provide rich detail on the boys' and their father, U.S. Marshal Jack Abernathy, it does not elaborate on the cause or circumstances of their mother's death.

Although our research, focusing on newspaper archives, did not reveal a lot of details, outside sources fill in some of the gaps. Thirty-year-old Jessie Pearl Abernathy died in Guthrie on May 7, 1907, just three months after giving birth to her sixth child. She left behind four daughters—Pearlie Mae, Kittie Joe, Vera Golda, and Johnnie "Jack" Martin—as well as the two young boys who would go on to capture the nation's imagination.

After her passing, Jack Abernathy's father and sister helped raise the children. Jack remarried the next July, eloping with Almira Pervaine, the teenaged daughter of a wealthy farmer near Guthrie. That union was short-lived; less than two years later, in April 1910—just weeks after the birth of their daughter Theodora Lucile, named for President Theodore Roosevelt—Jack filed for divorce. This brief and turbulent chapter added another layer to the backdrop of the Abernathy boys' daring adventures.[469]

The Father's Philosophy

For Jack, the world itself was the greatest classroom, and his sons were its eager students. Their unconventional upbringing captured the attention of newspapers and the public, sparking debates about parenting, education, and the nature of childhood.

Jack Abernathy firmly believed that life's challenges were the best teachers. While other parents of the era might have sought to shield their children from hardship, Jack encouraged Louis and Temple to embrace it. His parenting style emphasized independence and toughness, traits he felt were essential for survival in an ever-changing world.

> " Teach a boy self reliance from the moment he tumbles out of the cradle, make him keep his traces taut and work well forward in his collar and ninety-nine times out of a hundred his independence will assert itself before he is two years old. Then guide him with a firm but tender hand; instil into him the principles of right and wrong, and the rest is easy. If there is no taint in his blood and he doesn't possess a yellow streak he will develop into a fine man. That's my rule, and if you don't think I've taken the right tack talk to my boys for five minutes and they'll convince you that they are men in principles even if they are babies in years. God bless 'em."[470][471][472]

---

[469] Alexander, M.J. "The Astounding Adventures of the Abernathy Boys." *405 Magazine*, August 25, 2015. https://www.405magazine.com/the-astounding-adventures-of-the-abernathy-boys/.

[470] The *Omaha Evening Bee* (Omaha, Nebraska) June 17, 1910, Pg. 12.

[471] *Long Branch Record* (Long Branch, New Jersey) June 17, 1910, Pg. 7.

[472] *Aberdeen Herald* (Aberdeen, Washington) June 27, 1910, Pg. 2.

This belief often put Jack at odds with societal norms. Critics accused him of exposing his sons to unnecessary risks, but Jack dismissed these concerns, pointing to the boys' accomplishments as evidence of their capability. Many, however, agreed with him. Aunt Jean's Daily Talk, a column in The *Brooklyn Daily Eagle* when discussing the Abernathy boys stated:

> **Self-reliance is a fine quality in any boy, and should not be confounded with precocity. Boys who keep their heads level and learn to think for themselves are the kind that make the best American citizens. And they cannot begin too early to acquire these traits.**[473]

The Role of Schooling

Jack's approach to education was equally unconventional. Though the Abernathy boys attended formal schooling, their adventures often took precedence. Jack believed that the lessons learned on the road—navigating unknown territories, managing resources, and overcoming adversity—were just as valuable, if not more so, than those taught in a classroom.

The boys' tutors and schools were often temporary, arranged during lulls between their journeys. Temple, the younger of the two, was

---

[473] The *Brooklyn Daily Eagle* (Brooklyn, New York) July 9, 1910, Pg. 2.

reportedly more reluctant about formal education, preferring the excitement of the trail to the rigidity of a classroom. Louis, however, excelled when given the opportunity, balancing his academic studies with his love of adventure.

They also had a unique opportunity to attend school in different geographies at the end of their various trips. They are reported to have enrolled in schools in New York following their 1910 trip and San Francisco following their 1912 trip.

— *ABERNATHY BOYS IN SCHOOL.*
'Eat 'Em Alive' Father Is Busy Forming Roosevelt Clubs.
SPECIAL DISPATCH TO THE GLOBE-DEMOCRAT.
GUTHRIE, OK., January 28. —Louis and Temple Abernathy, sons of John N. Abernathy, former United States marshal, have entered a school in San Francisco.

The boys recently completed an overland trip with their father from New York City to Los Angeles, and prior to that time they took two other long-distance horseback trips.

Their father will return to Oklahoma soon to assist Ed. Perry of Coalgate and others in the organization of Roosevelt clubs.[474] [475] [476]

Criticism and Public Debate

"Their progress is going to be watched with all manner of interest for these boys are little more than well grown infants, comparatively speaking, and a ride such as they propose to make means the display of great bravery on their part."[477]

> The Abernathy boys are at last in school. That's better than being in the Associated Press reports every day.

[478]

I am one of the old-fashioned who fail to see anything brave, praiseworthy, clever, or commendable in the cross-country jaunt of those little Abernathy boys who left for Santa Fe Saturday morning after having ridden horseback from Guthrie, Okla., to Roswell. The oldest is seven and the youngest only five years old.[479] *Five years old! A child of five on such a pilgrimage, exposed to all sorts of weather and the manifold dangers of the trail, in the care of another child of*

---
[474] *St. Louis Globe-Democrat* (St. Louis, Missouri) Jan 29, 1912, Pg. 4.
[475] *Kansas City Weekly Journal* (Kansas City, Missouri) Feb 1, 1912, Pg. 9.
[476] *Hutchinson News* (Hutchinson, Kansas) Jan 29, 1912, Pg. 7.
[477] *St. Louis Post-Dispatch,* (St Louis, Missouri) February 14, 1911
[478] The Peoples Press (El Reno, Oklahoma) February 1, 1912, Pg. 2.
[479] The boys were 9 and 5 on the first trip. You see many slight variations of these ages.

seven! True, they came through all right, for God watches over children sometimes. If they get to Santa Fe, where for a few days they will enjoy their father's visit, it will be another miracle. But just think of it! Two little tots like that, who ought to be kept at home with the protecting arm of love around them, tackling a thousand-mile horseback ride! I have the privilege of acquaintance with Mr. Abernathy, and if he ever comes out of the country, I want him to understand that I am not making any new acquaintances of his type. Though it is no fault of his, how many are there who, with all that devotion and care can do, stand by empty cradles of those who were seven and five! And these little boys are allowed to play with death by the roadside, hundreds of miles of prairie and desert mountains. What kind of father must that be! Of course, there is no mother — that were impossible of belief.[480]

---

[480] *Carlsbad Current-Argus* (Carlsbad, New Mexico) September 3, 1909, Pg. 5.

The Abernathy boys have been heard of again. They have started to school. Awful glad to hear it. Hope they will pick up something useful. [481]

THIS world is replete with a variety of things, and we really do not need to hear anything further from the "Abernathy kids." [482]

One of the Abernathy boys was overcome by the heat in Kansas. Those youngsters ought to be put to bed and allowed to forget the stunt they did. [483]

Just as we were getting ready to enjoy a safe and sane Fourth the word comes that the Abernathy boys are contemplating another horse-back trip across the continent. [484]

---

[481] The News Chronicle (Scott City, Kansas) February 2, 1912, Pg. 5.
[482] *Chicago Tribune* (Chicago, Illinois) August 7, 1911, Pg. 6.
[483] *Record-Journal* (Meriden, Connecticut) July 29, 1910, Fri Page 6.
[484] The *Los Angeles Times* (Los Angeles, California) June 20, 1911, Pg. 20.

> It is a pleasure to note the hole in the atmosphere through which the Abernathy boys disappeared into the vastnesses of Texas.

486 487 488 489 490 491 492 493 494 495 496 497 498

> The Abernathy boys have started on another horseback ride. This time it is from New York to San Francisco. What a pity those boys are not put to work at something that will be a benefit to somebody.—Broken Arrow Ledger.

> The Abernathy boys have ridden across the continent on horseback. Now will they please go away back out of the limelight, like good little boys?

---

[485] The *Atchison Daily Globe* (Atchison, Kansas) October 8, 1910, Pg. 2.
[486] The *Topeka State Journal* (Topeka, Kansas) October 12, 1910, Pg. 4.
[487] The *Coffeyville Daily Journal* (Coffeyville, Kansas) October 14, 1910, Pg. 6.
[488] The *Hutchinson News* (Hutchinson, Kansas) October 15, 1910, Pg. 3.
[489] The *Chillicothe Constitution-Tribune* (Chillicothe, Missouri) October 21,1910, Pg. 3.
[490] *Ledger-Enquirer* (Columbus, Georgia.) October 23,1910, Pg. 1.
[491] The Journal (Meriden, Connecticut) October 27, 1910, Pg. 6.
[492] *Lincoln Nebraska State Journal* (Lincoln, Nebraska) October 29, 1910, Pg. 4.
[493] The Journal (Meriden, Connecticut) October 27, 1910, Pg. 6.
[494] The *Butte Miner* (Butte, Montana) November 10, 1910, Pg. 9.
[495] The *Norfolk Weekly* News-Journal (Norfolk, Nebraska) November 11, 1910, Pg. 4.
[496] The *Ottawa Daily Republic* (Ottawa, Kansas) November 14, 1910, Pg. 4.
[497] *Canon City Record* (Canon City, Colorado) November 24, 1910, Pg.11.
[498] The *Pomona Daily Review* (Pomona, California) November 25 1910, Fri Pg. 7.
[499] The *Guymon Herald* (Guymon, Oklahoma) August 24, 1911, Pg. 2.
[500] *Press-Telegram* (Long Beach, California) November 2, 1911, Pg. 4

SOMEBODY, if no one else than the truancy officers, should call in "the Abernathy kids," who ought to be making garden, or making ready to attend the fall and winter schools. It seems to be the set purpose and established policy of their father, "Catch 'Em Alive" Abernathy, to develop the tramp instinct in his boys to the utmost, and keep them strangers to work and study and home influences as long as possible. These children have just made a fair start toward riding horseback from New York City to San Francisco, and are pledged to not eat or sleep in a house during the trip. The oldest boy is 11 years old, the youngest 4 years younger.[501]

The Boys' Perspective

Louis and Temple themselves often spoke highly of their father's influence. Despite their youth, they displayed a level of maturity and

---

[501] *St. Joseph Gazette* (St. Joseph, Missouri) August 13, 1911, Pg. 12.

awareness about the value of their unique upbringing. Reporters frequently commented on the boys' eloquence, noting how they spoke with composure and clarity.

Temple, always quick with a quip, once told a reporter, "I might not know all my arithmetic, but I know how to find my way across the country and fix a broken wagon. That's gotta count for something."

Louis, the more serious of the two, emphasized the balance their father tried to maintain. "Pa makes sure we know how to read and write, but he also teaches us how to handle ourselves in the real world. We're lucky to have him," he said during a 1911 interview.

Success Despite Doubts

Jack's unorthodox parenting ultimately paid off. As the boys grew older, they demonstrated not only resilience and independence but also intelligence and poise. Louis eventually became a successful lawyer, while Temple found his path in the oil industry. Their achievements reflected Jack's conviction that life's greatest lessons are learned outside the classroom.

While Jack's methods might never have won universal approval, his sons' accomplishments silenced many of his critics. For Jack, the greatest reward was not the fame or notoriety that came with their adventures—it was the pride he felt in raising boys who could face the world with courage and confidence.

The debates surrounding Jack Abernathy's parenting style and the boys' education offer a fascinating insight into the era's evolving views on childhood, independence, and the purpose of schooling. Jack's approach, though unconventional, reflected the values of a frontier mindset, where survival skills and resilience were paramount.

For Louis and Temple Abernathy, their father's guidance gave them the tools to navigate both the literal and metaphorical trails of life. Their adventures were profound lessons that shaped them into men who could thrive in any circumstance.

His heritage as a father is intertwined with the legend of the Abernathy boys. His parenting proved that sometimes, the greatest lessons come from taking the road less traveled.

Chapter 14: After the Last Ride

Traffic conditions have changed so much in the last 30 years that these present day riders will find the traveling difficult," L. V. Abernathy said. "The men will endure the ride, but I doubt if the horses will be able to stand it.[502]

It was a fine little car," recalls Bud. "We sold our Brush a few months after we got back to Oklahoma. But when we got older, we were real sorry. We used to talk about buying another 'Wildcat' but we never did. I haven't seen one in years. But in its day, it was a fine car — none finer.[503]

From Headlines to Ordinary Lives

For a brief period in the early 20th century, Louis and Temple Abernathy were among the most famous young celebrities in America. Their cross-country horseback rides, daring motorized exploits, and resilience captivated the public, earning them a place in newspapers and hearts across the nation. Yet, as the years passed and their youthful escapades became distant memories, the brothers quietly stepped away from the limelight. Unlike many child celebrities, Louis and Temple chose normal lives over public adulation, becoming remarkable for how ordinary their adult lives appeared to be.

---

[502] *Times Record News* (Wichita Falls, Texas) March 4, 1939 Pg. 1.
[503] The *Herald-News* (Passaic, New Jersey) May 10, 1969 Pg. 26.

The Transition to Adulthood

As the Abernathy brothers grew older, their adventurous exploits faded into the demands of adult responsibilities. After their last documented journey in 1913—a motorcycle ride to New York—Louis and Temple began to focus on building their adult lives. News of their exploits faded into the "Remember When" sections of newspapers such as the following:

Two boys, Louis and Temple Abernathy, one ten years old and the other six, passed through here Monday en route from Frederick, Okla., to Springfield, a distance of 800 miles. They were on horseback and unattended. They had recently completed a trip of over 1,000 miles on horseback through New Mexico and were contemplating a trip from coast to coast. The younger child's stirrups were only seven inches long.[504]

TWENTY YEARS AGO
From The Sarcoxie Record of April 22, 1910.

Louis, the elder of the two, pursued higher education and eventually became a lawyer. He set up a legal practice in Wichita Falls, Texas. His reputation as a competent and fair attorney grew, though few of his clients realized they were being represented by one of the nation's most celebrated boy adventurers.

Temple followed a different path, entering the oil industry during its boom in the early 20th century. His outgoing nature and knack for

---

[504] The *Sarcoxie Record* (Sarcoxie, Missouri) April 17, 1930, Pg. 4.

building relationships likely served him well, and he found success in various ventures.

Life Out of the Spotlight

For all the public interest in their childhood, the Abernathy brothers showed little interest in capitalizing on their fame as adults. While their names occasionally surfaced in nostalgic newspaper articles, they rarely gave interviews or participated in events commemorating their youthful exploits. This retreat from the public eye may have puzzled many who had followed their early adventures so avidly.

We found nearly 5,000 total mentions of their travels, over 3200 of those were between the years of 1908 and 1913. After that there were few mentions of their exploits in the media. A news clipping from the 1914 *Pasadena Star* shows they were slipping from the spotlight.

> Anybody seen anything about the Abernathy boys lately? [505]

---

[505] *Pasadena Star* (Pasadena, California) July 14, 1914 Pg. 4.

You can find examples of them occasionally speaking in their local community reminiscing on the long trips the brothers took, sharing stories not covered in the newspapers at the time, such as one told by Louis at a Rotary Luncheon in Wichita Falls, Texas.

> *It seemed that when we crossed the border into New Mexico we had left civilization behind. We visited Roswell and Santa Fe and other points of interest. We struck into the forest covered mountains and soon realized we had lost our way. At nightfall we unsaddled our horses and built a fire, which seemed only to have the effect of drawing the denizens of the forest closer to us. We rode on the next day with nothing to eat and I think the most welcome sight I shall ever see was a solitary Mexican sheepherder upon whom we chanced the second afternoon. He couldn't understand our speech but he did understand that we were lost and hungry. He fed us and pointed us on our way.*[506]

> *Newness and excitement reached new high gear as the two travelers to "cancel" an engagement with the governor of New Jersey at Trenton, a fact regretted now by Mr. Abernathy, because the governor was Woodrow Wilson. Eight to 10 days after leaving Guthrie, Okla., they entered New York, and despite the protection of a police mounted patrol, the speaker declared curious women seekers pulled hair, tore slashes from their clothing.*[507]

Overall, however, there is not much else until years later when their story was told in books such as *"Bud and Me."*[508]

---

[506] *Times Record News* (Wichita Falls, Texas) April 18, 1929 Pg. 13.
[507] *Times Record News* (Wichita Falls, Texas) May 18, 1934 Pg. 14.
[508] Abernathy, Alta. *Bud & Me: The True Adventures of the Abernathy Boys*. Dove Creek Press, 1998.

Their choice to live quietly was perhaps influenced by their father. There are a few mentions throughout this text that indicate he may not have anticipated the fame that would follow his sons. Jack's parenting emphasized personal integrity over public approval, a lesson that clearly resonated with his sons.

Fading into History

By the mid-20th century, the Abernathy brothers had become footnotes in history, their childhoods overshadowed by the rapidly changing world. The rise of automobiles, airplanes, and other technologies made their extraordinary rides seem like relics of a bygone era. For younger generations, their names no longer evoked memories of daring long distance rides, but rather vague references in dusty newspapers.

While the Abernathy brothers' adult lives were far removed from the public eye, their childhood adventures left an indelible mark on American history. Their journeys captured the essence of a nation evolving from its frontier roots into a new era of modernity. They became symbols of resilience, courage, and the limitless possibilities of youth.

Temple's death in 1986 marked the end of the Abernathy brothers' story. He passed away quietly, leaving behind a life defined more by his oil ventures than his youth. Louis had preceded him, dying in 1979 after a long and successful career in law.

With their passing, the Abernathy boys became part of history, preserved in the fading pages of newspapers and the memories of those who marveled at their daring.

Yet, their disappearance into ordinary life serves as a poignant reminder of the transient nature of fame. The Abernathy brothers chose to let their accomplishments speak for themselves, avoiding the pitfalls of childhood fame and embracing the stability of normalcy.

Their fame may have faded, but their legacy endures as as a testament to the fearless energy of youth and the enduring value of living life on one's own terms."

Quiet Heroes

By stepping away from the limelight, they ensured that their adventures remained untainted by the complications of prolonged celebrity. Today, their story is remembered not only for the feats they accomplished but for the humility with which they chose to live the rest of their lives.

The Abernathy boys challenged societal norms, proving that age and circumstance could be surmounted with tenacity and resourcefulness. In an era of burgeoning technological change, they also highlighted the evolving face of transportation, from the enduring reliability of horses to the nascent rise of automobiles and motorcycles.

Perhaps most strikingly, their journey intersected with the birth of aviation itself. In Dayton, Ohio, the boys were welcomed by Mayor and Mrs. Edward F. Burkhart and taken on a "joy ride in the air" by none other than Wilbur Wright at Wright Aviation Field. This moment captured more than a thrill—it marked their place on the very threshold of modernity, as they quite literally soared into a new age.

Today, their story resonates as an inspirational tale for all ages. Their independence encourages modern readers to embrace challenges with vigor and resilience. Their story remind us of the importance of stepping outside comfort zones to explore and grow. The Abernathy boys' journeys remain a testament to the human capacity to overcome, adapt, and thrive, no matter the odds.

As their escapades are retold, they invite us to reflect on the enduring values of bravery, self-reliance, and an adventurous heart—qualities as relevant today as they were over a century ago. Through their lens, we glimpse a world brimming with possibilities and a future shaped by those daring enough to seize it.

The Abernathy boys remind us that the greatest stories often end quietly, as the heroes, Louis and Temple moved on to lives of quiet dignity.

Appendix 1 — Timeline of Trips

1908: Temple Visits the White House
At just three years old, Temple Abernathy accompanied his father, U.S. Marshal Jack Abernathy, to Washington, D.C., on official business. During the trip, Temple charmed the White House staff, dressed in a soldier's uniform, and received a personal tour of the residence. President Theodore Roosevelt himself ensured Temple was shown every detail of the historic mansion.

1909: Ride to Santa Fe
Louis (age 9) and Temple (age 5) embarked on their first major trip, riding over 1,000 miles on horseback from Frederick, Oklahoma, to Santa Fe, New Mexico. Traveling with minimal supplies, they relied on instructions from their father to cover no more than 35 miles per day. This journey demonstrated their independence and introduced them to national audiences through local newspaper coverage.

1910: Horseback Ride to New York City
In the spring of 1910, the Abernathy brothers set off on their most famous ride—2,500 miles from Oklahoma to New York City. Along the way, they made a stop in Washington, D.C., where they met President Taft and were introduced to Congress. Their journey culminated in New York City, where they greeted former President Theodore Roosevelt upon his return from an African safari. The ride was widely covered by newspapers, cementing their status as national folk heroes.

1910: Automobile Journey Back to Oklahoma
After arriving in New York, the boys decided to return home in a Brush Runabout, one of the earliest affordable automobiles. At ages 10 and 6, they became pioneers in long-distance car travel. Louis took

on most of the driving, managing breakdowns and the car's manual crank system, while Temple occasionally navigated using the spokes of the steering wheel.

1911 (January): Brush Automobile Exhibit at Madison Square Garden

The boys' Brush Runabout journey caught the attention of automobile enthusiasts and the press. In January 1911, they participated in an exhibit at Madison Square Garden, where they demonstrated their driving skills and captivated audiences with their charm. Temple, only six years old, gave an impromptu pantomime demonstration of how to operate a car, impressing both spectators and engineers.

1911 (Spring): Race to Washington, D.C., with Judy the Elephant

The Abernathy brothers participated in a whimsical race from New York to Washington, D.C., leading Judy the elephant and Jennie the donkey. The event was a publicity stunt but showcased their adaptability and sense of fun.

1911 (Summer): Cross-Country Ride from New York to San Francisco

In the summer of 1911, the boys undertook one of their most grueling trips—a cross-country ride from New York City to San Francisco. This 60-day journey, done entirely on horseback, required them to sleep outdoors and adhere to strict rules. Although they arrived two days late to claim the prize money, the journey solidified their reputation as fearless adventurers.

1913: Motorcycle Ride to New York

For their final documented adventure, Louis (14) and Temple (10) rode an Indian motorcycle from Oklahoma to New York City, accompanied by their stepbrother Anton. This trip marked the boys' transition from childhood explorers to young men, signaling the end of their moment in the spotlight.

Later Years: Post-Adventure Lives

Louis went on to become a successful lawyer in Wichita Falls, Texas, where he practiced until his death in 1979. Temple pursued a career in the oil industry and lived a quieter life, passing away in 1986. Both men remained proud of their adventures, which shaped their identities and left an enduring heritage of courage and resilience.

Appendix 2 — Significant 1910 News

This section includes additional excerpts from newspaper articles published in 1910 which were among our favorites and which help tell the story. In general these are not in the main text of the book.

Washington, June 3. — The young Abernathy boys, sons of Jack Abernathy, the rough rider, United States marshal and friend of Roosevelt, who have ridden 2,000 miles from Oklahoma to meet Roosevelt upon his arrival in New York, threw the house into confusion when they were brought upon the floor upon the suggestion of the speaker.

"You own as much of this city as Rockefeller or Carnegie," said Cannon, addressing the boys, as the members crowded about and questioned them about their long horseback ride.[509] [510] [511] [512]

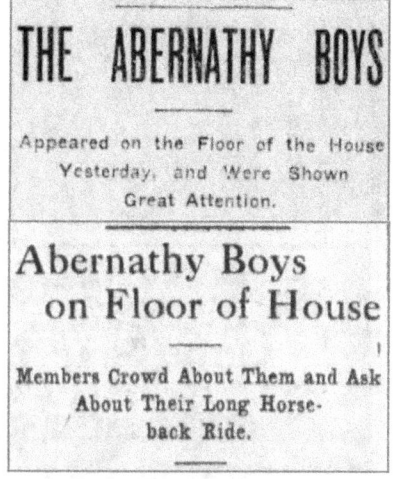

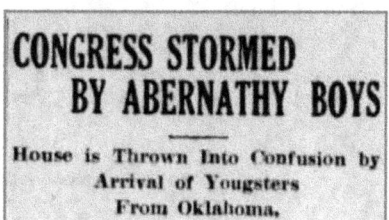

---

[509] The *Enid Morning News* (Enid, Oklahoma) June 4, 1910, Pg 1.
[510] The *Daily Review* (Decatur, Illinois) June 4, 1910, Pg. 7.
[511] *Omaha Daily Bee* (Omaha, Nebraska) June 4, 1910, Pg.1.
[512] *Lincoln Nebraska State Journal* (Lincoln, Nebraska) June 4, 1910, Pg. 1.

ABERNATHY BOYS SEE CINCINNATI'S SIGHTS

It is safe to say that the Prince of Wales on his local visit did not have so much fun as Louie, aged nine, and Temple Abernathy, aged six years, have encountered here the last three days.

These youthful scions of the great Southwest, who are riding horseback from Guthrie, Okla., to New York city, to greet Mr. Roosevelt, have had the Queen City from soup to nuts, from the point of the small boy.

Odd as it may seem, that part of the great city which appealed to them most was the inclined planes. Messrs. Small and Evans had the lads in tow Saturday, and that evening went out of their car line way several times to do the Mount Adams incline, with the Oklahoma boys standing on the front platform, their eyes popping with excitement.

Although they have ridden 1,300 miles this stretch, still they were "saddle hungry" at the Zoo. Superintendent Sol Stephan trotted out two of his spotted ponies, and the diminutive Louie and the still smaller Temple climbed on the ponies and went scooting around the oval smiling like Indians.

Saturday night, yesterday and last night the boys were guests of Thomas L. Evans, secretary to the mayor, and Mrs. Evans at their home on Taylor avenue. Yesterday they attended Sunday school, and later went out on the river for a spin in Dick Witt's fast motor boat, and for a change took a ride in the motor craft of John Wenner, secretary to Service Director Sundmaker.

They were conducted down into the iron bowels of the pump pit at the waterworks, and looked with fascinated eyes on that mechanical wonder. In the afternoon they visited Ft. Thomas with Mr. and Mrs. Evans. They attracted as great an amount of attention there as elsewhere about the city, their quaint attire serving at once to establish their identity. They had the freedom of the fort, and returned to the Evans home with their military spirit above the hundred mark.

The sole thing which has interfered with the spirit of Temple so far is that he is trying to stand up and see all that comes to the vision of Louie the Elder. But there are two black marks against him—both gained in this city. First, he went to sleep during the moving picture show at the Refuge Home, and was of necessity put to bed in the guest chamber of that establishment. Then after a call on The Enquirer, Temple again went into the Land of Nod while a passenger on an East End car. He was carried several squares toward Mr. Evans' home before he realized that Louie was laughing at him.

The boys have made a big hit with Mayor Schwab. This morning the mayor will arrive at the city hall in time to give the youngsters an official farewell before they leave on their long ride to the Atlantic coast. The little chaps will mount their horses about 9 o'clock this morning, on the Plum street side of the hall. The animals have the benefit of almost three days' rest, and the boys expect to get to Washington for their call on President Taft in great shape. They will have a police escort to the eastern boundary of the city today.

Louie remembers Mr. Roosevelt very well as a hunter of wild game in the southwest. John Abernathy, father of these precocious children, is one of Mr. Roosevelt's hunting companions, and is the hunter referred to in the ex-president's books as the man who can run down a coyote and kill it with his naked hands. During their presence in the Zoo both boys conversing with Superintendent Stephan, showed their thorough familiarity with game life of the west.

Last night Temple had busted himself financially by going against that sort of slot machine that peddles chewing gum and candy for pennies. As an institution of civilization, the youngster thinks these machines are second only to the incline planes. That is why Louie, the elder, is business manager of the tour.

Their way eastward will be along the line of the B. & O. S.-W. railroad. They are to reach New York city June 15, where they will be greeted by their father, who will make the journey across country to meet them. Thence they are to ship their faithful horses, Sam and Willie, homeward, and follow soon afterward.

Last year these small boys rode over half a dozen states in the southwest. Such an occurrence as a rainstorm or a big wind does not perturb them in the least. They are true sons of the out-of-door theory, and show their birthright by ability to take care of themselves although hundreds of miles from home and on their own resources excepting the remittances which they receive by drawing on their father by bank drafts.—Cincinnati Enquirer, May 3.

Abernathy Boys at Washington

Washington, D.C. – After riding on horseback most of the way across the continent to meet Col. Roosevelt on his arrival in New York, Louis and Temple Abernathy, aged 9 and 6, respectively, sons of "Jack" Abernathy of Oklahoma, the wolf catcher and friend of the former president, have arrived in the national capital.

Abernathy Boys at Washington.
Washington, D. C.—After riding on horseback most of the way across the continent to meet Col. Roosevelt on his arrival in New York, Louie and Temple Abernathy, aged 9 and 6, respectively, sons of "Jack" Abernathy of Oklahoma, the wolf catcher and friend of the former president, have arived in the national capital.

The *Kirksville Graphic* (Kirksville, Missouri) May 27, 1910, Pg. 9.
The *Prescott Daily News* (Prescott, Arkansas) May 30 1910, Pg. 1.
Payne County Farmer (Yale, Oklahoma) June 1, 1910, Pg. 5.
Potosi Journal (Potosi, Missouri) June 1, 1910, Pg 2.
The *Advertiser-Courier* (Hermann, Missouri) June 1, 1910, Pg. 2.
The *Kingfisher Times* (Kingfisher, Oklahoma) 2 June 2, 1910, Thu Page 2.
The *Weekly Progress* (Boley, Oklahoma) June 2, 1910, Pg. 2.
The *Marlow Review* (Marlow, Oklahoma) June 2, 1910, Pg. 2.
Jefferson County Record (Hillsboro, Missouri) June 2, 1910, Pg. 1.
The *Olustee Democrat* (Olustee, Oklahoma) June 2 1910, Pg.6.
The *Tupelo Times* (Tupelo, Oklahoma) June 2, 1910, Pg. 6.
The *Apachan* (Apache, Oklahoma) June 2, 1910, Pg. 2.
California Democrat (California, Missouri) June 2, 1910, Pg. 2.
Mexico Missouri Message (Mexico, Missouri) June 2, 1910, Pg. 2.
The *Bridgeport News* (Hydro, Oklahoma) June 2, 1910, Pg. 4.
Sweetwater Breeze (Sweetwater, Oklahoma) June 2, 1910, Pg. 6.
The *Coweta Times* (Coweta, Oklahoma June 2, 1910, Pg. 2.
Muskogee County Republican and Fort Gibson Post
(Fort Gibson, Oklahoma) June 2, 1910, Pg. 4.
Coweta Times-Star (Coweta, Oklahoma) June 2, 1910, Pg. 2.
Haskell News (Haskell, Oklahoma) June 2, 1910, Pg. 6.
The *Altamont News* (Altamont, Illinois) June 2, 1910, Pg. 2.
Marble Hill Press (Marble Hill, Missouri) June 2, 1910, Pg. 2.
The *Southern Standard* (Arkadelphia, Arkansas) June 2, 1910, Pg. 2.
Crawford Mirror (Steelville, Missouri) June 2, 1910, Pg. 2.
The *Jet Visitor* (Jet, Oklahoma) June 2, 1910, Pg. 2.

---

[513] The *Daily Oklahoman* (Oklahoma City, Oklahoma) May 11, 1910, Pg. 16.

The *Walters Herald* (Walters, Oklahoma) June 2, 1910, Pg. 7.
The *Osage Eagle* (Hominy, Oklahoma) June 2, 1910, Pg. 6.
The *Okemah Ledger* (Okemah, Oklahoma) 2 Jun 1910, Thu Page 6.
Edmond Enterprise (Edmond, Oklahoma) June 2, 1910, Pg. 2.
The *Helena Star* (Helena, Oklahoma) June 2, 1910, Pg. 7.
Iron County Register (Ironton, Missouri) June 2, 1910, Pg. 2.
Heavener Ledger (Heavener, Oklahoma) June 2, 1910, Pg. 2.
The Jet Visitor (Jet, Oklahoma) June 2, 1910, Pg. 2.
Moniteau County Herald (California, Missouri) June 2, 1910, Pg. 7.
Custer Courier (Custer City, Oklahoma) June 2, 1910, Pg. 2.
The *Sterling News* (Sterling, Oklahoma) June 2, 1910, Pg. 5.
The *Pittsburg Enterprise* (Pittsburg, Oklahoma) June 2, 1910, Pg. 1.
The *Inola Register* (Inola, Oklahoma) June 2, 1910, Pg. 1.
Beckham County Democrat (Erick, Oklahoma) June 2, 1910, Pg. 2.
The *Star-Gazette* (Sallisaw, Oklahoma) June 3, 1910, Pg. 6.
The *Vian Press* (Vian, Oklahoma) June 3, 1910, Pg. 5.
The *Checotah Times* (Checotah, Oklahoma) June 3, 1910, Pg. 3.
The Dewey *Sentinel* (Dewey, Oklahoma) June 3, 1910, Pg. 2.
Broken Arrow Democrat (Broken Arrow, Oklahoma) June 3, 1910, Pg. 2.
The *Porum Journal* (Porum, Oklahoma) June 3, 1910, Pg. 5.
The *Okarche Times* (Okarche, Oklahoma) June 3, 1910, Pg. 2.
The *Nowata Weekly Star-Times* (Nowata, Oklahoma) June 3, 1910, Pg. 2.
The *Sayre Headlight* (Sayre, Oklahoma) June 3, 1910, Pg. 2.
The *Canadian Valley News* (Jones, Oklahoma) June 3, 1910, Pg. 2.
The *Mobridge News* (Mobridge, South Dakota) June 3, 1910, Pg. 2.
The *Star-Gazette* (Sallisaw, Oklahoma) June 3, 1910, Pg. 6.
Weleetka American (Weleetka, Oklahoma) June 3, 1910, Pg. 4.
Miami Record-Herald (Miami, Oklahoma) June 3, 1910, Pg. 2.
The *Chickasaw Banner* (Wynnewood, Oklahoma) June 3, 1910, Pg. 2.
The Pioneer Express (Pembina, North Dakota) June 3, 1910, Pg. 2.
Lexington Leader (Lexington, Oklahoma) June 3, 1910, Pg. 6.
Adair County Democrat (Westville, Oklahoma) June 3, 1910, Pg. 2.
The Oklahoma Critic (Tulsa, Oklahoma) June 3, 1910, Pg. 2.
The Sisseton Weekly Standard (Sisseton, South Dakota) June 3, 1910, Pg. 6.
The Muldrow Press (Muldrow, Oklahoma) June 3, 1910, Pg. 5.
The Davidson Record (Davidson, Oklahoma) June 3, 1910, Pg. 3.
The Snyder Signal-Star (Snyder, Oklahoma) June 3, 1910, Pg. 3.
The Mustang Enterprise (Mustang, Oklahoma) June 3, 1910, Pg. 8.
Bridgeport Grit (Bridgeport, Oklahoma) June 3, 1910, Pg. 3.
The Bloomfield Vindicator (Bloomfield, Missouri) June 3, 1910, Pg. 2.
The Webbers Falls Record (Webbers Falls, Oklahoma) June 3, 1910, Pg. 1.

Haskell County Chant News (Chant, Oklahoma) June 3, 1910, Pg. 4.
The Gotebo Gazette (Gotebo, Oklahoma June 3, 1910, Pg. 6.
The Cleveland Enterprise (Cleveland, Oklahoma) June 3, 1910, Pg. 2.
The Checotah Times (Checotah, Oklahoma) June 3, 1910, Pg. 3.
The Headrick Leader (Headrick, Oklahoma) June 3, 1910, Pg. 1.
The Kiefer Searchlight (Kiefer, Oklahoma) June 3, 1910, Pg. 5.
McAlester Democrat (McAlester, Oklahoma) June 3, 1910, Pg. 4.
Cache Clarion & Indiahoma News (Cache, Oklahoma) June 3, 1910, Pg. 8.
The *Osage City News* (Osage City, Oklahoma) June 4, 1910, Pg. 4.
Wheatland Weekly Watchword (Wheatland, Oklahoma) June 4, 1910, Pg. 8.
The Semi-Weekly Leader (Brookhaven, Michigan) June 4, 1910, Pg. 2.

"Teach a boy self reliance from the moment he tumbles out of the cradle, make him keep his traces taut and work well forward in his collar and ninety-nine times out of a hundred his independence will assert itself before he is two years old. Then guide him with a firm but tender hand; instill into him the principles of right and wrong, and the rest is easy. If there is no taint in his blood and he doesn't possess a yellow streak he will develop into a fine man. That's my rule, and if you don't think I've taken the right tack talk to my boys for five minutes and they'll convince you that they are men in principles even if they are babies in years. God bless 'em."

This is the theory of John R. Abernathy, marshal of Oklahoma and father of Louis and Temple Abernathy, the two "kiddies," aged respectively ten and six years, who made a triumphal entrance into New

York astride the cow ponies they rode across country from their father's ranch to greet Roosevelt. There are five little Abernathys at home—all girls. And according to their daddy each and every one of them is just as "wonderful," just as self reliant and just as grown up as Louis and Temple.

Is Man of Strength.

Marshal Abernathy might best be described as a "great big little man." He is about five feet six, well set up and shows every inch of his height. He is broad of shoulder and tapers down to the perfect V. He shows power, great strength and determination in his every gesture and move. Aside from the wide brimmed, tan colored felt hat there is nothing about him to suggest the man who "catches wolves with his bare hands and strangles them to death."

"When Mrs. Abernathy died," said Captain Jack, "I called the children around me and had a heart to heart talk with them. They knew of my frequent and protracted absences from the ranch, so I mapped out the work and gave each his or her task. Each was made to feel that unless they lived up to their part of the work the ranch would go to the devil. Wild horses couldn't have held them back then."

Corral Their Kindergarten.

"Perhaps your boys would have had better educational advantages had they lived in the city?" was suggested.

"No, they wouldn't," the captain quickly answered. "They have lived close to nature and they have studied it. Their book learning hasn't suffered either, for they are just as well advanced in their studies, I find, as the average city child of their age.

"Their kindergarten course was obtained in the ranch corral. Horses, dogs, wolf and bear cubs were their playmates from infancy, and their knowledge of the traits and habits of each of these animals is as intimate as my own, and I have been studying them forty-five years.

"Each shall have a college education. Harvard will be their alma mater unless they suffer a change of heart. You know they fairly worship Colonel Roosevelt and he is a Harvard man. Anything the colonel does or has done is perfectly all right in their eyes, for next to their daddy he is the greatest man in the world."

Harder Trip Last Year.
Whereas the country at large is amazed at the feat of the boys in riding to New York, Captain Abernathy does not think it as hazardous an undertaking by one-half as the trip to Mexico the boys took last year.

"You see, nothing was written about that trip, and the boys were just as anxious to keep their present movements as secret as they did when going to and from Mexico. Those little chaps bunked in with Indians, brigands and outlaws all down through the alkali country, and not a hair of their little heads was harmed. They weren't afraid for a moment. They returned with more money than they started out with, and they made it all by swapping horses. Can you beat that?"[514]

---

[514] The *Bryan Democrat* (Bryan, Ohio) June 21, 1910 Pg. 8.

Appendix 3 — Brush Auto Ads

Full Text and References for the Aug 1910 Brush Auto Ads in the following issues:

The Inter Ocean (Chicago, Illinois) August 14 1910, Pg. 19.
The Inter Ocean (Chicago, Illinois) August 21 1910, Pg. 44.
Omaha Daily Bee (Omaha, Nebraska) August 21 1910, Pg. 11.
Omaha World Herald (Omaha, Nebraska) August 21 1910, Pg. 43.
The Kansas City Star (Kansas City, Missouri) August 21 1910, Pg. 41.
Buffalo Courier (Buffalo, New York) August 21 1910, Pg. 53.
Detroit Free Press (Detroit, Michigan) August 21 1910, Pg. 20.
The Washington Times (Washington, DC) August 21 1910, Pg. 17.
The Minneapolis Journal (Minneapolis, Minnesota) August 21 1910, Pg. 44
Star Tribune(Minneapolis, Minnesota) August 21 1910, Pg. 44.
The Herington Times (Herington, Kansas) August 24 1910, Pg. 44.
The *Indianapolis News* (Indianapolis, IN August 24 1910, Pg. 4.
The Indianapolis Star (Indianapolis, IN) August 24 1910, Pg. 20.
The *Boston Globe* (Boston, Massachusetts) August 28 1910, Pg. 55.
The *Daily Oklahoman* (Oklahoma City, Oklahoma) August 28 1910, Pg. 11

Ask Yourself This Question

"Would an Automobile that I Could Buy for $485.00 and Operate for Less than One Cent a Mile be a Good Investment for Me?"

The way to arrive at a sensible conclusion as to whether or not you should buy an automobile, is to base your answer wholly upon the needs of your own business. You know how you make your money. If you have much getting about to do, find out how much time it takes and what it costs you to do it. So you are the best judge of whether or not you would be wise to invest in an automobile to employ in the active use of an automobile.

If time is worth anything to you, the chances are you would save a great deal of it by the use of any automobile. But its first cost would have to be so low and the up-keep of it so small that the result would show a net profit.

The BRUSH RUNABOUT, because of its first low cost, because of the very small amount of money necessary to operate and maintain it, is the logical car for you to use as a basis for your investigation. If the BRUSH will not do the things you want it to do and show a profit, then no motor car built will. If you have much getting about to do, a BRUSH will do it for you cheaper than carfare. If you are now using a horse or horses, a BRUSH will enable you to cover much more ground, do more work, and raise you to a level of efficiency that you are now paying for feed and blacksmith bills. This may sound to you like a strong statement. The proof of it lies in the testimony of thousands of BRUSH owners who are proving it to their satisfaction every day. It is a simple matter of fact.

Think for a moment about the 2,500 mile trip of the Abernathy boys riding from Oklahoma City to New York and back, where they paid their respects to Colonel Roosevelt, those youngsters, whose combined ages do not form a bridge across the gap between babyhood and young manhood (they are 10 and 7 years old), chose a Brush Runabout for their journey because it is the only car which is so simple mechanically and so easy to handle that a boy of his age could run it as well as a professional driver operates a large machine. Louie Abernathy drove the BRUSH all the way himself. They "honked" up the main street of Oklahoma City just twenty-three days after they left New York. They stopped a day each in four of the larger cities to see the sights, so they made the run in nineteen days, averaging about 140 miles a day.

Louie Abernathy demonstrated in a way that admits of no argument that the BRUSH features which we have been telling you about in our advertising are actual features. He demonstrated that the BRUSH is simple to operate and easy to control. He demonstrated its easy-riding qualities when they left New York. He demonstrated that a 9-year-old boy could start it and stop it and that it was easy for him to keep it going.

If a BRUSH would not do what we say about it in the way, we know how long a journey, then it certainly is no motor car for you to use. But the strength and sturdiness of the BRUSH, its ability to do a big job at a small cost, has been set at the very high standard by that successful trip of the Abernathy boys who drove it about 140 miles a day for nineteen days.

We could go on enumerating BRUSH features and advantages. The car loans us to buy purely as an investment. The best we can do, however, in any piece of advertising, is to arouse your curiosity to the point of making a personal investigation of the BRUSH. The way to find out all about the BRUSH RUNABOUT, the way to prove to yourself that it does what we say about it are true, the way to know for yourself whether or not it is the car you may now buy at the lowest first cost, the car which needs no more than will show you a very considerable profit and net gain in your business, is to purchase a BRUSH for $485 and run it for less than one cent a mile. The Abernathy boys drove almost 140 miles a day for nineteen days.

We have been taking advantage of the Abernathy trip to call your attention to the utility of the BRUSH. This trip demonstrated, however, in just as big a way, the pleasure of this wonderful car. No car offers more as a pleasure vehicle than the BRUSH, except size and carrying capacity. No car in the world offers as much, combining both from the standpoint of utility and pleasure, as the BRUSH.

Ask yourself the same question which you did at the beginning of this advertisement, and remember that there is a BRUSH dealer near you who will be glad to show you how to prove what the BRUSH will do for you. If you are busy, he will be glad to come to you if you will write or telephone him.

Brush Runabout Company, Detroit, Michigan
Brush Chicago Motor Company
2328 Michigan Boulevard
Distributors for Chicago and Vicinity

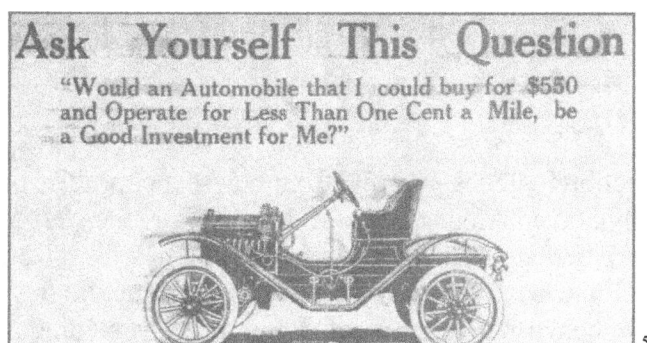

[515] The *Herington Times* (Herington, Kansas) August 25, 1910, Pg. 4.

Appendix 4 — Significant 1911 News

This section includes excerpts from newspaper articles published between July 30 and August 5, 1911, documenting the start of Louis and Temple Abernathy's historic horseback journey from Coney Island to San Francisco. These accounts capture the public fascination, colorful commentary, and unexpected moments—including a candy-induced delay at the starting line.

ABERNATHY KIDS BEGIN COAST TO COAST RIDE
Leave Coney Island, N.Y., for the Presidio, San Francisco —
NEW YORK, August 1. — Scarcely tall enough to reach their horses' heads, Louis and Temple Abernathy, eleven and seven years old respectively, at just 12:01 a.m. today started on the longest and hardest ride of their strenuous career, a jaunt of about 3,600 miles across the continent. An example of boy manhood, their ride will probably stand unmatched for a long time. The boys declared as they made final arrangements that the long ride looked easy compared to the grind they have just been through in helping to write the history of their to previous rides. It may not be telling too much to add that the boys' father, John R. Abernathy, of Oklahoma, better known as "Catch Em Alive Jack" from his wolf catching proclivities in the old days when he was United States Marshal in Oklahoma, and took President Roosevelt hunting also sighed with relief when the history of writing was finished and the action began again. "Catchin' wolves is isn't near so hard as catchin' typographical errors," admitted Abernathy.

The book, however, which treated the "The Ride of the Abernathy Boys" was actually written by their uncle Miles Abernathy, with the active solicitation of the boys and their strenuous father.

But no sooner had the Abernathys asserted that the last pages of proof had been sent them to Doubleday, Page and Company, their publishers, than they began final preparations for their long trip. Their book was run through the presses while these last preparations were made and their dad, Page and Co., delivered them a limited number of copies just as they were going away. Thus, while the boys are making history on the westward journey, they'll reach all the world by means of a read of their story of the earlier journey a year ago from Oklahoma to New York where they were they were a conspicuous part of the welcome to the homecoming Lion Hunter, and former president.

The program for the start, Tuesday morning, August 1, by the two youngest boys in the West, was very different from the start of the earlier trip that had its ending at Times Square when the 60,000 horse-enthusiasts cheered them on. Doubleday, "The Ride of the Abernathy Boys" is scheduled for their own April 5th, 1911, start. Crowds arose before daylight and cheered only by other readers and the copyreaders, rode away from their father's ranch at Frederick, Okla., near the Texas line, on their long ride to New York. That was a ride of about 2,200 miles.

"We're agon' to do it or bust," shouted the doughty Col. Jack to which his sons answered in unison, their childish voices shrilling above the noise of the thousands on the beach. "You bet we are."

THE RIDERS
Louie Abernathy, 11 years old.
Temple Abernathy, 7 years old

WHAT THEY WILL TRY TO DO
Ride from Coney Island, New York, to the Presidio, San Francisco, 3,600 miles in 60 riding days.

TERMS
To win a big money prize the boys must not ride on Sunday, must not sleep under a roof, must not eat under a roof, must average 60 miles a day for the whole distance, must deliver letters from New York officials to San Francisco officials, not later than Tuesday, October 10.

WHAT THE ABERNATHY BOYS HAVE DONE
In 1909 they rode from Guthrie, Okla., to Santa Fe, New Mexico, and return, 2,340 miles. Boys then aged 9 and 5 years respectively.

OTHER ENDURANCE FEATS OF HORSEBACK RIDING
Nan Aspinwall, "The Montana Girl," rode from San Francisco to New York in 180 riding days having ridden 4,500 miles. En route from September 1, 1910, to July 8, 1911. Claims world's long distance riding record.

"Cheyenne Bill" rode from Cheyenne to Chicago. Horse dropped dead at end of ride.

"Calamity Jane" rode from Pacific to Billings, Mont.

Then they were off at a good clip, through Brooklyn, across newspaper row and City Hall Square to Broadway, and up that metropolitan backbone to the Bronx. Before starting Abernathy declared that they would not stop until they got to Yonkers, soon after daylight, when they would rest a bit before starting for Albany.

Since spring the boys have been in and around New York and both of them, as well as their father, Col. Jack, have heard the call of the trail—the same call that is heard by the Boy Scouts, except that with these boys, it is inbred. So they're off to try to lower the only existing transcontinental horseback record, which was made by Miss Nan Aspinwall of Montana who rode from San Francisco to New York in 180 days. Miss Aspinwall started last September 1, and reached New York July 8. She rode a California mare, Lady Ellen. Miss Aspinwall's feat was a notable one and deserves a prize—it will take the hardest riding of their career to lower her record. If they succeed they win a large money prize.

Today the boys had a sendoff of soft gay Coney Island crowds that massed around them in such a way they would start at just one minute after midnight. No boisterous moments. The books were bound and the thrill lasted for hours nearer to see the start. The horses had already been groomed for their Sunday morning bath in the surf. They rode shortly before 12:00 and prepared to ride down Surf Avenue for a water wash. Their father, who decided to accompany them, rode beside Temple, the youngest, who had said at the beginning of the trip, "Father, you need the rest."

As the first picture cameramen flashed the trip by newspaper lighting, the crowds followed the cheering for almost blocks as they bathed their ponies in the surf. Then turned up, an officer signaled the boys that a halt would be necessary.

Temple had been in New York three months and needed the greatest caution for further adventures and carefully explained that, as their book told, the strawberry soda pop was just as good in small towns along the road as at Coney Island. Temple, though learning fast, does not talk entirely plainly yet, and when he wants to mount his horse, and his brother is not around to help him, he just shouts at the animal's foreleg. It matters not the name of the animal to a youthful expert. At the point of a straight session of bucking and pitching,

Temple was raised in the saddle, and when eighteen months old was being carried in the front of his father on the horn of the U.S. Marshal's saddle when the incident that gave Abernathy the reputation of catching wolves with his bare hands occurred. After going over an embankment for the wolf, an enhancement for the wolf, Abernathy was confronted by a cornered animal, the book "The Ride of the Abernathy Boys" describes the famous incident as follows: "Making a lightning grab, the hunter threw his bare hand into the mouth of the angry wolf and soon subdued him. Meantime, Temple succeeded in pulling out of the mud and sand and slush and instead of crying or being excited, he said triumphantly to his parent, 'Well, daddy, you shore dot him.'".

Louis is the responsible one. From having the care of his little brother on their other two rides, and their other two rides he has developed a great sense of his duties toward health, mind and soul. He highly interests the management by weathering their rule of never working nor riding on Sunday, and whenever it is down on Sunday, asks Temple to Sunday School.

"Yes," admitted their father Col. Jack, "It's a long hard trip and they were to do in the 60 days, but we are going to do our best. The boys wanted to go so bad I couldn't refuse 'em, but I want to ride at least 3 ways with 'em. Oh, they could take the entire expense all right, I was given the exercise."

After leaving New York the Abernathy boys will follow the east side of Hudson River, through Schenectady, Utica, Syracuse, Rochester and Buffalo, thence to Cleveland, Toledo and Chicago, through Illinois and from there to Des Moines and Omaha. They will then proceed on their trail westward to Cheyenne, across Wyoming and on through Utah, then to Nevada and California where they hope to finish well ahead of the time. The horses have been specially selected for their journey, and one of the saddles will be worn on Sunday when Louis will wear special shoes for the race. [516] [517] [518]

---

[516] The *Sandusky Register* (Sandusky, Ohio) August 2, 1911, Pg. 2
[517] *Albuquerque Journal* (Albuquerque, New Mexico) August 3, 1911, Pg 1.
[518] The *New York Times* (New York, New York) August 5, 1911.

THE ABERNATHY BOYS' GREATEST RIDE.

The Riders
Louis Abernathy, 11 years old.
Temple Abernathy, 7 years old.

What They Will Try To Do
Ride from Coney Island, New York, to the Presidio, San Francisco, 2,600 miles, in 60 riding days.

Terms
To win a big money prize the boys must not ride on Sunday, must not sleep under a roof, must not eat under a roof, must average 60 miles a day for the whole distance, must be liver letters from New York to San Francisco officials not later than Tuesday, October 10.

What the Abernathy Boys Have Done
In 1909 the rode from Guthrie, Oklahoma, to Santa Fe, New Mexico, and return, 2,240 miles. Boys then aged 9 and 5 years respectively.

NOTHING LIKE THIS UNTIL THEY REACH THE PACIFIC COAST. THE BOYS AGREE TO EAT OR SLEEP UNDER A ROOF DURING THEIR RIDE. ABOVE WAS TAKEN AFTER THE ABERNATHY'S FIRST TRIP TO CONEY ISLAND.

In 1910 they rode from Frederick, Oklahoma, to New York, 2,296 miles. Boys aged 10 and 6, respectively.

Other Endurance Feats of Horseback Riding

Nan Aspinwall, "The Montana Girl" rode from San Francisco to New York in 180 riding days, having ridden 4,500 miles. Enroute from September 1, 1910, to July 8, 1911. Claims world's long distance riding record.

"Cheyenne Bill" rode from Cheyenne to Chicago. Horse dropped dead at end of ride.

"Calamity Jane" rode from the Pacific to Billings, Mont.

New York, August 19.—Scarcely tall enough to reach their horses' heads, Louie and Temple Abernathy,

But no sooner had the Abernathys corrected the last pages of proof and sent them to Doubleday, Page and Company, their publishers, than they began final preparations for their long trip. Their book was run through the presses the long ride looked easy compared to the grind they have just been through in helping to write the history of their two previous long rides. (It says not in telling how much to add that the boys' father, John R. Abernathy, of Oklahoma, better known as "Catch 'em Alive Jack" from his well catching proclivities in the old days when he was United States Marshal in Oklahoma and until President Roosevelt hunting also sighed with relief when the history writing was over and the action began again. "Catchin' wolves isn't

from fee their ride when they delivered down Surf Avenue shortly before 17:00 and prepared to life their horses into the water. Their father who had decided to go with them, rode beside Temple, the youngest of the boys, and the contrast only served to accentuate the smallness of the plucky youngsters.

As the crowds cheered and the p—

RESTING THEIR "BRONCOS"

firemen tried to keep women and children from under the horses' hoofs the trip rode into the surf, bathed their horses in the Atlantic Ocean and then started for the Pacific coast. "We're again' to do it or bust," shouted the doughty Col. Jack to which his sons answered in unison, their childish voices shrilling above the noise of the thousands on the beach, "You bet we are."

Then they were off at a good clip, through Brooklyn, across the bridge, across newspaper row and City Hall Square to Broadway, and up that metropolitan harkway to the Bronx. Before starting Abernathy declared that they would not stop until they got to Yonkers, even after daylight; when they would rest a bit before starting for Albany.

Since Spring the boys have been in and around New York and both of them, as well as their father, Col. Jack, have heard the call of the trail — the same call that is heard in the Boy Scouts, except that wild horses it is inbred. So they're off to try to lower the only existing transcontinental horseback record, which was made by Miss Nan Aspinwall of Montana who rode from San Francisco to New York in 180 riding days. Miss Aspinwall started last September 1, and reached New York July 8. She rode a California mare, Lady Ellen. Miss Aspinwall's feat was a notable one, and the boys realize it will take the hardest riding of their careers to lower her record. If they succeed they win a horse money prize.

Col. Abernathy is riding a Virginia bred horse recently purchased in Philadelphia, while Temple rides the bay horse Sam that Louis rode from Oklahoma. Geronimo the Indian pony, went lame on that trip but was brought here later. He will not be ridden as Col. Abernathy has disposed of him for another white horse for Louie.

In preparing for the ride the greatest precaution as to the weight of mounts was used. It is part of the compact that the riders shall not cat nor sleep under a roof during their ride on they will have to carry two blankets, tarpaulins, slickers, grub, and a few cooking utensils with them making very heavy loads for the horses.

Both boys and their father are as brown as beach life savers, fit for any kind of a grind, and anxious for adventures.

"Are you glad to go?" Louie and Temple were asked. The elder of the two little boys replied, with his South-Western accent, "Sure we are. It's more fun ridin' than just stayin' around here."

"But don't you like New York and Coney Island?" he was asked.

"Oh, 'course we do; we like Temple, but you can't beat the fun o' gettin' out yonder an ridin' over those plains all day."

The seven-year old child who is to make the ride that nearly baffled a strong young woman whose whole life

has been spent in the saddle, looked askance and explained that, at their book told, the strangers and it—it was just as good in small towns short. He read as at Coney Island. Youngster, though learning fast, does not talk entirely plainly yet, and when he wants to mount his horse, and his brother is not around to help him, he just shins up the animal's foreleg.

THEY'RE OFF

eleven and seven years old, respectively, recently started on the longest and hardest ride of their strenuous career—a little jaunt, on horseback, of about 2,500 miles across the continent. As an example of how exciting their ride will probably stand unexcelled for a long time. The boys declared as they made final arrangements, however, which bears the title of "The Ride of the Abernathy Boys" was actually written by their uncle, Miles Abernathy, with the active collaboration of the boys and their strenuous father.

Louie and Temple arose before daylight and, cheered only by their relatives and the cowpunchers, rode away from their father's ranch at Frederick, Okla., near the Texas line, on their long ride to New York. That was a ride of about 2,500 miles.

The boys had spent a weekend so on gay Coney Island can give. It was known long in advance that they would start at just the minute after midnight so thousands, who otherwise would have left the resort before that hour remained to see the start. The boys had rested Monday and were

THEY WILL SLEEP WHEREVER THE DAY'S RIDING LEADS THEM

care of themselves all right. I just want the exercise.

After leaving New York the Abernathys rode up the East side of the Hudson to Albany, thence through Schenectady, Utica, Syracuse, Rochester, and Buffalo. Thence the route lays on the Cleveland and Chicago, and from there to Omaha. They will then ride Northwest over the great plains, more barren than any they ever rode in Oklahoma, through Cheyenne, and the mountains to Salt Lake City. From where they will shape their course to San Francisco.

[520] The *Omaha Daily News* (Omaha, Nebraska) Sep 7, 1911, Pg. 1.
[521] The *Omaha Daily News* (Omaha, Nebraska) Sep 7, 1911, Pg. 1.

Top—The arrival in Omaha over the Douglas street bridge.
Middle—The Abernathys, father and sons, eating breakfast on Harney street.
Below—The ponies of the boys getting their breakfast.

Louis and Temple Abernathy of Fredrick, Okla., the horseback scouts, 11 and 7 years of age, drew reins in Omaha this morning on their transcontinental junket from Coney Island, New York to the Presidio, San Francisco, Cal.

With their father, "Catch-'Em-Alive" Jack Abernathy, they breakfasted in the street at Sixteenth and Harney streets, as guests of Henry Kieser, manager of the Bennett book department, and the local troops of boy scouts.

Several hundred boys, and some grown-ups, were waiting to receive the young riders and gave a lusty cheer as the little tots rode in.

---

[522] The *Omaha Daily News* (Omaha, Nebraska) Sep 7, 1911, Pg. 1.

After "grub," which was a public exhibition of how plainspeople dispose of victuals when their appetites are keen, the trio was taken for an automobile spin about the city, then they departed merrily on their way west, expecting to cover at least fifty miles before nightfall.

The youngsters are riding on a wager, the conditions of which are that they cross the continent in sixty riding days, eating and sleeping outside. They are now four days behind schedule but expect to make up the loss in Nebraska and Wyoming, where they will not be delayed so much by the crowds of big cities.

If they fulfill the requirement of their wager, the two boys will receive $5,000 apiece. The management at Coney Island put up the stakes, and betting there now is 3 to 1 that the youngsters will not succeed.

The youngsters are hardened to the saddle. When the train was sighted this morning, the trio reached Omaha. The long jaunt is telling on Jack to some extent, and because he rides all of the time to safeguard his boys, Abernathy will buy an automobile soon for his own use on the rest of the trip.

Louis and Temple were in the best of spirits. They smiled and waived their hands as they passed a crowd of boys at the Union Station. Each tipped his hat just so, that it would be a lesson in politeness for most Omaha boys. When an older person spoke to him, each boy always answered, "Sir."

Likes Red Pop.

The younger of the midget scouts talks more and is a favorite everywhere. He could hardly wait for breakfast and a drink of red pop, which he affects. When the trio sat down to eat, he didn't wait for ceremonies, but pitched in in cowpuncher fashion.

The long ride so far apparently has not affected either of the lads. Both were anxious to get off, and the elder inquired many times about the route. He is the leader when the two are alone, and his word on most affairs goes. Temple, however, rides faster and would wear out a horse every day, if his brother would let him go.

"I like to ride horseback better than in an automobile," Temple said. "A car is alright for business, when you want to get there in a hurry, but horseback is the most fun.

"I sure got tired of New York; all the girls wanted to kiss me. That was fun for awhile, but it got tiresome.

"You ought to see my dogs. I got fifteen. Some are wolf hounds, and the fire chief at Fredrick keeps them for me. Then I got some game cocks, too. They licked everything in Oklahoma."

Louis takes most of the responsibilities on himself and tries to look after his little brother. He carries a calendar and a map in his hat and consults the map when in doubt about the route.

Besides their little riders, the two horses carried two blankets each, a knapsack filled with "grub," and a skillet. The horse used by the smaller lad was ridden by former President Roosevelt when he hunted in Oklahoma with the elder Abernathy. Both horses are toughened cow ponies. They are not good to look at, but can cover the ground.[523]

---

[523] The *Omaha Daily News* (Omaha, Nebraska) Sep 7, 1911, Pg. 1.

Appendix 5 — Summary of Abernathy Boys' Journeys

The journeys of Louis and Temple Abernathy captivated a nation during the early 20th century. This appendix summarizes their documented rides.

Year	Journey Name	Route	Ages	Mode of Travel	Key Highlights
1908	Before They Rode Alone	Oklahoma to Washington, D.C.	Temple (3)	With Father (Train)	Temple toured the White House; met Roosevelt
1909	The New Mexico Ride	Guthrie, OK to Santa Fe, NM	Louis (9), Temple (5)	Horseback	1,300 miles solo ride; national headlines begin
1910	From Oklahoma to New York	Oklahoma to NYC via D.C.	Louis (10), Temple (6)	Horseback	Met Taft and Roosevelt; national fame
1910	Journey Home in the Brush Auto	New York to Oklahoma	Louis (10), Temple (6)	Automobile	Bought car themselves; drove alone cross-country
1911	Elephant and Donkey Race	New York to Washington, D.C.	Louis (11), Temple (7)	On foot/with animals	Political stunt; traveled with Judy the elephant
1911	Coast to Coast	NYC to San Francisco	Louis (11), Temple (7)	Horseback	Nearly won $5,000/$10,000 prize; missed by 2 days
1913	The Indian Motorcycle Adventure	Oklahoma to New York	Louis (14), Temple (10)	Motorcycle	Final major journey; traveled with stepbrother

ABOVE: Undated historical public domain photograph of Bud and Temple Abernathy, in a Brush Runabout ca. 1910. The original image is believed to have been published in a U.S. newspaper around 1910 and is in the public domain.

Index

Africa, 31, 35, 40, 63, 64, 66, 78, 142, 174, 191, 233, 236, 247, 249
Amarillo, 20, 22
Brush runabout, 170, 178, 190, 191, 195, 196, 200, 202, 206, 306
Bud, 165, 169, 199, 236, 289, 327, 330
California, 27, 87, 132, 142, 223, 242, 262, 272, 273, 276, 277, 278, 281, 283, 286, 290, 322, 323, 329, 339, 340, 351, 352
Cannon, 90, 96, 161, 208, 209, 337
Catch 'Em Alive, 95, 260, 324
Central Park,, 131, 132
Columbus, 35, 53, 323
Coney Island, 134, 195, 208, 216, 217, 218, 224, 233, 235, 236, 237, 241, 242, 243, 247, 255, 256, 258, 259, 261, 262, 265, 271, 279, 281, 282, 287, 348, 351, 356, 357
Curry, 20, 26
Dayton, 52, 83, 302
Doubleday, 150, 229, 241, 244, 256, 349, 350
Elephant and Donkey Race, 208, 359
Frederick, 26, 36, 43, 64, 66, 100, 109, 113, 130, 140, 141, 149, 204, 241, 244, 281, 288, 295, 296, 299, 315, 328, 334, 350
Geronimo (horse), 12, 33, 100, 204, 315
Golden Gate, 221, 233, 235, 287
Gotham, i, iii, 197, 206
Guthrie, i, iii, 11, 20, 22, 23, 25, 26, 34, 35, 47, 84, 93, 117, 130, 148, 178, 204, 243, 254, 259, 288, 307, 320, 330, 359
Hotel Breslin, 110, 115, 117, 118, 131, 139
Indian motorcycle, 293, 295, 296, 299, 304, 335
Iowa, 51, 87, 153, 248, 250, 252, 255, 275, 282, 312
J.D.F. Jennings, 79
Jack Abernathy, 32, 90, 107, 162, 164, 203, 222, 226, 229, 233, 235, 268, 273, 291, 292, 296, 299, 304, 317, 325, 334, 337
Jennie the donkey, 210, 213, 335
Judy the elephant, 210, 213, 335, 359

Louis, 2, 11, 19, 24, 30, 31, 32, 33, 36, 39, 41, 43, 46, 54, 59, 64, 65, 67, 68, 74, 76, 77, 78, 79, 80, 81, 88, 89, 90, 91, 93, 97, 98, 101, 102, 103, 104, 107, 109, 110, 111, 112, 113, 114, 115, 116, 117, 118, 119, 120, 122, 130, 131, 132, 134, 138, 139, 141, 143, 145, 150, 158, 165, 171, 173, 174, 176, 179, 180, 190, 198, 204, 205, 206, 208, 209, 216, 217, 221, 222, 224, 225, 227, 230, 235, 238, 243, 246, 248, 251, 252, 254, 257, 259, 264, 267, 269, 273, 279, 280, 281, 283, 284, 289, 292, 294, 296, 297, 299, 300, 303, 304, 313, 314, 315, 317, 319, 320, 324, 325, 326, 327, 328, 330, 331, 334, 335, 336, 339, 348, 352, 359

Luna Park, 208, 209, 221, 222, 224, 226, 282

Madison Square Garden, 169, 197, 198, 199, 203, 335

Missouri, 33, 36, 37, 38, 40, 53, 60, 63, 75, 98, 104, 111, 136, 140, 150, 179, 205, 224, 225, 227, 276, 284, 289, 291, 294, 300, 301, 307, 320, 323, 324, 328, 339, 340, 344, 366

New Jersey, 112, 113, 114, 143, 159, 160, 161, 162, 204, 205, 211, 213, 317, 327, 330

New York, v, 4, 14, 31, 32, 35, 38, 40, 46, 47, 48, 57, 59, 60, 61, 63, 66, 67, 68, 69, 73, 74, 75, 76, 84, 85, 90, 92, 93, 95, 97, 99, 102, 103, 105, 106, 107, 108, 109, 112, 113, 114, 115, 116, 117, 118, 119, 120, 121, 122, 125, 126, 128, 129, 130, 131, 132, 134, 135, 136, 137, 138, 139, 140, 141, 142, 143, 145, 149, 150, 151, 158, 161, 163, 165, 166, 169, 171, 172, 174, 176, 178, 179, 182, 189, 190, 191, 192, 193, 194, 195, 196, 197, 198, 200, 202, 203, 204, 206, 208, 209, 210, 216, 217, 219, 221, 222, 223, 224, 225, 226, 227, 228, 229, 233, 234, 235, 236, 237, 238, 241, 242, 244, 245, 246, 247, 249, 250, 251, 253, 254, 255, 257, 258, 259, 264, 265, 267, 268, 270, 272, 275, 279, 280, 282, 283, 285, 287, 288, 289, 292, 293, 294, 295, 299, 303, 304, 306, 307, 310, 312, 315, 318, 319, 324, 328, 330, 334, 335, 337, 339, 342, 343, 344, 345, 349, 350, 351, 352, 356, 357, 359, 365

New York City, 31, 47, 115, 126, 134, 138, 139, 143, 165, 190, 191, 192, 193, 194, 195, 196, 197, 206, 210, 221, 222, 223, 227, 237, 238, 244, 255, 257, 267, 270, 288, 310, 319, 324, 334, 335

Ohio, 31, 48, 53, 55, 116, 205, 207, 229, 235, 244, 245, 272, 302, 332, 343, 352

Oklahoma, ii, vii, x, 2, 5, 7, 8, 10, 11, 12, 13, 17, 20, 21, 22, 23, 24, 25, 26, 28, 29, 31, 33, 34, 35, 36, 39, 41, 42, 43, 46, 48, 49, 53, 54, 55, 57, 58, 59, 60, 61, 63, 64, 66, 67, 68, 69, 70, 73, 74, 76, 79, 82, 84, 90, 93, 94, 100, 101, 102, 105, 107, 108, 109, 110, 111, 112, 113, 114, 115, 117, 132, 136, 137, 138, 139, 140, 141, 142, 143, 145, 149, 165, 166, 171, 174, 177, 178, 179, 180, 181, 188, 190, 191, 195, 197, 200, 202, 204, 206, 208, 211, 224, 226, 233, 235, 237, 238, 243, 244, 246, 247, 248, 249, 251, 252, 255, 257, 264, 265, 269, 270, 280, 283, 285, 287, 288, 289, 290, 292, 293, 294, 295, 298, 303, 306, 307, 308, 309, 320, 323, 327, 334, 335, 337, 339, 340, 341, 344, 345, 348, 349, 358, 359, 365, 367, 368

Oklahoma City, 17, 24, 25, 26, 28, 35, 43, 53, 57, 63, 107, 109, 115, 138, 141, 145, 174, 177, 178, 179, 181, 188, 190, 191, 195, 206, 211, 233, 247, 269, 280, 287, 292, 298, 303, 306, 344, 345

President Taft, 63, 65, 67, 68, 74, 76, 77, 78, 85, 107, 108, 161, 285, 334

Roosevelt, v, x, 3, 5, 7, 8, 9, 12, 14, 17, 22, 31, 32, 35, 38, 40, 46, 47, 48, 57, 63, 64, 65, 66, 67, 68, 74, 75, 78, 90, 93, 94, 103, 105, 106, 107, 108, 109, 111, 112, 113, 114, 116, 117, 120, 122, 123, 124, 125, 126, 127, 128, 129, 130, 131, 136, 137, 138, 139, 140, 142, 145, 158, 159, 161, 165, 171, 174, 175, 176, 177, 178, 189, 191, 200, 202, 206, 210, 225, 226, 233, 236, 238, 241, 244, 246, 247, 248, 249, 252, 254, 255, 260, 264, 265, 268, 269, 270, 280, 283, 285, 287, 288, 289, 290, 294, 295, 299, 303, 304, 315, 316, 319, 320, 334, 337, 339, 342, 345, 348, 358, 359, 365, 366, 367

rough rider, 17, 41, 128, 337

Sam (horse), 12, 33, 97, 100, 125, 198, 204, 225, 226, 254, 315

Santa Fe, ii, 11, 19, 20, 21, 22, 23, 26, 161, 191, 243, 246, 259, 283, 288, 320, 330, 334, 359

Shriner buttons, 65, 74

Smithsonian Institution, 78

Temple, 2, 7, 8, 9, 11, 16, 17, 19, 21, 23, 24, 26, 28, 30, 31, 33, 34, 35, 39, 40, 41, 43, 46, 54, 59, 63, 64, 65, 66, 67, 68, 73, 74, 76, 77, 78, 80, 81, 82, 83, 84, 88, 89, 90, 91, 93, 97, 101, 102, 105, 107, 108, 109, 110, 112, 113, 114, 115, 116, 117, 118, 119, 120, 121, 122, 123, 130, 131, 132, 134, 138, 139, 140, 143, 145, 148, 150, 158, 159, 161, 165, 166, 169, 171, 172, 173, 174, 175, 176, 178, 180, 189, 192, 193, 195, 196, 198, 199, 202, 206, 208, 209, 213,

216, 217, 221, 222, 224, 225, 226, 227, 229, 230, 231, 233, 235, 237, 238, 241, 242, 243, 246, 248, 249, 252, 254, 255, 257, 258, 259, 260, 261, 264, 265, 267, 269, 270, 273, 274, 279, 280, 281, 283, 284, 285, 286, 287, 288, 289, 290, 292, 294, 295, 296, 297, 299, 301, 303, 304, 313, 314, 315, 317, 318, 319, 324, 325, 326, 327, 328, 331, 334, 335, 336, 339, 348, 351, 352, 359

The Abernathy Kids to the Rescue, 143

Threadgill Hotel, 29, 367

Uncle Joe, 161, 208, 209

Utah, 87, 130, 271, 274, 280, 352

Washington, D.C, 7, 10, 62, 63, 78, 79, 80, 88, 91, 115, 208, 209, 269, 334, 335, 339, 359

White House, 7, 8, 9, 65, 74, 75, 76, 77, 78, 79, 80, 81, 84, 96, 108, 139, 208, 216, 285, 334, 359

Wilbur Wright, 52, 189, 333

Wiley (horse), 12, 198, 204, 225, 226, 254, 280

William Howard Taft, 63, 81

wolf hunting, 226, 254

Glossary

Abernathy Boys
Louis and Temple Abernathy, young brothers from Oklahoma famous for their daring long-distance horseback and automobile journeys across America in the early 1900s.

Barehanded Wolf Hunting
A method used by Jack Abernathy, catching live wolves without weapons, which earned him the nickname "Catch-'Em-Alive Jack."

Brush Runabout
A small, early automobile purchased by the Abernathy boys in 1910, which they drove unassisted from New York back to Oklahoma.

Catch-'Em-Alive Jack
Nickname for John "Jack" Abernathy, father of Louis and Temple, noted for catching wolves with his bare hands and his friendship with Theodore Roosevelt.

Endurance Riding
Long-distance horseback riding where riders cover hundreds or thousands of miles, a central element of the Abernathy boys' fame.

Indian Motorcycle
The brand of motorcycle used by the Abernathy boys in later adventures, notably their 1913 trip.

Indian Territory
Region before Oklahoma's statehood, heavily associated with frontier life and home to Native American tribes.

Letters Series
Multiple historical letter compilations by Kent Brooks about various states during the 19th century.

Moving Picture Shows
Early cinema performances; the Abernathy boys often attended these in towns during their travels.

Old Santa Fe Trail
A historic 19th-century trade route connecting Missouri to Santa Fe, New Mexico, which the Abernathy boys traveled along in part.

Pioneering Spirit
Courage and determination associated with frontier exploration, embodying the Abernathy boys' adventures.

Rough Riders
A volunteer cavalry unit famously led by Theodore Roosevelt during the Spanish-American War; connected to Jack Abernathy through Roosevelt.

Sam (Horse)
Louis Abernathy's faithful mount during the early journeys, previously used in Roosevelt's wolf-hunting expedition.

School of the Open Road
Phrase used to describe the life-learning and self-reliance lessons the Abernathy boys acquired through their adventures.

Shriner Buttons
Badges worn by the Abernathy boys indicating their father's membership in the Shriners, a fraternal organization.

Smithsonian Institution
Museum in Washington, D.C. where the Abernathy boys visited exhibits, including animals sent back by Roosevelt from Africa.

Steering Wheels (1910s)
Automobile control mechanisms the Abernathy boys learned to use during their pioneering drive across America.

Temple Abernathy
Younger of the Abernathy brothers, known for his youthful spirit and fearless participation in their expeditions.

Theodore Roosevelt
26th President of the United States, Rough Rider, and close friend of Jack Abernathy, whom the boys admired and sought to meet.

Threadgill Hotel
Historic Oklahoma City hotel where the Abernathy boys were honored during their 1909 return reception.

Toughening Up
A philosophy advocated by Jack Abernathy, meaning building resilience through exposure to hardships and challenges.

White House Visit
Refers to the Abernathy boys' visit to meet President Taft after riding on horseback from Oklahoma to Washington, D.C.

Wright Brothers
Inventors of the airplane; the Abernathy boys visited Wright Field and were shown airplanes during their travels.

Youthful Audacity
The combination of bravery, innocence, and determination shown by the Abernathy boys throughout their journeys.

The Writer

Kent Brooks is a writer, researcher, historian, and technologist whose work brings forgotten stories to life through the lens of place, persistence, and the power of the press. A native of Springfield, Colorado, Brooks grew up hearing tales of broomcorn harvests, Dust Bowl survival, and the cowboys of the big cattle outfits that once roamed Southeast Colorado. These formative stories sparked a lifelong passion for preserving local history.

For nearly 30 years, Brooks has led Information Technology and Distance Learning initiatives in New Mexico, Oklahoma, and Wyoming. While living in Southwest Oklahoma, he came across the tale of the Abernathy boys—two young adventurers whose solo rides across the country captivated early 20th-century America. That discovery led to *Guthrie to Gotham*, a narrative drawn directly from the newspaper headlines that once made the boys national heroes.

He currently lives and works in Casper, Wyoming, continuing to explore the rich intersections of community memory, the settling of the American West, and journalistic legacy.